The Art of

Kiltmaking

The Art of

Kiltmaking

Step-by-Step Instructions for
Making a Traditional Scottish kilt

Barbara Tewksbury • Elsie Stuehmeyer

Celtic Dragon Press

Pellon is a registered trademark of Freudenberg Nonwovens
Tailor's Pride is a registered trademark of Handler Textile Corporation
Q-tip is a registered trademark of Cheseborough-Pond's USA Inc.
Era is a registered trademark of Proctor and Gamble
Ott-Lite is a registered trademark of Environmental Lighting Concepts, Inc.

Published by Celtic Dragon Press
P. O. Box 244
Deansboro, NY 13328

Additional copies of this book may be ordered at
www.celticdragonpress.com

Printed by Canterbury Press
Rome, NY

Front cover: Ancient Duncan kilt under construction; Shaker box by Gordon Jarvis (photo by Dave Tewksbury).
Title pages & page 142: Carolyn Tewksbury, Tioram Castle, Scotland (photos by Barbara Tewksbury).
Back cover, clockwise from upper right: Mohawk Valley Frasers with Drum Major John MacNeill and Pipe Major
*   James Clough, tartan Modern MacGillivray (photo by Barbara Tewksbury); Alec Duncan and Carolyn*
*   Tewksbury, tartans Ancient Duncan and Weathered Ferguson (photo by Dave Tewksbury); Highland dancer*
*   Lorna Stuehmeyer Brown, tartan Dress Glasgow (photo by Bonnie Kamin).*

Table of Contents

Acknowledgements

We are indebted to the following people who have read and used various versions of this manuscript and whose careful reviews and insightful comments helped make this a much better book: Sandi Burton, Margaret Cook, Helen Jarvis, Gordon Jarvis, Lynn Murray, Christina Ramsey, Jean Ritchie, Carolyn Tewksbury, Jean Tewksbury, and Dave Tewksbury.

Commercial photographer Dave Tewksbury was instrumental in producing the images for this book, and we are deeply grateful for his design insights, skill in scanning, and photographic acumen. We are grateful to Sandra at Lochcarron of Scotland and Angie at D.C Dalgliesh, Ltd., who patiently answered questions and sent off samples and odd lengths of tartan to be considered for illustrations in the book. We also thank Robert Allers, who guided us toward sources of information on kilts in the 18th century Highland regiments in North America.

We would also like to thank our models: piper and Highland dancer Carolyn Tewksbury, Professor of Religious Studies Dr. Stephenson Humphries-Brooks, and geologist-to-be Captain Alec Duncan. We are grateful for their good cheer, patience, and willingness to appear in this book.

The family of an author puts up with a lot, particularly near the end of a project when getting the book done becomes an all-consuming effort. Deepest thanks must go to Dave and Carolyn Tewksbury for their patience, good humor, and encouragement throughout the entire project.

Preface

We were inspired to produce this book, because we were acutely aware that people in North America have had essentially no effective way of learning how to make traditional Scottish kilts, short of taking one of Elsie's five-day kiltmaking courses. Furthermore, few people outside of Scotland have the knowledge and experience in traditional kiltmaking that Elsie has, and we felt that a step-by-step instruction book was the best way to preserve her half century of experience as a kiltmaker.

Who is this book for? First and foremost, this book is for those of you who would like to make a kilt in proper and traditional fashion. Text and figures are designed to be detailed enough to guide you in planning, laying out, and successfully constructing a kilt from start to finish, regardless of the tartan chosen or the size of the person.

This book is also for those of you who are endlessly fascinated by all hand crafts and who, like us, have bookshelves crammed to the top with books on all sorts of hand crafts. While we've not tried all the crafts on our bookshelves, we feel somehow enriched by knowing more about how they are done. And there's always the future for trying them!

And finally, this book is for those of you who are enamored of all things Scottish, who have wondered what's inside a kilt (and not just what's underneath it!). We hope that this book will give you a new appreciation of the national dress of Scotland by helping you understand more about proper kilt construction and the hallmarks of fine workmanship.

Happy kiltmaking!

Barb Tewksbury and Elsie Stuehmeyer

Introduction

Those who sew are familiar with modern garment construction. Assembling even a simple garment involves joining pieces with complex shapes, compound curves, notches, and darts. Shaping and sizing are accomplished at the time of cutting, and only the truly experienced, bold, or creative person can confidently create a garment without a pattern.

As plans for this book began to take shape, several people asked how we would include the pattern for making a kilt. The remarkable thing about a kilt, though, is that it requires no pattern! All a kiltmaker needs to know are the wearer's waist and hip measurements and the length of the kilt in order to turn out a shaped and tailored kilt that fits the wearer perfectly. A kilt is constructed from a rectangle of cloth a little less than two feet wide and six to eight yards long. Rather than shaping and fitting by cutting out and assembling an assortment of complex pieces, a kiltmaker works with the rectangle of cloth and shapes it to fit during the sewing process, eliminating the need for a pattern. Even interfacings and linings are shaped to fit from rough, rectangular pieces of fabric, and facings are folded and shaped without cutting.

Kiltmaking methods have remained essentially the same for over a century. Making a kilt will put you in touch not only with Scottish tradition but with a tailoring and hand sewing tradition that has been almost entirely lost as we begin the 21st century.

The instructions in this book

This book provides detailed instructions for constructing a kilt in traditional fashion, by hand. Don't expect modern shortcuts or sewing machine speed. Unlike many garments that *could* be hand sewn but that are more quickly and easily constructed largely by machine, a kilt *cannot* be properly constructed except by hand.

If you have made a kilt before, or if you have read other materials on kiltmaking, you may find that our methods differ from those that you have previously used or encountered. The method for making kilts that we present in this book is the one that Elsie learned 50 years ago as an apprentice and kiltmaker with the renowned firm Thomas Gordon's of Glasgow. Our instructions include a superior method for stitching pleats, details for achieving a superb fit, and steps for all of the interior construction necessary for making a kilt that will hold its shape for a lifetime.

How to use this book

If you want to evaluate the fit and construction of an existing kilt, read the tips and guidelines in Chapter 2, and consult the color figures and captions.

If you want to understand the basic principles before beginning a kilt, read Chapters 1 through 4. If you understand *why* kilts are designed and sewn as they are, the construction process will make more sense. We think you'll save time in the long run if you work through these introductory sections before plunging into the instructions.

But, if you want to plunge directly into making a kilt, go to Chapter 5, where the step-by-step instructions for kilt construction begin.

Chapter 1

A brief history of kilts and tartan

Modern kilts represent the legacy of evolution of traditional Highland dress that stretches back over a thousand years. In this chapter, we will briefly trace the development of kilts and tartan, and we hope that you will be intrigued by the history of the marvelous garment you are about to make!

Kilts and tartan stand among the world's most recognizable symbols of cultural affinity and kinship and represent without question one of the most distinctive and well-known examples of national dress. Few people fail to recognize a kilt and to associate it with Scotland. Much of this comes from the fact that kilts are currently remarkably popular. Few western cultures can count as many people who frequently wear a traditional garment whose style has changed little in nearly two centuries. And, whereas interest in traditional dress in many cultures is dying as we begin the 21st century, interest in traditional Scottish dress is actually on the rise, particularly in North America, and more and more people of Scottish descent are commissioning and wearing kilts.

Origin of Highland Dress

While we have little direct historical record of early dress in Scotland, we do know that striped and checked woolen fabric was woven and worn as early as the third century. A cloth fragment of this date excavated at Falkirk, west of Edinburgh, shows a familiar check and stripe pattern produced by weaving alternating cross-stripes of two natural colors of wool across a similarly striped warp. Such pattern weaving was certainly not unique to Scotland and was common in all early cultures, whether for weaving fabric or baskets.

What is unique about the evolution of Highland dress is that check and stripe patterns woven as twill evolved to become *the* traditional fabric for garments in the Highlands of Scotland. In a twenty-volume history of Scotland published in 1582, scholar George Buchanan describes Highland dress for men as consisting of a tightly-woven, cross-striped woolen length of cloth used as a garment by day and a blanket by night.[1] Over the centuries, dyes from native plants and lichens had supplanted natural wool colors, and Buchanan notes that blues and purples had become the favorite colors.

By 1600, the word *tartan* was used to describe the distinctive cross-striped fabric of Highland dress, and contemporary paintings and literature of the 17th and early 18th centuries give us a very clear picture of Highland dress.[2] Men wore a belted plaid (pronounced *played*) of wool tartan which came to be called the *feileadh mór*, or great kilt, the word *feileadh* derived from the word *eileadh*, meaning folding, and the word *mór* meaning big. The *feileadh mór* was an immense piece of wool tartan two yards wide and four to six yards long that was loosely pleated, wrapped, and secured with a belt around the wearer. Unlike a modern kilt, the *feileadh mór* had no stitched pleats. Each time the wearer wished to don his kilt, he spread the piece of tartan on the ground with a belt lying underneath.[3] Next, he folded the plaid into pleats on top of the belt, leaving an unpleated portion at each end. He then lay down on top of the pleated portion, wrapped the free sides across the front of his body, and buckled the belt to secure the plaid around his middle. The lower edge hung down to his knees, and, because the plaid was two yards wide, a considerable width of fabric extended above his waist as well. The fabric above the waist could be tucked under the belt, worn wrapped around the shoulder or over the head for warmth, or pinned fashionably with a brooch (as in Color Figure 1). At night, this immensely practical garment could be used as a blanket or even a tent. Anyone who has seen the movie *Rob Roy* has seen great kilts in action.

A plaid kilted above the knees with short hose or bare legs below seems to have evolved as a practical solution to the cold, damp moors of Scotland.[4] Clothing soaked by walking through the low brush of the Highlands did not dry readily in damp and chilly dwellings, and the kilted plaid was a healthy alternative to long wet robes or sodden trousers. Traditional Highland footwear, laced leather *ghillie brogues*, was equally practical, having holes punched in the top to let the water out as the wearer tramped through the oozy terrain of the Highlands.

A more stylized version of the old ghillie brogues is still worn not only by pipers but also by fashionable western men, who don't have the faintest idea of the origin of the decorative pattern of holes on their wing-tip shoes!

What did women wear in the 17th and 18th centuries in the Highlands? The *feileadh mór* was strictly a man's garment. Women wore an ankle length dress under a tartan *earasaid* (anglicized to *arasaid*) that was worn as a long shawl, commonly draped over the head.

Multi-colored tartan made sense in terms of the limitations of 17th and 18th century home dyeing and weaving. Wool was dyed using vegetable materials in small dye pots. Because it was virtually impossible to match dye lots from pot to pot, fabric woven in stripes from small amounts of yarn produced an attractive fabric in which color mismatches were less obvious.

The notion that 17th and 18th century tartan was woven only in muted shades of brown, brownish-red, black, khaki, and muddy green is far from the truth. Contemporary artwork shows a wide range of colors, many of them quite bright, although not as bright as colors that can be achieved using modern chemical dyes. Reds and purples came from many sources, including lichens, tormentil root, ladies' bedstraw, bramble, dandelion root, spindle, and St. John's wort. Blues came from imported indigo, although gray-blue was dyed directly using yellow flag. Yellows came from lichen, birch leaves, broom, and bog myrtle, with a particularly bright shade of yellow coming from flowering heather. Black was dyed using alder bark, and browns came from various plants. Most greens were produced by overdyeing yellow yarn with indigo, although greens were also dyed directly using nettles, ling, and sorrel.[5]

The Evolution of Modern Highland Dress

The modern association that we make between tartans and specific clans simply did not exist in the 17th and 18th centuries. People wore whatever tartan pattern took their fancy. The lack of association between clans and specific tartan colors and patterns is driven home most compellingly by formal paintings of the period. A famous 18th century painting of Sir James and Sir Alexander MacDonald of Sleat as children[6] shows one of the children wearing three different red and black tartans, one each for jacket, vest, and great kilt. A different 18th century painting of Charles Campbell in full Highland dress[7] portrays him wearing one tartan for his plaid and another for his jacket, both in black and red and neither one a known modern tartan nor a tartan bearing any resemblance at all to any of the modern Campbell tartans!

The first official, regularized tartan appeared, ironically enough, in fabric issued for uniforms by the British Army, and the tartan chosen had a profound influence on the eventual evolution of clan tartans. The first events in that evolution began in 1724, when the British Army mustered six companies of Highlanders primarily from Clans Campbell, Grant, and Munro. These independent companies were known informally as the "Black Watch", in reference to the "black" or undercover activities engaged in by the companies in keeping watch on suspected Jacobite clans and in rooting out Jacobite activities. All members of the Highland companies wore belted plaids, although little effort was made to standardize tartan.

In 1739, the British government formed the Highland companies into a regiment, the 43rd Highland Regiment, and issued uniforms that included a belted plaid in a standard, dark-colored tartan of blue, green, and black, which became known as the "government pattern". The tartan quickly came to be called by the nickname of the regiment, the Black Watch, and was virtually identical to the Black Watch tartan that is so familiar around the world today in everything from kilts to stadium blankets (Color Figure 20). The only difference between the modern Black Watch and the 18th century Black Watch is the size of the check and the depth of the colors. The original Black Watch had a smaller check size and softer colors. The vegetable dyes of the period did not produce colors as deep as modern dyes, and the original Black Watch was dominated by softer blues and greens.

Why the government chose this particular tartan over others that were worn at the time is not entirely clear. The choice may have been partly influenced by a desire to have a dark tartan that contrasted with the red jackets issued along with the plaids. The choice may also have been influenced by what some of the independent companies were wearing at the time. The early Black Watch companies included significant numbers of Campbells, and some have suggested that some of the Campbells may have worn this tartan at an early date.[8] But this predates the association of a particular tartan with a specific clan, and the tartan was undoubtedly worn by individuals from other clans at the time as well.

Six years after formation of the first Highland regiment, the last of the Jacobite Wars ended with defeat of the Scots at the Battle of Culloden. Because kilts and tartan were such powerful and recognizable symbols of Highland loyalty and independence, the British banned the wearing of kilts and the display of tartan as part of the Disarming Act of 1746. For over 35 years, kilts and tartan could be legally worn *only* in the Highland regiments. During this time, the British Highland regiments fought in Highland dress in the War of Austrian Succession (1743-1748), the Seven Years War (1756-1763), the French and Indian War (1754-1763), and the American Revolution (1775-1783). Virtually all regiments wore the standard government tartan, although a 1759 painting of the 78th (Fraser's) Highlanders shows members wearing brown kilts and an officer wearing a tartan with broad buff and green stripes. The explanation may lie in the fact that the regiment was raised in rather a hurry and may not have received its government tartan until after the end of the French blockade of Québec.[9]

With kilts banned for over a generation in Scotland, credit for survival of Highland dress goes to the Highland regiments. Highland dress not only survived but also evolved in the regiments, because the traditional belted plaid was not overwhelmingly practical for a soldier, particularly in North America. No one knows precisely who made the first *feileadh beag,* or little kilt, in which the plaid wrap was separated from the kilted lower part and in which the pleats were permanently stitched in the kilted part (Color Figures 2 and 3). It *is* clear, however, that the *feileadh beag* had replaced the traditional great kilt in the Highland regiments in North America by the time of the American Revolution. The early military *feileadh beag* (anglicized to *philabeg*) was simply the lower half of the traditional *feileadh mór* with stitched but not pressed box pleats, rather than with the sharply creased knife pleats that we associate with modern kilts. Each kilt was made from three to three and a half yards of material, rather than the eight yards in a modern kilt. Separate plaids became ceremonial additions that were left behind on campaigns. Regimental uniforms were completed with hose (or, sometimes, with Iroquois-style leggings), red jackets with facings color-coded for the regiment, and a regimental bonnet.[10]

While the Disarming Act was in force, all Highland regiments wore the Black Watch tartan. Toward the end of this period, the first new official tartan was developed for the Seaforth Highlanders, who were raised in 1778 by MacKenzie, Earl of Seaforth. The standard government tartan was modified by adding a red stripe bordered by narrow black to the middle of the blue, and a white stripe bordered by narrow black to the middle of the green (Color Figure 21). The modified Black Watch of the Seaforth Highlanders officially began as a regimental tartan

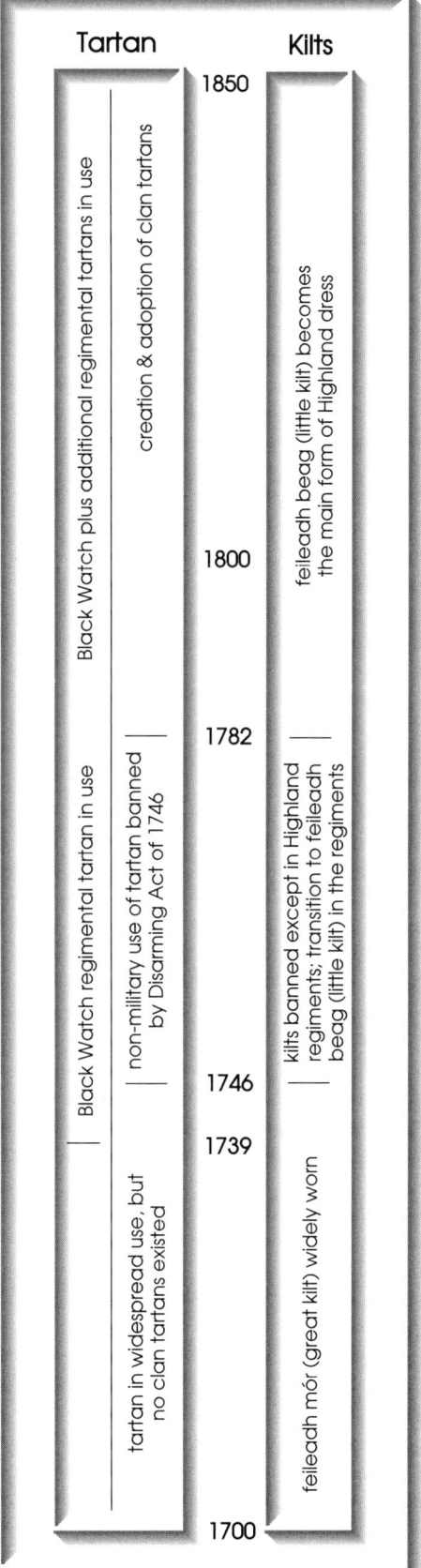

but was adopted much later as the tartan of Clan MacKenzie.

Interest in preserving and promoting Highland dress, music, Gaelic language, and Gaelic literature rose in the latter part of the 18th century, as British fears of renewed Jacobite uprising dimmed. Efforts by the Highland Society of London, formed in 1778, resulted in the 1782 repeal of the Disarming Act of 1746, and Highland dress was once more permitted in Scotland. By the time the ban was rescinded, however, nearly a generation had passed, and Highlanders had grown used to wearing the same dress as other Scots. Many showed little enthusiasm for returning to tartan clothing, and, contrary to what one might have guessed, kilts and tartan did not make an immediate and universal come-back in Scotland. Significant revival of interest in kilts and tartan did not, in fact, occur until the 19th century. When it did, the style of dress was drawn from that of the Highland regiments at the time, which included a tailored jacket and a buckled, close-fitting kilt with pressed knife pleats and a separate plaid for dress occasions.

Additional regimental tartans were the first new tartans developed after repeal of the Disarming Act. The Cameron Highlanders created a new tartan for their regiment in 1793, and the Gordon Highlanders modified the government Black Watch for their regiment in 1794 by adding a yellow stripe to the green (Color Figure 22).

So, when did the familiar association between clans and tartans develop? Curiously enough, particular tartans were not associated with specific clans until well into the 19th century. One of the initiatives that helped stimulate the movement occurred in 1815, when the Highland Society of London began the first systematic collection of extant tartans by asking all clan chiefs and heads of families to send samples of the "tartans of their clans". Few clans at the time had distinct tartans, and the request clearly puzzled many of the clan chiefs. The Chief of Clan Donald, for instance, was anxious to comply but wrote back promptly to the Highland Society, saying, "Being really ignorant of what is exactly the Macdonald Tartan, I request you will have the goodness to exert every means in your power to obtain a perfectly genuine pattern, such as will warrant me authenticating it with my arms."[11] Despite some confusion, the Society made headway in collecting tartan samples and, more importantly, encouraged the clans to think in terms of clan tartans.

A widespread romantic revival of Highland dress began in the 1820s, when King George IV visited Edinburgh in 1822. The occasion was stage-managed by Sir Walter Scott, a dévoté of reviving Gaelic culture and Highland dress. When invitees were asked to attend functions wearing full Highland dress, the rush was on to acquire tartan regalia. Weaving houses such as William Wilson and Sons of Bannockburn were deluged with requests, for which there were not only limited supplies of fabric but also of registered tartans, and few varieties belonged to specific clans.

The Wilsons maintained a book of tartans for order, with many tartans listed simply by number, and others with names such as "Caledonia", "Robin Hood", "Large Gipsy", and "White Wellington". Still others were listed by the name of the person who had recently ordered a bulk lot (e.g., a tartan sometimes referred to as "Kidd" by the Wilsons, after a man named Kidd who had bought a bulk lot several years earlier so that he could clothe his West Indian slaves). This latter tartan was the one selected several years later to become the tartan of Clan MacPherson! As another example, the tartan made by the Wilsons and listed as "New Bruce" was eventually adopted by Clan Grant.[12] Many other clans selected what were to become their clan tartans from the tartans in the Wilsons' book. Wilson and Sons also invented new tartan patterns for their clients, and some of these were eventually adopted as clan tartans.

Still other clans adopted or modified the old regimental Black Watch tartan. The Campbell tartan (Color Figure 30), for example, is virtually identical to the Black Watch. Clan Gordon adopted the regimental tartan of the Gordon Highlanders, which was the Black Watch with a yellow stripe instead of single black in the green (Color Figure 22). Many others also modified the old government tartan. Several clans chose to replace the black stripes in the green of the Black Watch, creating tartans that include the Lamont (white stripe), Forbes (white stripe with narrow black edge, also called a *guarded white*), Cheape (azure stripe), and Campbell of Argyll (yellow stripe in green alternating with white stripe in the next green, Color Figure 31). Still other tartans were created from the Black Watch by adding stripes to both the blue and the green, including Farquharson (yellow stripe in the green and red stripe in the blue), Hunting Robertson (guarded red stripe in the green and guarded white stripe in the blue), and Murray of Atholl (red stripe in the green and guarded red stripe in the blue). It's no wonder that many blue, green, and black tartans look so much alike! They're all based on the Black Watch! Even the red and blue MacLachlan is basically a Black Watch tartan in which red replaces blue and blue replaces green (Color Figure 27).

Other clans have tartans related to one another. The Gunn and Morrison, for example, share the same basic structure as the MacKay, but the Gunn has a red stripe in the green and the Morrison has a red stripe in the blue. We could go on, but we won't!

Clans adopted and registered specific tartans over the middle decades of the 1800s. Tartan had become so popular in both the Highlands and Lowlands of Scotland by the 1850s that no well-dressed lady would dream of being seen without her tartan arisaid.

Clans and families continued to adopt and register tartan in the late 19th century and throughout the 20th century. Some clans based their tartans on ancestral portraits or relics associated with the family. The sett for the Lennox tartan, for example, was taken in 1893 from a 16th century portrait of the Countess of Lennox. As another example, the colors and thread counts for the Gordon of Abergeldie tartan (the Red Gordon) were taken in 1953 from a scarf in a 1723 portrait of Rachel Gordon. In a very recent example, Lochcarron of Scotland designed a tartan for the Young family in 1991 based on the Christina Young arisaid, a beautifully-preserved arisaid dating from 1726.[13]

Other tartans have been designed wholly from scratch using colors of some significance to the family. D.C. Dalgliesh, Ltd., for example, designed the Teall of Teallach tartan in 1966 using colors that represent the associations of the Teall family: yellow for association with the House of Gordon, red for association with the Singer Sewing Machine Company, blue for the merchant navy, and black for the Priory Independent Schools.[14]

Highland Dress Today

As is clear from the brief history outlined in this chapter, a kilt is traditionally a man's garment. The view expressed in Robert Bain's 1938 book *The Clans and Tartans of Scotland* that "The kilt is male attire and should never be worn by ladies"[15] was a nearly universal sentiment until well into the 20th century, and many traditionalists still frown on women in kilts. When more and more women began to compete in Scottish Highland dancing after World War II, however, women were eventually allowed to compete in Highland dances wearing the traditional kilt. With the large number of girls and women competing in Highland dancing, and with increasing numbers of women in pipe bands, one now sees many women dressed in kilts at Scottish games and gatherings.

[1] Alexander Fulton, *Clans and Families of Scotland: The History of the Scottish Tartan* (Edison, NJ, Chartwell Books, 1999) p. 20.
[2] Fulton, pp. 19-21.
   Hugh Cheape, *Tartan: The Highland Habit* (Edinburgh, National Museums of Scotland, 1995), pp. 13-31.
[3] The following web site provides pictures and instructions for donning a great kilt:
   http://www.tartanweb.com/tweb/greatkilt/index.htm
[4] Fulton, p. 20.
[5] Fulton, p. 20.
[6] Cheape, p. 37.
[7] Cheape, p. 37.
[8] Blair Urquhart (ed.) *Tartans: The Illustrated Identifier to Over 140 Designs* (London, The Apple Press, 1994), p. 28.
[9] Stuart Reid and Mike Chappell, *18th Century Highlanders* (London, Reed International Books, Ltd., 1993), p. 37.
[10] Reid and Chappell, pp. 16-17.
[11] Urquhart, p. 18.
[12] Fulton, p. 42.
   Cheape, pp. 52-54.
[13] Urquhart, pp. 39, 45, 79.
[14] Urquhart, p. 77.
[15] Margaret O. MacDougall, *Robert Bain's The Clans and Tartans of Scotland* (London, William Collins Sons and Co., Ltd., 1973), p. 31.

Ancient Malcolm tartan

Color Figure 1. Front and back views of a modern interpretation of a *feileadh mór* or great kilt. Tartan: Ancient Malcolm, an asymmetric tartan.

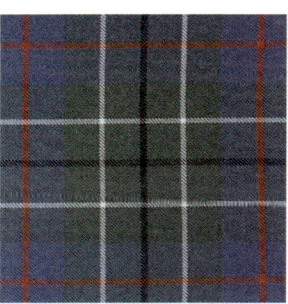

Ancient Duncan tartan

Color Figure 2. Front and back views of a modern kilt pleated to the sett. Pleats are folded to repeat the tartan pattern across the back of the kilt. Tartan: Ancient Duncan.

Weathered Ferguson tartan

Color Figure 3. Front and back views of a modern kilt pleated to the stripe (military pleating). Each pleat is folded to show the same stripe. Tartan: Weathered Ferguson.

Fit of a kilt

length

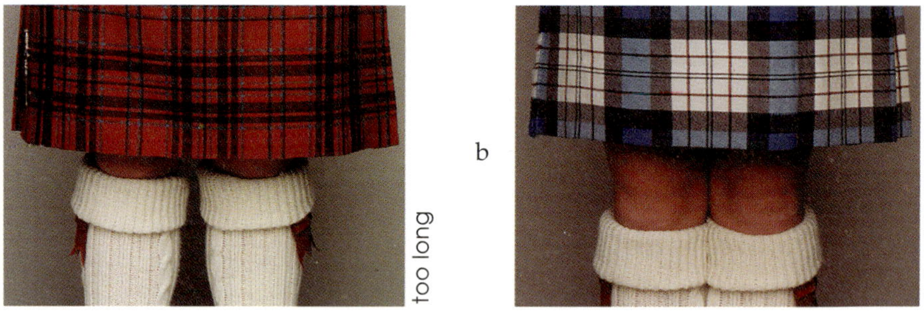

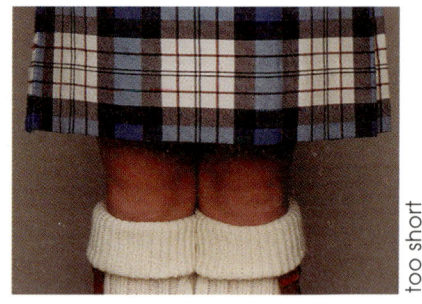

too long   too short

Color Figure 4. Proper length: a kilt should come to the top of the knee. The kilt in (a) is too long, whereas the kilt in (b) is too short. Tartans: MacGillivray (a), Dress Ferguson (b)

size

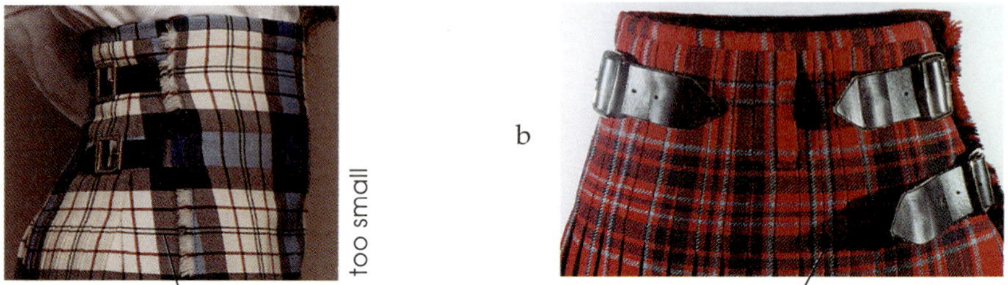

too small — underapron shows here   center back stripe — too big

Color Figure 5. Proper size: the fringe edge of the apron should just cover the right hand edge of the underapron. The kilt in (a) is too small, and the apron does not cover all of the underapron. The kilt in (b) is too big. The apron comes too far over the pleats, forcing the center back stripe off center. Tartans: Dress Ferguson (a), MacGillivray (b).

shaping in back

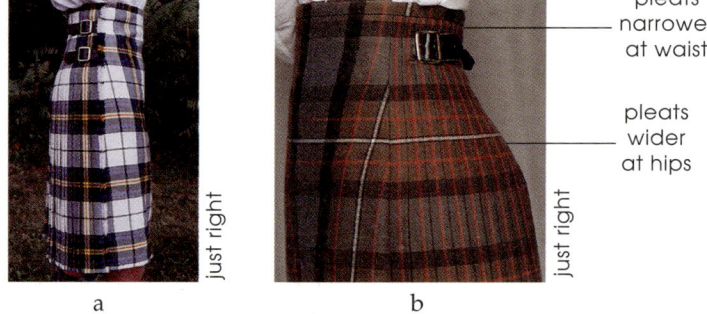

pleats narrower at waist

pleats wider at hips

just right   just right

a   b

Color Figure 6. Proper shaping in the back: a kilt should snug into the small of the back and flare out over the buttocks, leaving the apron edge straight up and down, as shown in (a). Shaping in the pleats is accomplished by making the pleats wider at the hips than at the waist (b). Tartan: Dress Nova Scotia (a), Weathered Ferguson (b).

length of fell

bottom of fell   bottom of fell

fell too short   fell too long

a   b   c

Color Figure 7. Proper length of fell: pleats in a kilt should be stitched from the top of the kilt to the flare of the buttocks, about one third of the length of the kilt, including the rise. The fell (the stitched portion of the pleats) in kilt a & b is much too short; the fell stops well above the flare of the buttocks (a) and extends only about one quarter of the length of the kilt (b). This kilt is also too small around. The fell in (c) is much too long. The pleats are stitched more than one third of the length of the kilt, and the fell extends well below the flare of the buttocks. Tartans: Dress Edinburgh (a & b), Dress Wine Sutherland (c).

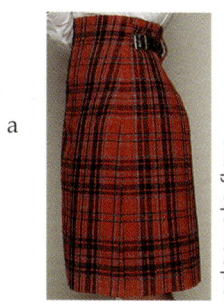  

a — adequate flare

b — inadequate flare

c — inadequate flare

Color Figure 8: Proper shaping in the front: the edges of the apron should have an A-line flare. If the flare from hip to bottom is adequate, the left apron edge will lie flat as it does in kilt (a) and won't open forward. If the edge of the apron does not flare enough, the left edge will open forward (b & c). Tartans: MacGillivray (a), Dress Nova Scotia (b), Weathered Henderson (c).

dart

a — improper shaping

b — proper shaping

shaping in front

Color Figure 9. Proper shaping in the front: a kilt must never have darts in the apron, as the kilt in (a) does. All of the shaping in the apron must be accommodated at the edges of the apron, as in kilt (b). Tartans: Dress MacLeod of Harris (a), Dress Wine Sutherland (b).

a — good rise

b — skimpy rise

rise

Color Figure 10. Proper rise: a kilt should extend at least two inches above the waistline. The kilt in (a) has an adequate rise, whereas the kilt in (b) has a skimpy rise. Tartans: Dress Wine Sutherland(a), Dress MacLeod of Harris (b).

kilt flares above the waist

a — good shaping

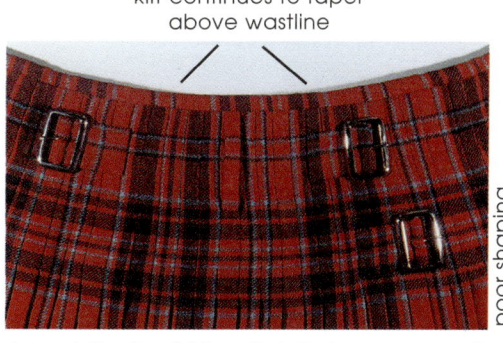

kilt continues to taper above wastline

b — poor shaping

flare above waist

Color Figure 11. Proper flare above the waist: a kilt should be slightly larger around at the very top than it is as the waistline, where the buckles lie. Kilt (a) will buckle tightly at the waist, because it is slightly larger around at the top and can accommodate the flare of the rib cage above the waist. Kilt (b) will not buckle tightly at the waist and will tend to sag, because the kilt tapers toward the top and is smallest around at the top of the kilt, not at the waistline. Tartans: Dress Blue Arisaid Hebridean (a), MacGillivray (b).

Workmanship

stitching

Color Figure 12. Stitching: pleat stitching should be essentially invisible (a). The stitching in kilt (b) shows because the stitches are too large, too far apart, and are sewn with non-matching thread. Tartan: Dress Wine Sutherland (a).

matching stripes

Color Figure 13. Matching stripes: stripes in a well-made kilt match perfectly across the back of the kilt, as they do in kilt (a). The mismatched stripes of kilt (b) are unsightly. Tartans: Dress Nova Scotia (a), Dress Royal Cunningham (b).

problems with mismatched stripes

Color Figure 14. Mismatched stripes are not only unsightly, but they can contribute to poor kilt hang. Because each pleat is offset upward by about $1/16$", the back of the kilt shown in (a) is about $3/4$" higher at the right hip than at the left hip. The apron cannot go straight across the front of the kilt but must rise from left hip to right hip, causing the apron to be skewed in an unsightly fashion (b).

poor pleats

Color Figure 15. Accurate pleating: pleats must taper smoothly from hip to waist, as they do in kilt (a), and must not pinch and swell, as they do in (b). Tartan elements that appear in a pleat must be straight and should not wander around in the pleat, as they do in kilt (c). Tartans: Dress Royal Menzies (a), Dress Merrilees (b), Dress Edinburgh (c).

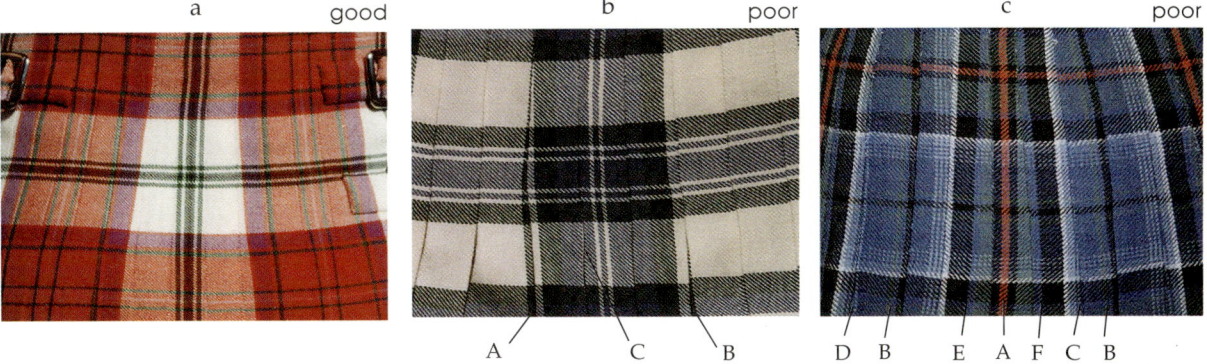

Color Figure 16. Proper pleating to the sett: a kilt pleated to the sett must reproduce the tartan accurately in the back of the kilt, as in kilt (a), without extra or missing stripes. The kilt in (b) has several extra stripes (at A, B, and C) that do not appear in the tartan but that appear in the pleats, because the pleats were not folded in the right place. The kilt in (c) has an astounding number of errors described in the text on page 27, including several missing or partially missing stripes (at B, C, and D) and lack of symmetry in the pleats (E and F). Tartans: Dress Crieff (a), Dress Arisaid Fraser (b).

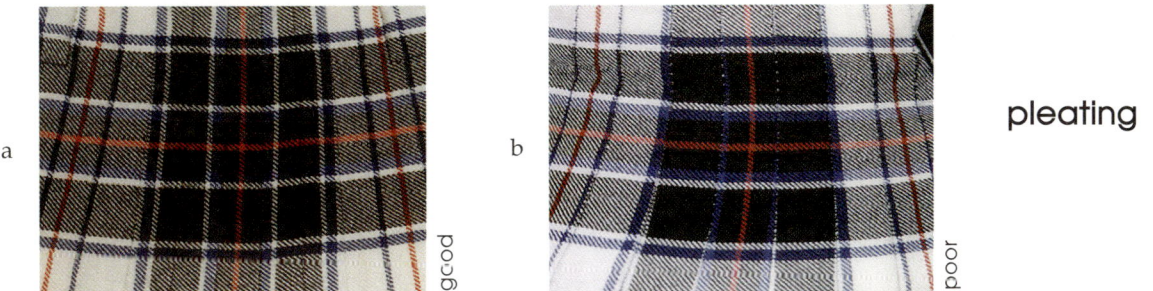

pleating

Color Figure 17. Some pleating choices are better than others. The kilt in (a) has the pleats folded in such a way that the prominent white stripes are preserved as the pleats taper toward the top of the kilt. The kilt in (b) loses the prominent white stripes as the pleats taper. Tartan: Dress MacRae.

Color Figure 18. Proper pleating to the stripe: a kilt pleated to the stripe must have the featured stripe centered in each pleat, as does the kilt in (a). The kilt in (b) is beautifully and uniformly pleated, but the light tan stripes are all off-center. The kilt in (c) is poorly pleated, and the white stripe is not centered in each pleat. Tartans: Fraser of Lovat (a), Weathered Henderson (b), MacGregor (c).

hems & buckles

Color Figure 19. Proper hem: if a kilt is hemmed, the hem should be essentially invisible, as it is in kilt (a). The hem should never make a ridge or bulge at the bottom of the kilt, as it does in kilt (b). The hip buckle in kilt (a) is placed correctly, about 5" below the kilt top; the hip buckle in kilt (b) is placed much too low. Tartan: Dress Wine Sutherland.

Color Figure 20. Black Watch tartan.

Color Figure 21. MacKenzie tartan (Black Watch sett with guarded red and white stripes in the overcheck).

Color Figure 22. Gordon tartan (Black Watch sett with yellow stripe in the overcheck).

|full repeat = 7 1/4"|

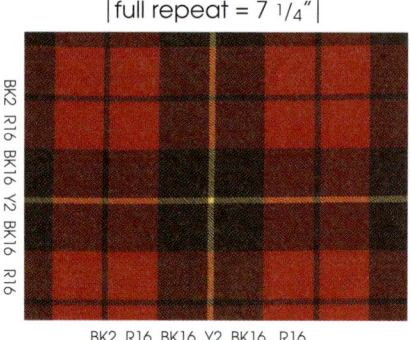

BK2 R16 BK16 Y2 BK16 R16

BK2 R16 BK16 Y2 BK16 R16

pivot (line of symmetry)

Color Figure 23. Wallace tartan; notice that the sett is the same in the warp and weft, which is characteristic of all true tartans.

Color Figure 24. Generic plaid fabric; notice that the sett is not the same in the warp and the weft. This is not tartan.

236 threads
| full repeat = 5 1/2" |

Color Figure 25. Cunningham tartan; symmetric, with a sett of 5 1/2".

|← full repeat = 8 1/2" (308 threads) →|

Color Figure 26. Weathered Ferguson tartan; symmetric, with a sett of 8 1/2".

|← full repeat = 12" (478 threads) →|

Color Figure 27. MacLachlan tartan, symmetric, with a sett of 12".

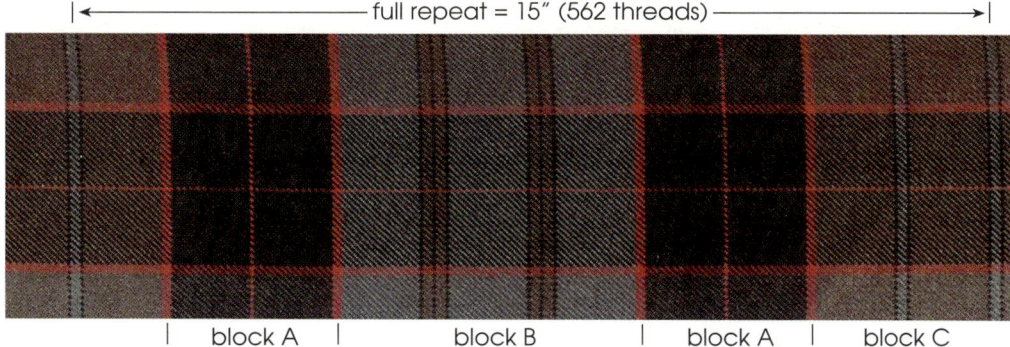

full repeat = 15" (562 threads)

block A | block B | block A | block C

Color Figure 28. Weathered Stewart Old Sett, symmetric, with a sett of 15".

Color Figure 29. Weathered MacKenzie tartan in two different weights, 12 ounce (left) and 16 ounce (right) The size of the sett increases with the weight of the fabric.

pivot (line of symmetry)

block A   block B   block A   block C

Color Figure 30. Ancient Campbell tartan; symmetric, with sett identical to the Black Watch in slightly lighter shades of blue and green.

NOT a line of symmetry

block A block B block C block D

Color Figure 31. Ancient Campbell of Argyll; asymmetric, with sett nearly identical to the Campbell. The additional yellow and white stripes are placed in such a way that no portion of the tartan is a mirror image of any other portion.

Color Figure 32. Color variations in the MacLean of Duart tartan. From left to right: Modern, Ancient, Weathered, Dress.

Color Figure 33. Color variations in the Hunting Ross tartan. From left to right: Modern, Ancient, Weathered, Dress.

Tartans

| a | b | c | d |

Color Figure 34. Wallace tartan (a) pleated to the sett (b) and to the stripe in two variations (c and d). Pleating to the black stripe in red produces a kilt that looks very different from one pleated to the yellow stripe in black!

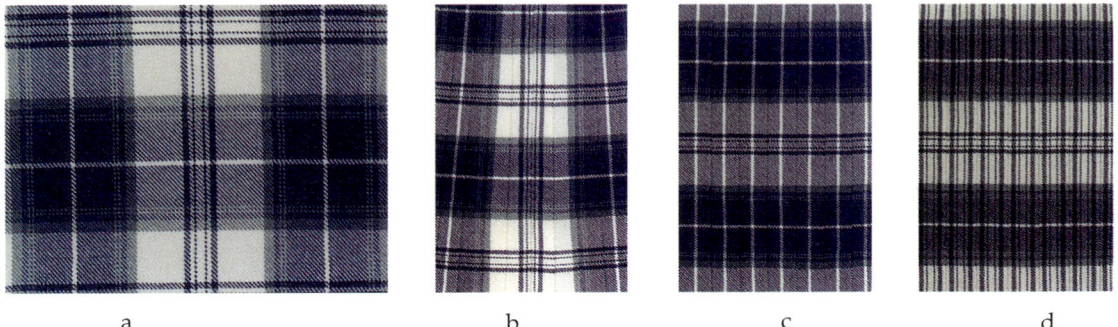

| a | b | c | d |

Color Figure 35. Dress Royal Menzies tartan (a) pleated to the sett (b) and to the stripe in two variations (c and d). While more than one option exists for pleating a tartan to the stripe, not all are pleasing. The variation in (d), for example, is terribly busy.

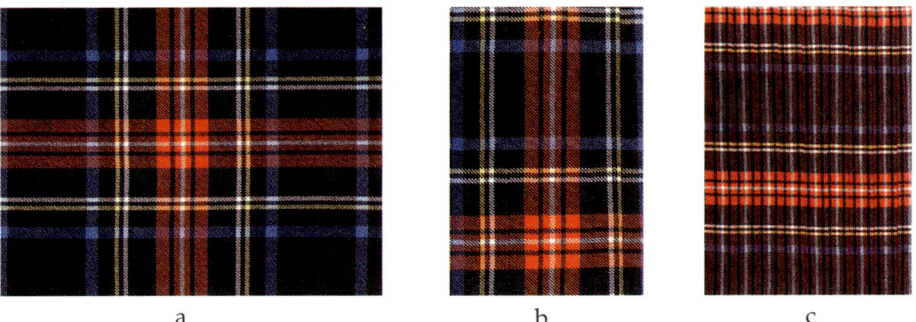

| a | b | c |

Color Figure 36. Black Stewart tartan (a) pleated to the sett (b) and to the stripe (c). The kilt pleated to the stripe in (c) would look reddish-purple from the back and black from the front.

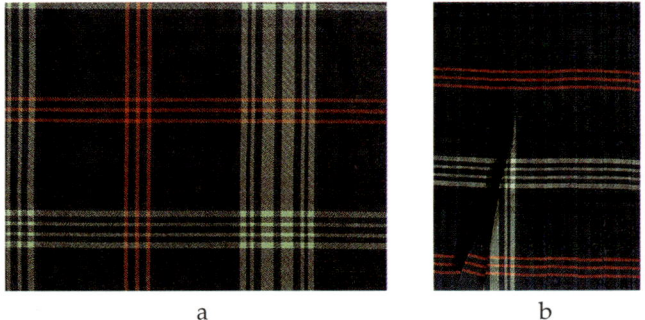

| a | b |

Color Figure 37. Hunting Ross tartan (a) pleated to the stripe. By pleating to the black and dark green stripe, the back of the kilt will look very dark but will open up to bright green as the wearer walks.

Chapter 2

A well-fitting, well-made kilt

Even a cursory examination of kilts at Highland games reveals that not all kilts fit well, nor are they all well-made. Because this book is designed to teach you how to construct a properly-fitting and well-made kilt, we ought to start with a discussion of what is and isn't a kilt, how a kilt should fit, and what a well-made kilt looks like.

What is a kilt?

A traditional kilt is a knee-length, hand-made garment of hard, worsted wool twill that wraps around the wearer and buckles at the waist. Only the back is pleated, and the front has two overlapping unpleated layers, the apron and the underapron. A kilt always wraps toward the right hip, and the fringe or open edge of the apron is always on the wearer's right side (Color Figures 2 and 3).

A kilt extends above the wearer's waist in a rise of at least two inches, a custom which originated as a way of keeping the wearer's midsection warm when a kilt was worn with the short jacket of the time. The rise means that the top of a kilt is designed to lie *above* a person's true waistline, which is significantly above the level at which many men wear their trousers.

Pleats in the back of a kilt are stitched part way down the back. The bottom of the fell (the stitched portion of the pleats) lies at the widest part of the buttocks so that the open part of the pleats falls straight and true from the buttocks to the bottom of the kilt.

A folklore of untruths exists about kilts. You may hear people say, "A woman's kilt opens on the left." *Not true.* All kilts open on the right. What these folks are undoubtedly referring to as a "woman's kilt" is, in fact, a kilt skirt. A kilt skirt, sometimes known as a hostess kilt, is not a kilt. Rather, it is a woman's pleated skirt made in lightweight tartan with machine-stitched pleats. Kilt skirts are commonly worn below the knee with the fringe edge at the wearer's left, rather than at the right. A kilt skirt requires much less cloth than a kilt and has wide, shallow pleats, no rise, and none of the interior construction of a kilt.

You may also hear people say, "A man's kilt is longer in the back than a dancer's kilt." *Not true.*

There's no such thing as a "dancer's kilt", and kilts for dance competitions are measured and laid out exactly the same way as a kilt for a man. This particular myth undoubtedly originated from the fact that many men wear their kilts buckled too loosely at the waist, with the result that the kilt sags in the back!

The bottom line is that there is really only one kind of kilt. Anyone who wears a kilt wears a garment that is laid out, stitched, and constructed by hand in exactly the same way, regardless of whether the wearer is a woman or a man, a piper or a dancer. While you might be able to guess from the measurements whether someone is making a kilt for a man or not, a kiltmaker would not do anything differently in making the kilt for a man or for a woman. The only differences from kilt to kilt involve size, amount of cloth, and style of pleating.

Pleating to the Stripe versus Pleating to the Sett

Color Figures 2 and 3 show the two different styles of pleating that can be used for a kilt. Color Figure 2 shows an Ancient Duncan kilt pleated to the sett. In a kilt pleated to the sett, the tartan in the back of the kilt is folded in such a way as to repeat the tartan pattern across the back of the kilt. A kilt pleated to the sett looks much the same from the back as it does from the front.

The Weathered Ferguson kilt in Color Figure 3 is pleated to the stripe, and every pleat has an identical stripe running down the center. This style of pleating is commonly called military pleating. The color figure shows clearly that a kilt pleated to the stripe looks very different from the back than it does from the front.

How should a kilt fit?

A kilt is a custom-made garment that should fit perfectly. In this section, we'll explore the elements that constitute good fit.

Length

The bottom of a kilt should come just to the top of the knee. Some prefer shorter kilts, but no one advocates longer ones. A kilt that is too long (Color Figure 4a) doesn't have enough bare leg between the top of the kilt hose and the bottom of the kilt. A kilt that is too short (Color Figure 4b) has too *much* bare leg between hose and kilt.

Size

The fringe of the apron edge should just cover the edge of the underapron. If the kilt is too small around (Color Figure 5a), the unpleated fabric of the underapron shows between the fringe and the pleats and looks unsightly. If the kilt is too big (Color Figure 5b), the apron edge covers part of the pleats. While this is less noticeable than having the underapron show, the center back stripe won't be centered in the exposed pleats if the apron edge extends over the pleats.

Shaping in the back

A well-fitting kilt snugs into the small of the back and flares over the buttocks while keeping the edge of the apron straight up and down (Color Figure 6a). Color Figure 6b shows how the shaping in the back is accomplished – by having pleats that are wider at the hips and narrower at the waist.

Pleats should be stitched from the top of the kilt to the widest part of the buttocks, about one third of the way down from top of the kilt. The stitched portion of the pleats is called the fell. Color Figures 7a and b show a kilt with a fell that is too short, only about one quarter the length of the kilt. The stitching clearly stops above the widest part of the buttocks, making the fell too short to control the swing of the kilt adequately. The fell in this kilt was originally one third of the length of the kilt. When the hem was let down as the child grew, however, the fell was not lengthened as well.

Color Figure 7c, on the other hand, shows a kilt with a fell that is much too long, extending nearly half the length of the kilt and well below the widest part of the buttocks. This kilt will not swing enough.

Shaping in the front

The apron of a kilt flares from waist to hem in a subtle A-line shape. If the apron has enough flare, the first pleat will lie closed and won't flap open (Color Figure 8a). If the apron doesn't have enough flare, the first pleat will tend to open even when the wearer is standing still (Color Figures 8b and c). For some body types, nothing can prevent the first pleat from flapping open. Any wearer with thick thighs will likely have a problem with the first pleat opening up regardless of the amount of flare.

Making a kilt for a woman with a small waist and wide hips demands significant shaping of the apron between hips and waist, and some kiltmakers solve the problem of shaping the apron by putting darts in the apron (Color Figure 9a). **A kilt should never be made with darts.** Darts are glaringly obvious in a kilt even from a distance and cause an unsightly bend in the tartan of the apron. All shaping in the apron should be done at the edges of the apron where the apron meets the fringe on the right and the pleats on the left (Color Figure 9b). Darts are, in fact, completely unnecessary if you follow the instructions given in this book.

Rise above the waist

A kilt should be made with a two inch rise above the waist. Because the buckles lie exactly at the waist, this means that the top of the kilt should be at least two inches above the center of the buckle. Color Figure 10a shows a kilt with an adequate rise. Color Figure 10b shows a kilt with a skimpy rise. If a dancer were to wear the latter kilt, her blouse would likely show above the top of her kilt as her vest pulled up when she raised her arms.

Flare above the waist

A kilt is buckled at the waist, which is the narrowest part of the torso. Everyone's torso, even that of a chubby person, flares above the buckle line of a tightly-buckled kilt. The top edge of a kilt should also flare slightly above the buckle line so that the kilt is slightly larger at the top edge than it is at the buckle line (Color Figure 11a). Such a kilt will stay put at the waist when it is buckled tightly.

A kilt that tapers above the buckle line, on the other hand, will be slightly smaller at the top edge of the kilt than at the waistline (Color Figure 11b). Because the smallest part of the kilt will tend to seek out the smallest body dimension, a kilt that is smaller at the top band than at the waist will be impossible to buckle tightly at the waist – it will tend to sag until the top band of the kilt rests at the waist.

What does a well-made kilt look like?

Workmanship is crucial to a sharp-looking kilt. In this section, we'll explore how to recognize top quality workmanship so that you know what to strive for in making your kilt!

Stitching

Pleats are stitched from the outside, and the stitches should be nearly invisible. Thread must match the pleat to be stitched, and stitches must be tiny and close together, catching only the very edge of the pleat. In a well-made kilt, you should be able to hear the stitches if you run your fingernail down the edge of a pleat, but you should not be able to see them (Color Figure 12a). The stitches in the kilt shown in Color Figure 12b are visible because they are too large, too far apart, and sewn with non-matching thread.

Matching stripes

Stripes must match perfectly across pleats in the back of the kilt. The instructions in this book will teach you how to match stripes precisely so that your finished kilt looks like Color Figure 13a, rather than like Color Figure 13b. There is no excuse for stair-step stripes.

Not only are mismatched stripes unsightly, but the resulting systematic offset can produce a cock-eyed kilt, particularly if the kilt is small. Color Figure 14a shows a small kilt with 21 pleats across the back. Each pleat is offset upward relative to its neighbor to the left by nearly $1/16$", making the back of the kilt a complex parallelogram about $3/4$" higher at the right hip than at the left hip. Although the child in the picture is standing completely straight, the kilt lies skewed across his back. Color Figure 14b shows that, not only does the kilt look odd from the back, but the apron hangs cock-eyed in the front. The apron top band starts at the left hip and must rise $3/4$" across the front of the body to meet the kilt at the right hip, which is higher because of the parallelogram shape of the kilt back. Viewed from the front, the top of the kilt is conspicuously lower at the left hip, and the apron is skewed in the front. The wearer is, in fact, standing straight, and the cock-eyed character of the kilt results directly from the fact that the kiltmaker did not match the stripes across the back of the kilt. No amount of tugging and smoothing can solve this problem.

Accurate pleating

Uniform width. Each pleat must taper smoothly in width from the bottom of the fell to the waistline (Color Figure 15a). The kilt shown in Color Figure 15b has several pleats that bulge and thin in an unsightly manner.

Straight tartan elements. Stripes and color boundaries must be absolutely straight and even in the pleats (Color Figure 15a). Color Figure 15c shows a poorly pleated kilt with several pleats in which stripes are wiggly or wander around within a pleat.

Accurate pleating to the sett. Repeating the tartan pattern across the back of a kilt requires careful planning and precise folding for each pleat (Color Figure 16a). Color Figure 16b shows a kilt that has not been pleated to reproduce the tartan pattern accurately, and additional stripes appear in various pleats. The narrow green stripes (at A and B) are not part of the tartan and represent errors in pleating, adding a narrow green and white pair that does not appear in the tartan. Both of these blocks were folded in the wrong place and should have been folded so that only white showed in each block. The narrow white stripe (at C) also does not belong and results from inaccurately folding the pleat.

Color Figure 16c shows a kilt with an astounding number of errors, all of which can be avoided by careful planning and workmanship. 1) The stripes are mismatched across the pleats. 2) The red stripe in the center back pleat (A) is centered at the top of the pleat but not at the bottom. It should be centered all the way down. 3) The pleat at B is folded in the wrong place, and the narrow green stripes to the right of the black stripe are missing. 4) The pleating also fails to reproduce other aspects of the tartan, which is a symmetric tartan. The pleats should show a set of three narrow white stripes on each side of the blue block. These stripes are entirely missing at C and mostly missing at D. 5) Pleats E and F should be identical, with the blue/black boundary in the same place in both pleats. 6) The twill line reverses in the middle of the back of the kilt! To the left of the red stripe, the twill line is correct, slanting from lower right to upper left. The right hand side, however, has the twill line slanting from lower left to upper right, which means that the right hand side of the kilt was pleated with the wrong side of the tartan facing up.

Some choices for pleating are more satisfactory than others. The tartan in the kilts shown in Color Figure 17 has four prominent narrow white stripes in the black block. The kilt in 17a has pleats folded in such a way as to preserve the prominent white stripes all the way up the pleats as they taper toward the top of the kilt. The kilt in 17b, however, has pleats folded in such a way that the white stripes disappear as the pleats taper. The kilt in 17b would have looked sharper had it been pleated to preserve this prominent tartan element.

Accurate pleating to the stripe. A kilt pleated to the stripe should have the prominent stripe *centered* in each pleat (Color Figure 18a). Color Figure 18b shows a beautifully pleated kilt with nice straight stripes, but the stripes are not centered in each pleat. They should be. Color Figure 18c shows a kilt in which the stripes were intended to lie in the centers of the pleats, but few stripes are actually centered. The kiltmaker did not take enough care to make sure that each pleat was precisely folded.

Hem

A kilt may be made with a hem. This may be merely desirable (*e.g.*, if the kilt is made for a growing child) or downright necessary (*e.g.*, if the tartan has a crummy selvedge). If a kilt has a hem, it should be carefully stitched so that the hem is not obvious. The instructions in this book will teach you how to make an invisible hem such as the one in the kilt in Color Figure 19a. There is no excuse for making a kilt with a conspicuous hem, such as the one in Color Figure 19b.

Buckle location

Some kilts have a hip buckle to hold down the fringe side of the apron. A man's kilt that will have a kilt pin does not need a hip buckle, nor does a small child's kilt. A larger kilt for a dancer benefits from a hip buckle to help keep the apron edge from flapping, because a dancer does not wear a kilt pin. A hip buckle should not be placed at the bottom of the fell, but somewhat higher, about five inches below the top edge of the kilt (Color Figure 19a). Color Figure 19b shows a kilt with a hip buckle located several inches too low.

Chapter 3

Understanding tartan

Most kilts are made from tartan, and understanding the language and structure of tartan is essential to working your way through this book. This chapter provides the basic information about tartan and the terminology that we will use throughout the book.

Tartan looks complicated but has, in fact, a very simple weave. The warp consists of a repeating pattern of stripes in various colors. The weft has the same stripes in precisely the same order. Intersections of warp and weft stripes produce the familiar color blocks, horizontal stripes, and vertical stripes of a tartan. Kilting tartan is traditionally woven as a straight twill in which each weft thread passes over and under two warp threads at a time, producing a diagonal weave pattern in the fabric threads. This diagonal weave pattern is referred to as the *twill line*. Tartan woven as plain weave does not have a diagonal weave pattern, because each weft thread passes over and under only one warp thread at a time.

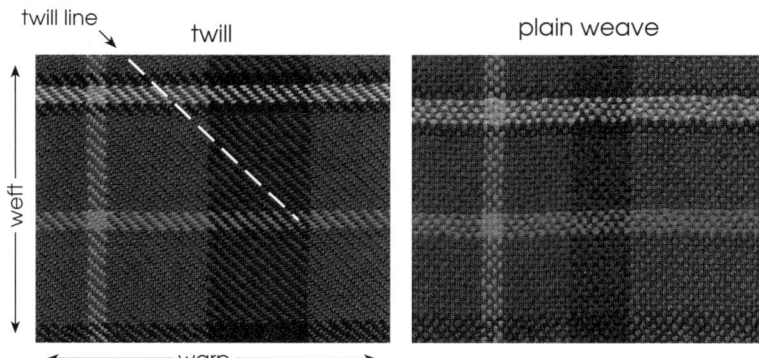

Sett

One way of describing a particular tartan is to list the precise proportions and sequence of colors in the tartan. This is called the sett, and it is unique to each tartan. The sett is very easily specified. The Wallace tartan in Color Figure 23, for example, has a sett that can be represented as BK2, R16, BK16, Y2, BK16, R16 which means a tartan woven with proportions of 2 black, 16 red, 16 black, 2 yellow, 16 black, 16 red. The sett is the minimum number of threads that completely defines the tartan, and a piece of fabric is created by repeating the sett in both the warp and weft of the fabric.

To be a true tartan, the sett must be identical in both warp and weft. Color Figure 23 shows that the proportions and sequence of colors for the Wallace is the same in both the warp and the weft. However, not all "plaid" fabric that one can find in fabric stores is actually tartan. Take for example the cotton fabric pictured in Color Figure 24. The sett is not the same in the warp and the weft, so this is not an example of tartan.

Recognizing the sett for a tartan is nothing more complicated than studying the tartan to determine where the tartan repeats itself. In Color Figure 25, the Cunningham repeats itself after 236 threads. The Weathered Ferguson (Color Figure 26) repeats itself after 308 threads, and the MacLachlan (Color Figure 27) after 478 threads. The Weathered Stewart Old Sett (Color Figure 28) repeats itself only after 562 threads! It's easy to make a mistake identifying the sett in the Stewart Old Sett. Block A, the prominent black block with a narrow red stripe, repeats every 280 threads, which could be mistaken for the repeat. The blocks *between* the A blocks, however, are not identical and, in fact, a full repeat consists of A-B-A-C, which stretches for 562 threads! Other tartans, including the MacLachlan (Color Figure 27) and the other members of the Black Watch family of tartans, have either an A-B-A-C or an A-B-C-D pattern in the large blocks (see, for example, the Ancient Campbell tartan in Color Figure 30 and the Ancient Campbell of Argyll in Color Figure 31). For tartans such as these, it pays to study the sett carefully in order not to make a mistake with the repeat.

The *size of the sett* is the number of inches in one full repeat. In the example of the Wallace tartan in Color Figure 23, the sett is 7 $^1/_4$". In other words, the pattern of stripes repeats itself identically every 7 $^1/_4$" in both the warp and the weft.

It's clear that different tartans will have different sett sizes because different tartans have different numbers of threads in the sett. The Cunningham in Color Figure 25 has a small sett measuring about 5 $\frac{1}{2}$". The Weathered Ferguson in Color Figure 26 has a medium sett of about 8 $\frac{1}{2}$". The MacLachlan in Color Figure 27 has a large sett of about 12", and the Weathered Stewart Old Sett (Color Figure 28) has a sett that is a whopping 15"! **The size of the sett is not simply a matter of academic interest**. As you will see in Chapter 4, the size of the sett governs how many pleats can be put into a kilt.

The size of the sett also varies with the weight of the fabric. Because the proportions in the written sett do *not* denote a particular size, "2 black" could mean 2 threads as fine as sewing thread or 2 threads as coarse as knitting yarn. "2 black" could also mean 2 inches of black, or even 2 *feet* of black. Woven in the proper proportions, the tartan with the sett shown in Color Figure 23 would still be Wallace, regardless of the scale of the tartan.

Color Figure 29 illustrates how the size of the sett varies with the weight of the fabric. The sett itself for each piece is identical, but the *size* of the sett increases with increasing weight of individual threads in the fabric. The lighter threads produce the smaller sett, while the heavier threads in the same proportions produce the larger sett. The general result is that heavier weight tartans commonly have larger setts than lighter weight tartans, because the threads are thicker.

In perfectly woven tartan, the twill line lies at a 45° angle to the warp and weft threads, because not only is the sett the same but each thread is exactly the same distance from its neighbor in the warp and in the weft. In a perfect 45° weave, the repeat measured parallel to the warp is therefore identical to that measured parallel to the weft. In reality, virtually all tartans are not perfect 45° weaves, and the repeat parallel to the warp is slightly longer than the repeat parallel to the weft. **This is important any time you want to match two pieces of tartan exactly**. Weft-wise pieces must be matched with weft-wise pieces, and warp-wise pieces with warp-wise ones. A piece cut parallel to the warp will have the same stripes in the same order as those in a piece cut parallel to the weft, but the width and spacing of stripes won't be quite the same.

Analyzing tartan components

The main component or background of a tartan is called the undercheck. The undercheck constitutes the large areas of color underlying the smaller stripes and bands of a tartan. Most tartans have a simple undercheck of two or three main colors. The Wallace (Color Figure 23) has a two-color undercheck consisting of alternating black and red.

The Black Watch (Color Figure 20) and all of its relatives that we've mentioned previously in several contexts have a three-color undercheck consisting of wide blue and green separated by narrower black.

The overcheck of a tartan consists of thinner stripes that break up and modify the large areas of color in the undercheck. The Wallace (Color Figure 23) has an overcheck with a black stripe centered in the red area of the undercheck and a yellow stripe centered in the black area of the undercheck. If we omitted the Wallace overcheck from the black and red undercheck pattern, we would have the Rob Roy tartan, one of the simplest tartans in existence. The Cunningham (Color Figure 25) has a different overcheck than the Wallace, but the undercheck is identical.

As mentioned above, every tartan in the Black Watch family has an identical undercheck. The overcheck is what distinguishes one tartan from another. Take the Gordon (Color Figure 22) and the Campbell (Color Figure 30) for instance, both of which have Black Watch underchecks. Replacing the yellow stripe of the Gordon overcheck with black gives us the Campbell overcheck.

Tartan symmetry

Most tartans have symmetrical setts. Symmetrical tartans have symmetry lines, called pivots, across which the colors repeat identically in both directions. The sett for a simple symmetrical tartan such as the Wallace, illustrates the concept of symmetry. In Color Figure 23, Y2 (yellow) represents a pivot, and it's easy to see that the tartan has identical stripes in both directions from the Y2 element. Color Figure 30 shows the Ancient Campbell tartan, which is also symmetrical. Although the sett is more complicated than that of the Wallace, the blue stripe in the center of block B represents a pivot with stripes repeating identically in both directions from that element.

The sett for the Ancient Campbell of Argyll, on the other hand (Color Figure 31), illustrates an asymmetric (non-centering, non-matching) tartan, in which the tartan does *not* repeat identically in each direction from an apparent line of symmetry. While the blue stripe in the center of block B *appears* to be a line of symmetry in the tartan, all color elements are mirror images *except* the white stripe to the left and the yellow stripe to the right. This makes the tartan asymmetric – it can't be folded along any single tartan element to match identically.

Of the hundreds of registered tartans, only a few are asymmetric, and those include Buchan, Buchanan and Hunting Buchanan (but not Old

Buchanan or Dress Buchanan), Campbell of Argyll, Dress Campbell, Drummond of Strathallen, MacAlpine, Dress MacDonald, Old Macmillan, Malcolm, Hunting Stewart, and the Ontario and Québec provincial tartans.

Types of tartan

The Official Registry of All Publicly Known Tartans, maintained by the Scottish Tartans Society in Pitlochry, Scotland[1], is a record of all recognized tartans, which numbered over 2500 by the year 2000. Many of the tartans are the familiar ones of the clans of Scotland, such as MacBeth, Douglas, Campbell, Ferguson, and MacDonald. District tartans have been created and adopted for places such as Edinburgh, Glasgow, and Dundee. The clergy have a tartan, as do many military units, such as the former RCAF, the U.S. Marine Corps, and the U.S. Navy. Some U.S. States and all of the Canadian provinces have tartans, such as the New Hampshire and Nova Scotia tartans. The U.S. even has a bicentennial tartan, which is red, white, and blue (*quelle surprise...*). New tartans are added to the registry at the rate of 25-35 per year. Appendix F lists a number of sources for good color images of tartans, including catalogs and web sites.

Registered tartans fall into the following groups:

Clan tartans: A clan tartan is the official registered sett of a clan or family. Technically speaking, only those affiliated with a clan or who have clan ancestry should wear a particular clan tartan, although practical usage in the modern world does not proscribe wearing a tartan that is not your own. Use your own good sense when choosing a tartan, and recognize that a clan tartan is a very strong symbol of kinship. The chief's tartan, on the other hand, is a personal tartan, and it is exceedingly poor taste for anyone but the chief to wear it. The clan chief's tartan commonly differs from the clan tartan by the addition of a stripe or stripes.

Hunting tartans. Hunting versions of tartans were created with darker colors so that the wearer would blend in more easily with the Scottish countryside. In a hunting tartan, one or more of the colors in the undercheck is replaced with a darker color by substituting, for example, brown for a red portion of the undercheck. Hunting tartans are a 19th century invention. Even as late as 1839, only one hunting tartan was listed in Wilson and Sons "Key Pattern Book" of tartans, the Hunting Stewart, and that tartan is now recognized as neither a hunting tartan nor a Stewart tartan. In fact, the Hunting Stewart,

despite its name, is considered a universal tartan, one that anyone can wear.

Regimental tartans: As discussed in Chapter 1, the first official, regularized tartan was the regimental tartan of the Black Watch Highland Regiment. Other tartans have been created, adapted, or adopted for various regiments, including the Dress Erskine for the Royal Scots Fusiliers, the Leslie for the King's Own Scottish Borderers, and the Royal Stewart for pipers in the royal regiments. The Black Watch regimental tartan is considered a universal tartan, and anyone can wear it.

District tartans. A district tartan is one that can be worn by someone who has an affiliation with a district, regardless of clan affinity. Some district tartans are probably quite old. Wilson and Sons of Bannockburn's 1819 Pattern Book includes a tartan labeled as the Mull or Glen Lyon District tartan that may quite genuinely have been associated with the region. Having one or two patterns that seemed to have genuine district affinities, though, Wilson and Sons happily named a range of new tartans after towns, cities, and districts, and it is difficult to tell which tartans may have had genuine original affinities. Other officially adopted district tartans are quite new, and still other tartans with district names have been introduced as trade tartans (see below) in the hopes that the district, town, or region will adopt them in the future.

Royal tartans. Many tartans are closely connected with the British Royal Family. The bright red Royal Stewart, without doubt the best known of all Scottish tartans, was first worn by King George IV on his visit to Edinburgh in 1822. The tartan was later adopted for the House of Windsor by King George V, who is reputed to have said that it could be worn by all members of his family. At the time, his "family" was interpreted as all people in the British Empire,[2] which undoubtedly contributed to the wide commercial use of the tartan. Other royal tartans, such as the Balmoral, should never be worn by someone outside the Royal Family.

Corporate tartans. A corporate tartan is a tartan invented for a corporation. "Corporations" include businesses, societies, associations, etc. Many corporate tartans have been created since the first corporate tartan was registered in 1987 for Highland Spring. For the past two years, new corporate tartans have been added to the Tartan Registry at the rate of over 30 each year. New corporate tartans also include State tartans from the United States (*e.g.*, the New Hampshire tartan), regional tartans from New Zealand (*e.g.*, the Glenfalloch tartan), and commemorative tartans (such as the Diana, Princess of Wales commemorative tartan).

Trade tartans. Trade tartans are created by weaving houses and commercial concerns, are given names, and are recorded with the Tartan Registry. These tartans become official tartans in the sense of having been recorded. Regardless of their names, however, they have no official affiliation with a clan, district, or organization until they are officially adopted by that entity, in which case they cease to be trade tartans and become, for example, an official district tartan. The Irish District tartans introduced in 1996 by House of Edgar are a good example of trade tartans that are not official district tartans but that may become so in the future if officially adopted by the Irish Districts. The Scottish National tartan and the new McLlennium (Scottish Millennium) tartan are examples of trade tartans.

Color variations in tartans

Many tartans are currently woven in modern, ancient, weathered or reproduction, and dress color variations. Color Figures 32 and 33 compare the MacLean of Duart and the Hunting Ross in each of these variations. Note that the setts for the variations of each tartan are the same but that the colors of the undercheck and overcheck vary.

- **Modern tartan:** Tartans woven in modern colors have the strong colors of modern dyes and are woven according to modern registered setts.

- **Ancient tartan:** Tartans woven in "ancient colors" are created to look like tartan woven with vegetable dye stuffs before the advent of modern dyes.

- **Weathered and reproduction tartan:** Tartans woven in weathered and reproduction colors are typically dominated by muted browns, khaki, slate blues, mustard yellows, and faded reds. These tartans go further than the ancient tartans in attempting to reproduce the effect of vegetable dyes after they have faded naturally.

- **Dress tartan:** Dress tartans are those that have been created from clan tartans with a dark undercheck by replacing portions of the undercheck with white (*e.g.*, the Dress Hunting Ross, as shown in Color Figure 33) or with a brighter color (*e.g*, the bright yellow of the Dress Barclay and the Dress MacLeod, fondly nicknamed the Loud MacLeod). Like hunting tartans, dress tartans are a 19th and 20th century invention. Not a single dress tartan is listed in Wilson and Sons of Bannockburn's 1839 "Key Pattern Book" of tartans. So, how were dress tartans developed? Before the adoption of clan tartans, tartan with substantial white in the undercheck was commonly used in the arisaids worn by Highland ladies. The 19th century revival in Highland dress produced a desire to have "evening dress" tartans that differed from the dark clan tartans adopted earlier in the century. The idea of a white-based sett patterned after traditional arisaid colors was combined with the dark clan tartans to produce dress versions with substantial white in the undercheck. Dress tartans also may eliminate one or more of the overchecks in the regular clan sett. Because dress tartans are something of a modern amalgamation of recognized clan tartans with an arisaid-type design, some clan chiefs do not recognize the dress versions of their tartans.

Dress tartans are very popular among Highland dancers, because dress tartans generally stand out better on stage than darker clan tartans. The demand for tartan by dancers has resulted in the recent creation of many color variations of the same dress tartan. The Dress Cunningham, for example, is available in regular dress colors (red), plus Royal (Color Figure 13b), Green, Purple, and Burgundy variations. The Dress Menzies, as another example, is available in Royal (Color Figure 35), Red, Purple, Green, Blue, and Black variations.

---

[1] The Official Registry of All Publicly Known Tartans, Port-na-Craig Road, Pitlochry, Scotland, PH16 5ND, Scotland; Tel: 011-44-1-796-474079; Fax 011-44-1-796-474090; e-mail: info@tartans.scotland.net; web site: http://www.tartans.scotland.net/

[2] Blair Urquhart (ed.), *Tartans: The Illustrated Identifier to over 140 designs* (London, Apple Press, 1994), p. 73.

Chapter 4

Understanding the structure of a kilt

We hope that you'll take a little time to understand kilts and pleats before you embark on making your kilt. In this chapter, we'll help you understand how the tartan you've chosen and the size of the person you're making the kilt for influence how many pleats a kilt will have, how wide those pleats will be, and how deep.

The general structure of a kilt

In order to understand the structure of a kilt, start by visualizing a gathered skirt. The waistband fits the wearer snugly, and 2, 5, or even 10 yards of fabric are fitted to the waistband by gathering the fabric and stitching it to the waistband.

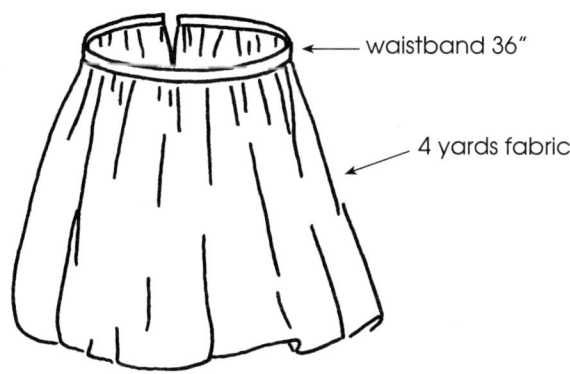

waistband 36"

4 yards fabric

A kilt is, many respects, the same type of garment. Think of a kilt as a length of cloth that is pleated, rather than gathered, to a waistband of the right length to fit the wearer. The differences between a kilt and a gathered skirt are that, in a kilt, the waistband overlaps in the front, and virtually all of the cloth is fitted to the *back* part of the waistband by folding the fabric into pleats instead of gathers.

Suppose that we wanted to make a kilt to fit someone who is about 36" around at the waist. Because only the back of the kilt is pleated, half the circumference (18") will be pleated, and half (18") won't. Because the front section is overlapping, the finished kilt will have an 18" wide unpleated section in the front (the underapron), an 18" pleated section in the back, and another 18" wide unpleated section in the front again that will completely overlap the underapron section. If this were a gathered skirt, the total waistband length would have to be

36". Because this is a kilt with an overlapping front, however, the total waistband length will need to be 36" + 18", or 54" total.

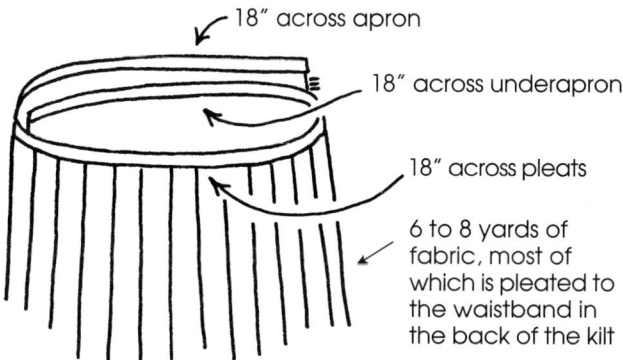

18" across apron

18" across underapron

18" across pleats

6 to 8 yards of fabric, most of which is pleated to the waistband in the back of the kilt

Well, where does that leave us? Let's think about the yardage and pleating of our hypothetical kilt. A kilt is typically made from a 6- to 8-yard length of fabric. Each apron front will need 18" of fabric, so the total length of fabric in the aprons will take up 36", or 1 yard of fabric stitched flat to 1 yard of waistband split in half on either side of the pleats in the back. You'll also use up about a yard in various facings and underfolds on each side of the apron and underapron (shown schematically as the shaded areas below).

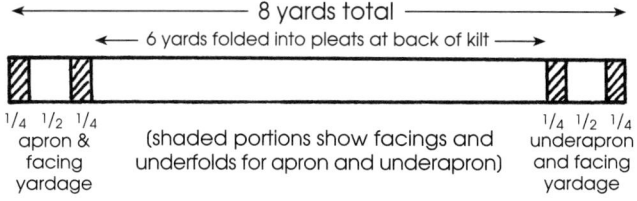

8 yards total

6 yards folded into pleats at back of kilt

1/4 1/2 1/4 apron & facing yardage

(shaded portions show facings and underfolds for apron and underapron)

1/4 1/2 1/4 underapron and facing yardage

The entire remaining length of kilt fabric, regardless of whether it is 4 yards, 5 yards, 6 yards, or 7 yards, must be folded into pleats and stitched to 18" ($\frac{1}{2}$ yard) of waistband in the back. The number of inches of fabric in the back of a kilt is typically *10 times* the length of the waist band in the back of the kilt!

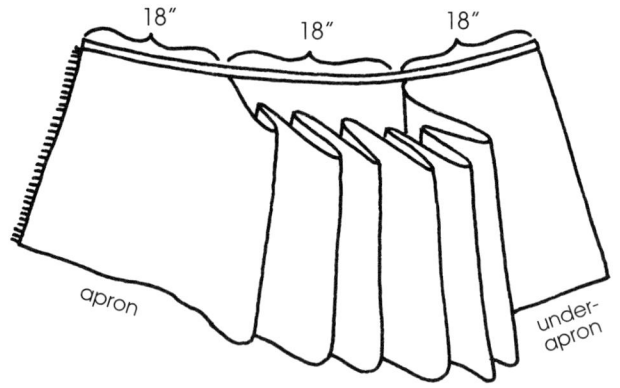

The diagram at the bottom of this page shows a complete "parts diagram" for a finished kilt, with the terms used to describe the major elements of a kilt. Wrapped around the wearer, the apron laps to the *right* over the underapron, with the pleats in the back, and the kilt is secured by buckles at the waistline. The extension of the kilt above the waistline is called the *rise*. Pleats are always folded toward the right hip and are stitched from the top of the kilt to the bottom of the fell, about ⅓ of the way down the kilt. A deep pleat underlies the left apron edge, and a box pleat (the inverted pleat) underlies the right underapron edge.

Understanding Pleats in a Self-Color Kilt

In order to understand the structure of a kilt, we'll start by examining a self-color (solid color) kilt, so that the presence of a tartan pattern does not confuse the picture for the moment. Kilts are, in fact, sometimes made in solid colors, and some pipe bands and military regiments have self-color kilts. Navy, green, khaki, or saffron are commonly used.

Let's suppose that our self-color kilt will be an 8-yard kilt for a person with a waist of about 36". If 1 yard goes into the two aprons and 1 yard goes into facings and such, that leaves us with 6 yards to fit into 18" across the back (that's 216" to compress into a distance of 18"!). There's more than one way to do this. Here are some of the possible choices:

- Choice 1: We might choose to make only a few big pleats. If we divided the fabric evenly into

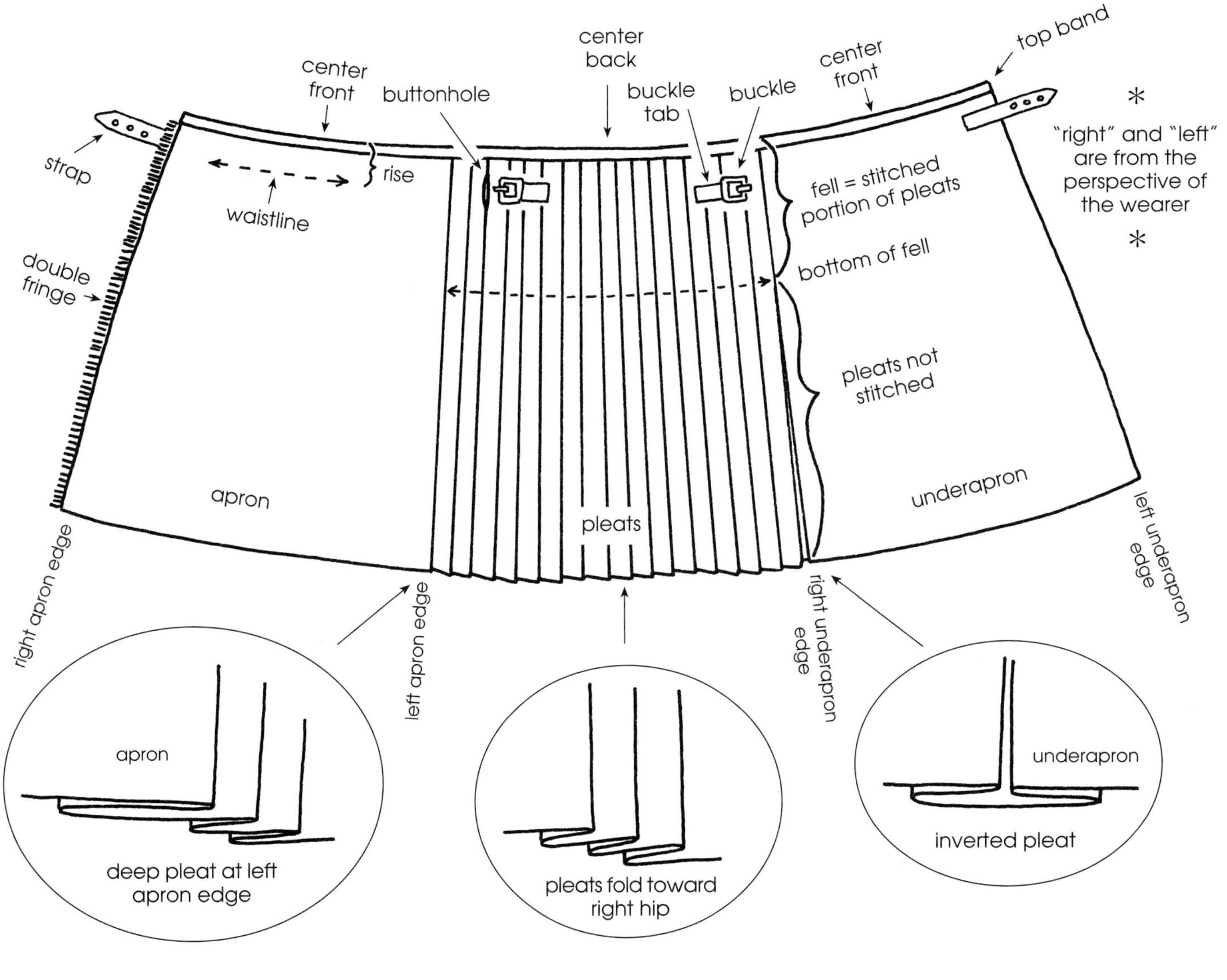

center front
buttonhole
center back
buckle tab
buckle
center front
top band
strap
rise
waistline
double fringe
right apron edge
apron
left apron edge
pleats
fell = stitched portion of pleats
bottom of fell
pleats not stitched
right underapron edge
underapron
left underapron edge

* "right" and "left" are from the perspective of the wearer *

apron
deep pleat at left apron edge

pleats fold toward right hip

underapron
inverted pleat

34

10 pleats, for example, each pleat would be about 10" deep, and each pleat would be almost 2" across.

- Choice 2: We might choose to make lots of little bitty pleats. If we divided the fabric evenly into 50 pleats, each pleat would be less than 2" deep, and each pleat would be only about $3/8$" across.

- Choice 3: We might choose to make an intermediate number of medium size pleats. If we divided the fabric evenly into 25 pleats, each pleat would be about 4" deep and would be about $3/4$" across.

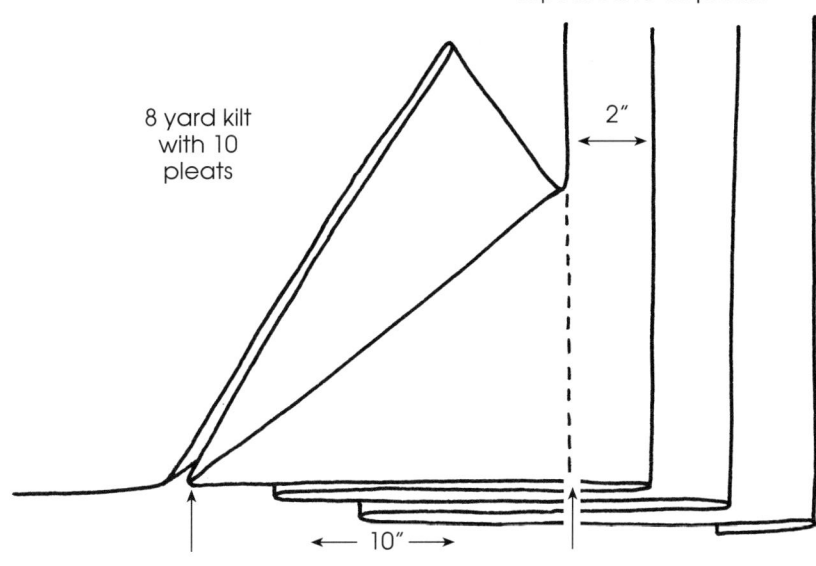

8 yard kilt with 10 pleats

repeated to 10 pleats →

What's crucial to understand at this point is that the same amount of solid color cloth can be divided into different numbers of pleats.

If a kilt has more pleats, each pleat will be shallower in depth and smaller across for a given amount of fabric. If a kilt has fewer pleats, each pleat will be greater in depth and bigger across for a given amount of fabric.

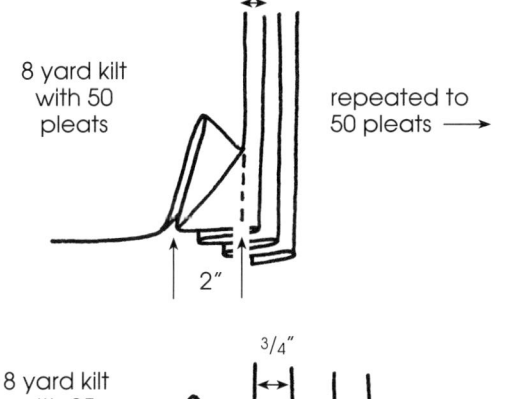

8 yard kilt with 50 pleats

repeated to 50 pleats →

What do pleat size and pleat depth mean??

In talking about a kilt, we need to be able to specify how big across the pleats are and how deep the underfold is for each pleat. The picture below illustrates the terms that we'll use throughout this book:

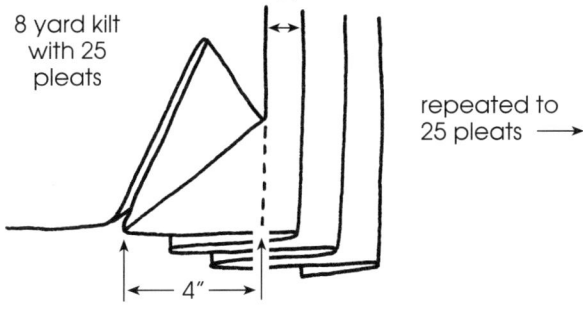

8 yard kilt with 25 pleats

repeated to 25 pleats →

- **pleat size.** The width of the pleat that you see when you look at the back of a kilt.

- **pleat depth.** The extent of the underfold for a pleat. You cannot see the depth of a pleat when you are looking at the back of a kilt unless you open up the pleat.

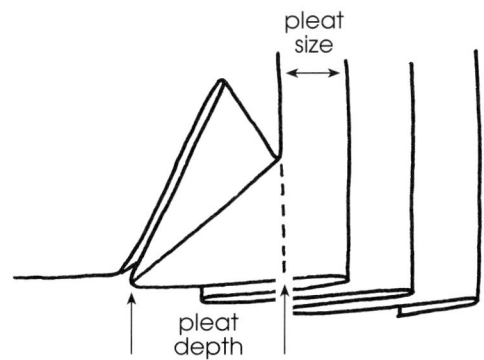

pleat size

pleat depth

Here's a common misunderstanding.

Someone comes to you and says, "I had a kilt made, and they put 7 $1/2$ yards of material into it, and it's *still* too small. I wish they'd put 8 yards into my kilt." Well, hogwash! The problem lies not in the amount of cloth but in the overall size of the kilt. If the size at the waistband is too short, cramming another six yards into the pleats isn't going to make the kilt fit better, any more than adding fabric to a gathered *skirt* will make the skirt fit if the waistband is too tight. The *only* solution is to make the kilt larger at the waistband.

Determining the number of pleats in a self-color kilt

Suppose that you were to go ahead and make your self-color kilt. Without a tartan to constrain the pleating, you simply need to pick the number of pleats that will make a reasonable pleat size and depth given the amount of fabric you have. The Goldilocks principle applies here – you don't want pleats that are too big, and you don't want pleats that are too small. A kilt should have pleats that are just right. **Pleats no smaller than $1/2$" and no larger than 1" look best.**

The relationship between the amount of cloth, pleat size, and pleat depth in a self-color kilt

Let's see what happens if we change the amount of material in our self-color kilt **but keep the same number of pleats.** Let's use the same person with a circumference of 36". As discussed above, any kilt we devise for this person will have roughly 18" of fabric in each of the aprons, or one yard total devoted to the aprons plus another yard in facings and such. The remaining fabric will be folded into 25 pleats and attached to 18" of back waistband. Here are some examples of what will happen if we change the yardage in the kilt but keep the number of pleats the same:

- Example 1, an 8-yard kilt: This was our original example above. With one yard taken up in the aprons and one yard in facings and such, we have 6 yards left over for the pleats. If we divided the fabric evenly into 25 pleats, each pleat would be about 4" inches deep and would be about $3/4$" across.

- Example 2, a 7-yard kilt: With one yard taken up in the aprons and one yard in facings and such, we have 5 yards left over to fold into 18" across the back. If we divided the fabric evenly into 25 pleats, each pleat would be about $3 1/4$" inches deep and would be about $3/4$" across.

- Example 3, a 6-yard kilt: With one yard taken up in the aprons and one yard in facings and such, we have 4 yards left over for the pleats. If we divided the fabric evenly into 25 pleats, each pleat would be about $2 1/2$" inches deep and would be about $3/4$" across.

If we arbitrarily set the number of pleats, as we would in a self-color kilt, the size of each pleat remains the same, even though we add more cloth to the kilt. What changes is the depth of each pleat.

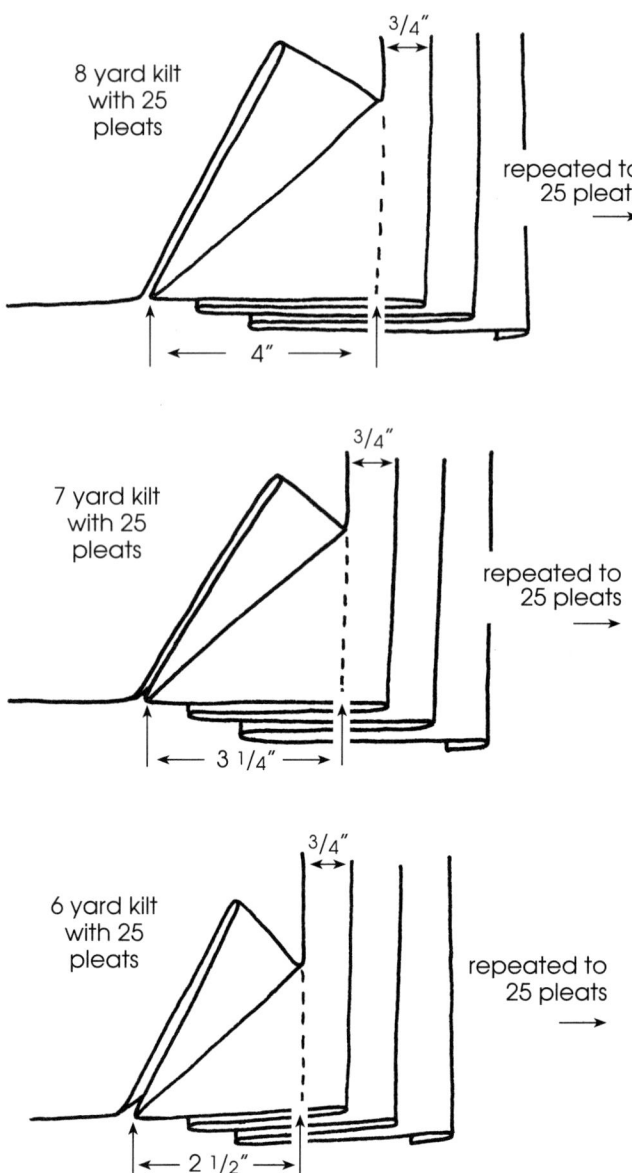

Understanding how tartan influences pleating a kilt

In the previous section, we began to look at the structure of a kilt, and we used a simple example of a self-color kilt. You learned that a self-color kilt could be pleated arbitrarily anywhere along the fabric to give as many pleats as desired. The presence of a tartan repeat, however, introduces complexities in pleating that aren't present in the self-color kilts that we've considered so far.

In the course of this section, we will show you that:

- the pleats in a tartan kilt cannot be located arbitrarily, as they can in a self-color kilt. In a tartan kilt, pleats are located at certain places in the sett in order to produce a pattern across the back of the kilt. In other words, the tartan dictates the location of pleats.

- the presence of a tartan repeat means that the size, number, and depth of pleats are not infinitely adjustable, as they are in a self-color kilt (as discussed previously).

- in a tartan kilt, the issues of how many pleats a kilt will have, what size they will be, and how deep they will be are complicated and inter-related. In this section, we will explore the structure of a tartan kilt by looking at the inter-relationships among the following six factors:

  - the number of pleats – the size of the kilt
  - the size of pleats   – yardage in the kilt
  - the depth of pleats   – the size of the sett

- the following interrelationships apply to tartan kilts:

  - **The number of pleats is determined by a combination of how much material you have (yardage) and by the size of the tartan sett.**

  - **The depth of the pleats is determined solely by the tartan sett.**

  - **The size of the pleats is determined by a combination of the size of the kilt and by how much material you have.**

Influence of yardage and sett on the number of pleats in a kilt

How *many* pleats will a kilt have? In a self-color kilt, you can simply choose the number of pleats arbitrarily, as you saw earlier in this chapter. In a kilt made from tartan, however, the number of pleats depends on how much cloth you have (the yardage) and on the size of the sett of the tartan. Let's see why this is the case by working through an example.

Suppose that we want to make a military-pleated kilt out of the Weathered Ferguson tartan. Military-pleated kilts are pleated to the stripe, meaning that the same stripe runs down the center of every pleat in the back of the kilt (Color Figure 3).

Let's imagine making a kilt for a hypothetical person who is about 36" around at the waist. As illustrated on page 34, half the circumference of the kilt (18") will be pleated, and half (18") won't. With an overlapping apron, we will need to reserve 18" of fabric for the apron and another 18" for the underapron, or one yard total. We'll also need to reserve 1 yard for facings and underfolds at the apron. The rest will be folded into pleats across the 18" back of the kilt.

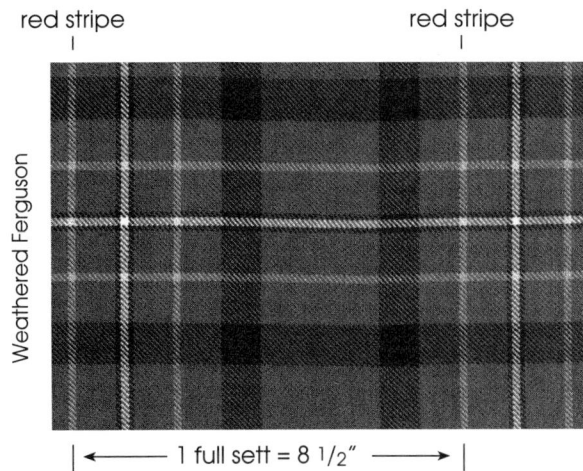

red stripe   red stripe

Weathered Ferguson

| ←———— 1 full sett = 8 ½" ————→ |

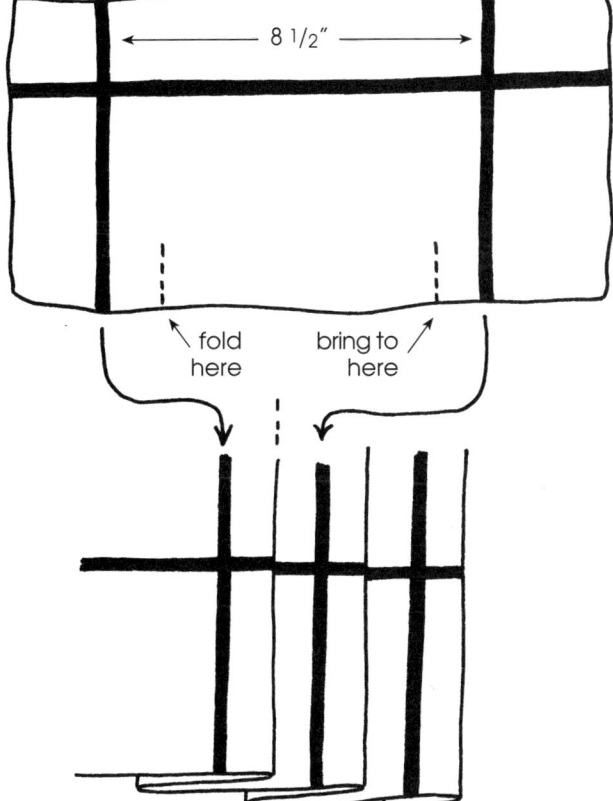

←——— 8 ½" ———→

fold here   bring to here

Let's start by looking at the Weathered Ferguson tartan itself (shown above in black and white and in color in Color Figures 3 and 26). One full sett can be measured from the center of one red stripe to the next. In this case, the sett is about 8 ½".

Suppose that we decide to put a prominent red stripe down the center of each pleat. We would fold the tartan to place a red stripe down the center of each pleat.

How many pleats will the kilt have? **It depends upon how much material we have.** Here are three examples to illustrate why this is so:

- Suppose we put 8 yards of Weathered Ferguson tartan into the kilt. With one yard taken up in the aprons and one yard in facings and such, we will have 6 yards left over to fold into 18" across the back. With an 8 1/2" sett, we will have 25 red stripes in the material that we will have available for pleating. This means that we will have 25 pleats, one for each red stripe.

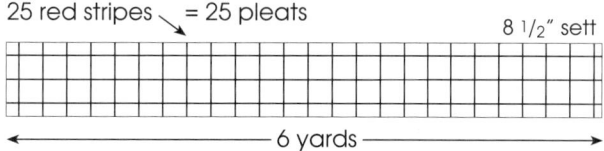

- Suppose we put 7 yards of Weathered Ferguson tartan into the kilt. With one yard taken up in the aprons and one yard in facings and such, we will have 5 yards left over to fold into 18" across the back. With an 8 1/2" sett, we will have 21 red stripes in the material that we will have available for pleating. This means that we will have 21 pleats, one for each red stripe.

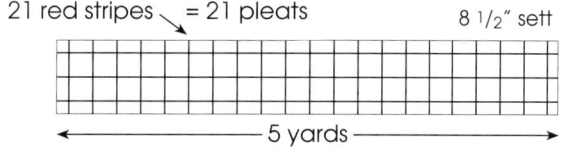

- Suppose we put 6 yards of Weathered Ferguson tartan into the kilt. With one yard taken up in the aprons and one yard in facings and such, we will have 4 yards left over to fold into 18" across the back. With an 8 1/2" sett, we will have 17 red stripes in the material that we will have available for pleating. This means that we will have 17 pleats, one for each red stripe.

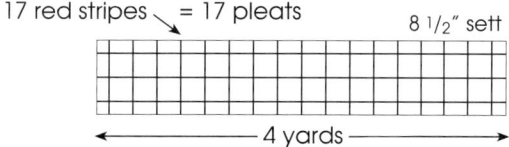

It is clear from these examples that the number of pleats is not arbitrary when pleating a tartan, as it would be in a self-color kilt. The tartan governs the size of the repeat, and the length of the fabric governs the number of repeats, and hence the number of pleats. Another way of saying this is that **the size of the sett and the amount of yardage determine the number of pleats.** The same thing holds true for a kilt pleated to the sett as it does for our

military-pleated example, although the pleating is a bit more complicated (which we deal with in chapter 7).

Let's look at two other examples to consolidate this point.

- Suppose that we wanted to make a military-pleated kilt with the Cunningham tartan (Color Figure 25) with a double red stripe centered in each pleat. The sett, 5 1/2", is much smaller than that of the Weathered Ferguson. We'll use the same amount of material as we did for our hypothetical Weathered Ferguson kilt, and we'll make the kilt the same size. With one yard taken up in the aprons and one yard in facings and such, we will have 6 yards left over to fold into 18" across the back. With a 5 1/2" sett, we will have 39 double red stripes in the material that we have available for pleating. This means that the kilt will have 39 pleats.

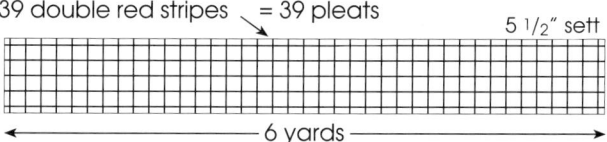

For the same amount of material, the Weathered Ferguson tartan would have made only 25 pleats, because the sett is larger.

- Suppose that we wanted to make a military-pleated kilt with the Weathered Stewart Old Sett (Color Figure 28), and we'll center a gray stripe in each pleat. The sett is huge – nearly 15". We'll use 8 yards of material and make the kilt the same size as the one in the Weathered Ferguson and Cunningham examples above. With one yard taken up in the aprons and one yard in facings and such, we will have 6 yards left over to fold into 18" across the back. With a 15" sett, we will have only 14 gray stripes in the material that we have available for pleating. **This means that the kilt will have only 14 pleats.**

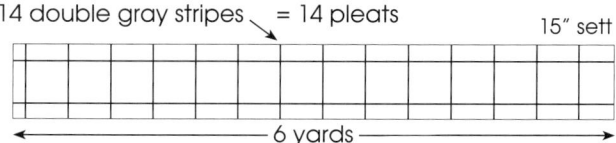

For the same amount of material, the Weathered Ferguson tartan would have made 25 pleats, and the Cunningham would have made 39 pleats.

In summary, then, if a kilt is made from tartan, the number of pleats depends upon the size of the sett and the amount of cloth you have. With the same amount of cloth in two kilts of the same size, the tartan with the larger sett will make fewer pleats than the tartan with the smaller sett. With a gigantic sett, even 8 yards of material may not be sufficient to make enough pleats for the kilt to look attractive.

Influence of sett on the depth of pleats

What governs how deep the pleats will be in a kilt? Remember that pleat depth is the extent of the *hidden underfold*.

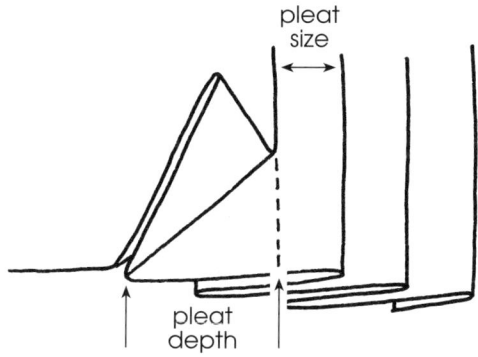

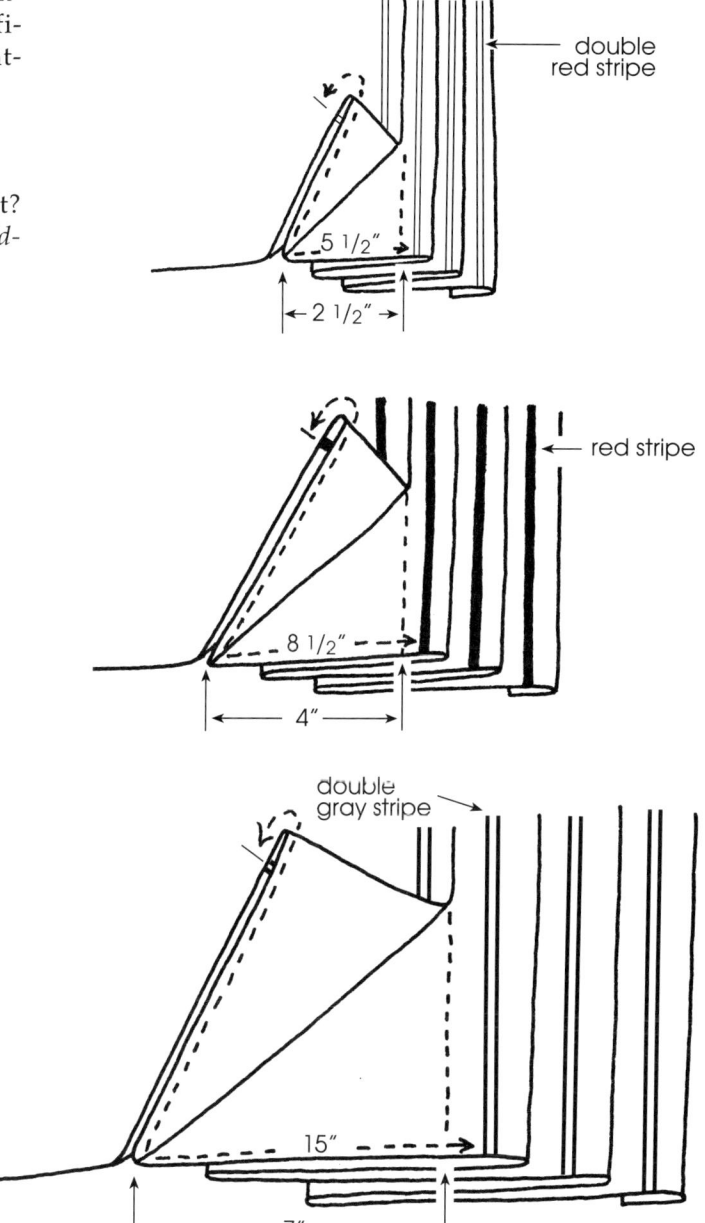

In a self-color kilt, you can simply choose to make a pleat as deep as you want, as you saw earlier in this chapter. In a tartan kilt, however, pleat depth depends *solely* on the size of the sett and is *independent* of how much cloth goes into a kilt. Let's explore an example to see why this is true.

Suppose we were to make a military-pleated kilt for our hypothetical person who is about 36" around at the waist. Let's look at a kilt made for this person in three different tartans, with three different setts. Each kilt will be the *same size* and will have the *same amount of yardage* (8 yards). Let's assume for each kilt that we will need to pleat 6 yards into 18" across the back of the kilt:

- Example 1, a kilt made from Cunningham tartan, with a 5 $^1/_2$" sett: 6 yards of cloth in the back of the kilt will have 39 repeats of the sett, giving 39 pleats each with a a pleat size of just under $^1/_2$" and a depth of about 2 $^1/_2$".

- Example 2, a kilt made from Weathered Ferguson tartan, with an 8 $^1/_2$" sett: 6 yards of cloth in the back of the kilt will have 25 repeats of the sett, giving 25 pleats each with a pleat size of $^3/_4$" and a depth of about 4". Pleats are deeper in the

Weathered Ferguson than in the Cunningham, because the sett is bigger in the Ferguson.

- Example 3, a kilt made from Stewart Old Sett, with a 15" sett: 6 yards of cloth in the back of the kilt will have only 14 repeats of the sett, giving 14 pleats each with a pleat size of 1 $^1/_4$" and a depth of about 7".

Here's a common misunderstanding.

Someone asks, "How many pleats should a kilt have?" Well, there's no answer to that question! In the example above, it's clear that the same amount of fabric will make a different number of pleats in the Weathered Ferguson, the Stewart Old Sett, and the Cunningham, because the number of inches in the repeat of the tartan varies from tartan to tartan.

In summary, then, if a kilt is made from tartan, the depth of the pleats is governed by the sett, not by the yardage.

Influence of a person's measurements on the size of pleats

What governs the size of pleats in a kilt? Remember that pleat size is the width of the pleat that can be seen when looking at the back of the kilt.

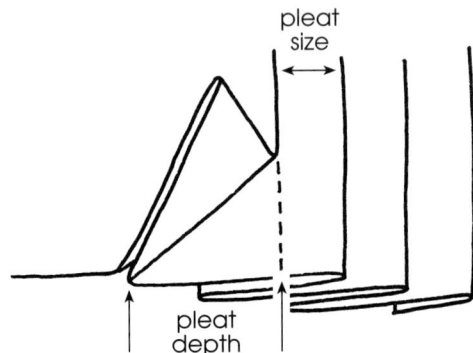

Will a kilt have $^1/_2$" pleats? $^5/_8$" pleats? $^3/_4$" pleats? It turns out that the size of the pleats is a combination of the size of the kilt and how much cloth you have. Let's explore an example to see why this is true.

Let's look at three military-pleated kilts – a small kilt 15" across the back, a medium kilt 18" across the back, and a large kilt 22" across the back. We'll assume that all three kilts will have 6 yards of cloth across the back of the kilt, and we'll use the MacLean of Duart tartan, which has a 7 $^1/_4$" sett (Color Figure 32). Because the three kilts have identical amounts of material in the backs, all three kilts will have 29 repeats of the sett, which means that all three kilts will have 29 stripes to use in 29 pleats.

- Example 1, the small kilt: In order to fit 29 pleats into 15" across the back of the kilt, each pleat will have to be about $^1/_2$" in size (15÷29≈$^1/_2$").

- Example 2, the medium kilt: In order to fit 29 pleats into 18" across the back of the kilt, each pleat will have to be about $^5/_8$" in size (18÷29≈$^5/_8$").

- Example 3, the large kilt: In order to fit 29 pleats

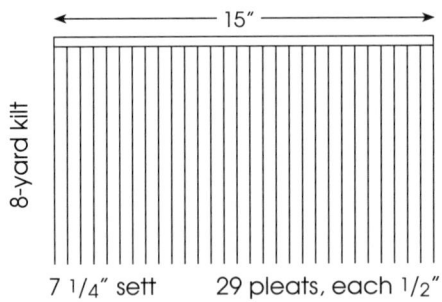

8-yard kilt

7 1/4" sett   29 pleats, each 1/2"

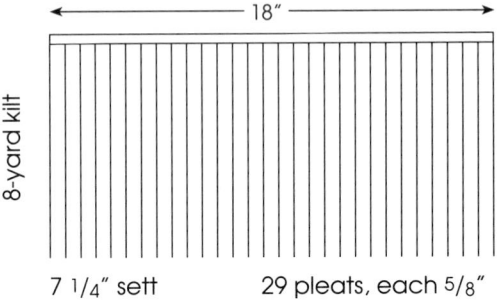

8-yard kilt

7 1/4" sett   29 pleats, each 5/8"

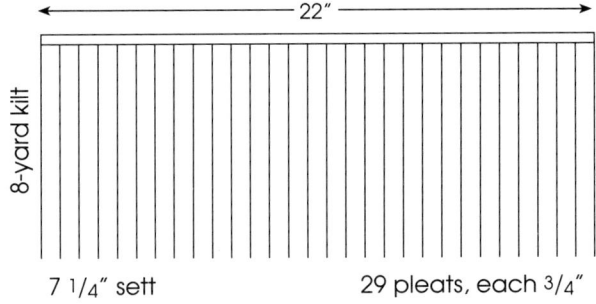

8-yard kilt

7 1/4" sett   29 pleats, each 3/4"

into 22" across the back of the kilt, each pleat will have to be about $^3/_4$" in size (22÷29≈$^3/_4$").

The pleat size in the large kilt is bigger, despite the fact that the large kilt and the small kilt have *identical* amounts of fabric and *identical* numbers of pleats. The pleat depth in each will be essentially the same (being only $^1/_8$" larger in the smallest kilt than in the largest). **In short, for an identical amount of material and an identical number of pleats, the size of the pleats is governed solely by the measurements of the person wearing the kilt.**

Here's a common misunderstanding.

Someone comes to you and says, "I wish that the pleats in my kilt were deeper. Can you make me another one with deeper pleats?" Regardless of whether a kilt is pleated to the sett or to the stripe, the depth of pleats is governed by the *size of the sett*. The only way to make someone a kilt with deeper pleats is to have the person choose a different tartan with a larger sett, or choose a heavier weight of the same tartan, which will have a larger sett and therefore deeper pleats. It is simply not an option to "make deeper pleats" in the same tartan.

Another way of looking at pleat size is to see what happens to pleat size as you buy more material. Let's take our hypothetical person again. Let's imagine three military-pleated kilts all of the same size (18" across the back, as in several of our previous examples). We'll make all three kilts out of the same fabric but we'll vary the amount of fabric. We'll use the Dress Hunting Ross tartan, with a 6" sett (Color Figure 33).

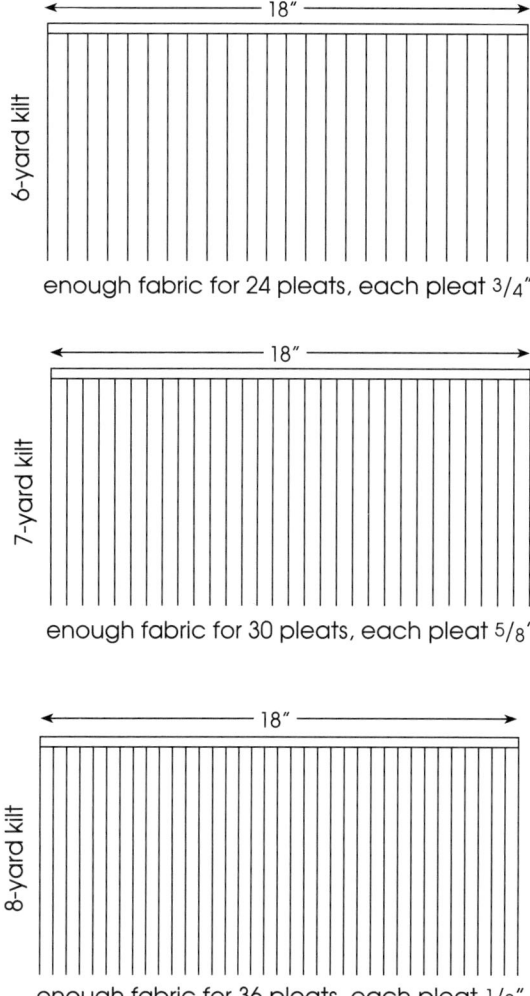

enough fabric for 24 pleats, each pleat 3/4"

enough fabric for 30 pleats, each pleat 5/8"

enough fabric for 36 pleats, each pleat 1/2"

- Example 1, a 6-yard kilt: 1 yard will go into the apron and underapron, and we'll use another yard in facings and such. This leaves 4 yards to pleat into 18" across the back. With a 6" sett, there'll be 24 repeats to put into 24 pleats. In order to fit 24 pleats into 18" across the back of the kilt, each pleat will have to be about $^3/_4$" in size.

- Example 2, a 7-yard kilt: 1 yard will go into the apron and underapron, and we'll use another yard in facings and such. This leaves 5 yards to pleat into 18" across the back. With a 6" sett, there'll be 30 repeats to put into 30 pleats. In order to fit 30 pleats into 18" across the back of the kilt, each pleat will have to be about $^5/_8$" in size.

- Example 3, an 8-yard kilt: 1 yard will go into the apron and underapron, and we'll use another yard in facings and such. This leaves 6 yards to pleat into 18" across the back. With a 6" sett, there'll be 36 repeats to put into 36 pleats. In order to fit 36 pleats into 18" across the back of the kilt, each pleat will have to be about $^1/_2$" in size

It's clear, then, that the more tartan you have for a kilt, the more pleats you will be able to make. And, the more pleats you are able to make, the smaller each pleat will be.

Here's a common misunderstanding.

Someone comes to you to order a kilt and says, "I want an 8-yard kilt, because I've heard that the more cloth in a kilt, the better it looks." Your answer should be, "I may not be *able* to put 8 yards of cloth into your kilt, and you'd be wasting your money to buy 8 yards." If the person is small, there may simply not be enough room across the back to fit in all the pleats that you could possibly make with an 8-yard piece of kilt fabric. Take the 8-yard example above. Suppose the person needed a kilt only 14" across the back (which would be typical for a woman with a 28-29" waist), and you had 6 yards of cloth to cram into those 14" (remember that the remaining 2 yards would be in the apron, facings, and such). The tartan would still give 36 pleats, but you would have to make each pleat about $^3/_8$" in size in order to use all the material (14÷36=0.38"). Pleats don't look good if they are less than $^1/_2$" in size, and it would be better to discard 1 $^1/_2$ yards, make only 27 pleats, and make each pleat about $^1/_2$" in size.

So, in summary of Chapter 4:

- The presence of a tartan repeat introduces complexities in pleating that aren't present in the self-color kilts, and the pleats in a tartan kilt cannot be located arbitrarily, as they can in a self-color kilt. In a tartan kilt, pleats are located at certain places in the sett in order to produce a pattern across the back of the kilt. In other words, the tartan dictates the location of pleats.

- The presence of a tartan repeat means that the size, number, and depth of pleats are not infinitely adjustable, as they are in a self-color kilt.

- In a tartan kilt, the issues of how many pleats a kilt will have, what size they will be, and how deep they will be are complicated and inter-related.

  1 **The number of pleats is determined by a combination of how much material you have (yardage) and by the size of the tartan sett.**

  2 **The depth of the pleats is determined solely by the tartan sett.**

  3 **The size of the pleats is determined by a combination of the size of the wearer and by how much material you use.**

Chapter 5

Preparing to make a kilt

I n this chapter, we'll outline what you need to make a kilt, offer advice on selecting tartan, and teach you how to take a person's measurements By the end of this chapter, you'll be ready to start laying out and marking your kilt.

List of materials[1]

5 to 8 yards of wool tartan (see Chapter 3 and this chapter)

$^3/_4$ yard to 1 yard of hair canvas (Tailor's Pride® or red edge) (see tips and hints on page 94)

1 yard cotton lining material (see tips & hints on page 109)

thread (see tips & hints on page 73)

    1 spool white basting thread

    high quality 100% polyester thread in colors matching the tartan

    1 spool each of black and white carpet (button) thread

2 or 3 silver-colored buckles and black or brown leather straps (see tips & hints on page 105)

several short, fine needles

a thimble, preferably a tailor's thimble with an open top

tape measure, with inches divided to sixteenths

a chunk of beeswax

a piece of tailor's chalk (see tips & hints on page 52)

several common pins

pressing ham and pressing cloth (an old pillow case works fine)

spray bottle

Selecting tartan

Tartan weights

Tartan for kilts is woven in 100% wool in a number of types and weights. Appendix F lists a number of suppliers of tartan.

- **Ultra heavy weight (regimental) worsted (up to 21 oz. per yard):** This is very heavy stuff and only available in regimental tartans. If you're a soldier, fine, but, if you're not, you'd be better off with something lighter!!

- **Heavy weight worsted (16 oz. per yard):** Tartan of this weight makes a superb kilt. The fabric holds an excellent crease and is heavy enough for a beautiful swing. This is the ideal fabric for a man's kilt but makes up into a kilt that is too heavy for a child or a dancer or for wearing in hot weather. Setts tend to be large to very large (8-10" or more). Tartan in this weight is woven with a kilting selvedge.

  - **hard finish:** Most tartan mills make heavy weight worsted with a hard finish. The fabric has a stiff "hand" and makes up into a beautiful kilt. At Dalgliesh, Ltd., the hard finish,

---

[1] Appendix F lists suppliers for tartan, tailoring supplies, notions, and Highland regalia.

16 oz. tartan is called "K/1 worsted"; at Lochcarron, it is called "Strome". House of Edgar simply refers to it as "heavy weight tartan".

- **soft finish:** Dalgliesh, Ltd. also weaves a 16 oz. worsted with a softer finish. Although it has the same weight as their K/1 worsted, the Dalgliesh F/1 worsted feels a bit lighter, because it is less stiff. F/1 worsted makes up into a beautiful kilt that many men find more comfortable than stiffer worsted.

- **Medium weight worsted (13 oz. per yard):** Tartan of this weight is very popular and makes an outstanding kilt that holds a good crease but that isn't as heavy or as hot as a kilt made with 16 ounce worsted. Setts tend to be medium in size. Lochcarron of Scotland calls their medium weight worsted "Braeriach"; House of Edgar refers to it as "medium weight tartan". Tartan in this weight is woven with a kilting selvedge.

- **Light-medium weight worsted (11-12 oz. per yard):** Dalgliesh, Ltd. weaves tartan intermediate in weight between light and medium weight tartan. Tartan of this weight makes an ideal kilt for a child or a dancer, because it does not make up into a kilt that is as heavy as one made with 13 or 16 oz. worsted. Dalgliesh, Ltd. stocks a fairly large number of tartans in this weight in double width and are particularly known for their very large selection of dress dancers' tartans. While light-weight worsted does not hold a crease as well as the heavier tartans, the Dalgliesh tartan is heavy enough to look nice and swing well for a dancer. Setts tend to be medium to small in size (5-8"). This tartan typically does not have a good enough selvedge for making a kilt without a hem.

- **Light weight worsted (10-11 oz. per yard):** Several mills make light weight tartan that can be used for kilts. At the 11-ounce end of the range, the tartan compares reasonably well to the slightly heavier Dalgliesh tartan described above, although it is a bit softer and doesn't hold a crease quite as well. At the 10-ounce end of the range, the tartan is on the light side for a kilt and makes a kilt that wrinkles easily. 10-ounce worsted is best reserved for kilt skirts and other sewing projects. Lochcarron of Scotland calls their 10 ounce fabric "Reiver". Light weight worsteds are not woven with a kilting selvedge.

- **Wool saxony:** This fabric has a very soft "hand" and doesn't hold a crease well. Saxony has a tendency to fuzz and pill. It is the cheapest fabric on this list. If you should find a bolt of tartan in a U.S. fabric store, it will likely be saxony.

Tartan widths

Tartan is woven either in single width (27-29") or double width (54-60"). "Single width" refers to the fact that the fabric is only wide enough for cutting a single kilt width. An 8-yard kilt would require 8 yards of single-width fabric. "Double width" refers to the fact that the fabric is wide enough for cutting two kilt widths. An 8-yard kilt would require only 4 yards of double-width fabric (or, if you bought 8 yards of double width fabric, you could make two kilts). Always be sure when you order tartan that you know whether the fabric comes in single or double width!!

How much tartan will I need?

The chart on the next page offers general guidelines for how much fabric to buy in order to make a kilt.

The table provides only general guidelines, because tartans vary a great deal in the size of the sett (the number of inches in a full repeat of the pattern). A kilt with a small sett will have more pleats than a kilt with a large sett for an equal amount of yardage, although each pleat will be deeper in the kilt with the larger sett. If you have a tartan with an extremely small sett (less than 5", such as the Dress Menzies Special Sett, a common tartan for a dancer's kilt), you may find that you have left-over material that can't be fitted into the kilt even with half inch pleats at the waistline. This is particularly true if the hip measurement is at the lower end of the size range on the chart at right. If you have a tartan with a large sett (more than 6"), you may wish to purchase a bit extra in order not to make the pleats too big at the hips, particularly if the hip measurement is at the upper end of the size range on the chart at right.

A kilt is a case where more is usually not better. You might be tempted to buy extra cloth so that your kilt can have more fabric in it than the chart at right recommends. Don't bother. Buying extra fabric can give you so many pleats that each pleat will have to be unacceptably narrow in order to fit in all the extra cloth. For example, if you bought enough cloth to make 29 pleats and your back waist measurement were only 12", each pleat would be less than $7/16$" across (12"÷29 pleats = 0.41" per pleat). Because pleats do not look good if they are less than $1/2$" wide, you'd need to decrease the number of pleats to 23 in order to make the pleats at least $1/2$" wide (12" ÷ 23 pleats = 0.52" per pleat). You would end up simply cutting off and wasting 6 pleats worth of material, which could be as much as a yard or more of cloth! At the price of tartan, who needs that?!?

hip measurement	kilt	yards of 27-29" (single width) fabric needed	yards of 56-60" (double-width) fabric needed[2]
less than 30"	5 yard	5 yards	$2 \frac{1}{2}$ yards
31-35"	6 yard	6 yards	3 yards
36-40"	7 yard	7 yards	$3 \frac{1}{2}$ yards
40-44"	8 yard	8 yards	4 yards
more than 44"	9 yard	9 yards	$4 \frac{1}{2}$ yards

Warning!!! Asymmetry can introduce problems during kiltmaking, if you plan to use a double width of fabric. To achieve a long, narrow piece of cloth from which to make the kilt, you would normally split the cloth down the middle lengthwise and rotate the second piece of fabric 180° to match the selvedges and join the second piece to the first.

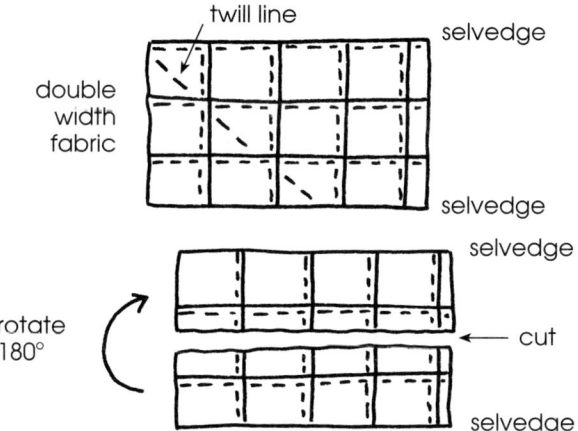

But! If you were to do this with an asymmetric (non-centering or non-matching) tartan, you would find that the tartan doesn't match across the center back join after you've rotated it! You wouldn't be able to solve the problem by simply flipping the piece over, because the twill line would then run the wrong way on the second piece of fabric and the repeat would still be a mirror image across the center back seam.

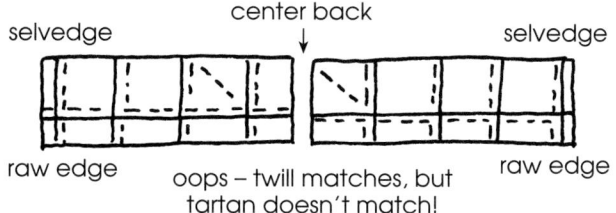

The only way to deal with the problem is not to rotate the second piece (which means that the selvedges will be on opposite edges) and to put a hem in the kilt. With a very large sett, you may also have trouble matching the setts horizontally, and you may have to offset the pieces so much that you may not have enough width to make the kilt.

How can you entirely avoid the problems introduced by asymmetric (non-centering) tartans?

- Strategy 1: If you have a choice of tartan, do the sensible thing and avoid choosing one of the rare ones with an asymmetric sett (see footnote below).

- Strategy 2: If you simply must have an asymmetric tartan, invest in a single width piece of fabric 8 yards long, rather than a double-width of fabric 4 yards long. This may require ordering a custom-woven piece of fabric (see Appendix F for a list of suppliers).

- Strategy 3: If you must have an asymmetric tartan, find a second person who wants a kilt made from the same tartan. Buy 7 or 8 yards of double width fabric, rip the fabric in half lengthwise, and make each kilt from a single width 7 or 8 yards long.

If, despite the advice above, you find yourself with only enough double width asymmetric tartan to make one kilt, be sure to read Appendix E carefully before proceeding.

Taking a person's measurements

While only three measurements are necessary for making a kilt, accuracy and care in measuring is crucial to the difference between a kilt that looks

---

[2] *Asymmetric (non-centering, non-matching) tartans are discussed in Chapter 3 and include the Buchan, Buchanan and Hunting Buchanan (but not Old Buchanan or Dress Buchanan), Campbell of Argyll, Dress Campbell, Drummond of Strathallen, MacAlpine, Dress MacDonald, Old Macmillan, Malcolm, Hunting Stewart, and the Ontario and Québec provincial tartans.* We strongly urge first time kiltmakers to avoid asymmetric tartans altogether unless the tartan can be bought in single width. If you have a double width piece of asymmetric tartan, be sure to work through Appendix E in order to determine whether, in fact, you will be able to make your kilt from the piece of fabric that you have.

sharp and one that looks a mess and feels awkward to wear. Here's how to measure for each:

– waist: measure the person's circumference at his/her natural waistline, and pull the measuring tape snug. One way to find the waistline is to have the person lean sideways. His/her waist is located where the side goes in the most between the ribs and hip bone. You can measure over lightweight clothes, but don't measure over a belt or heavy clothing. Don't let yourself be misled by a man who claims that the waist size you just measured is bigger than the pants size he wears. Many men wear their pants low, particularly those with a bit of a corpulence. A kilt is worn at the waist, and the waist measurement must be made at the waist.

– hip: measure the person's circumference at the widest part of the buttocks. In order not to embarrass a man, be sure to do this measurement from the side. The tape should be on the loose side. Measuring over a pair of pants is fine.

– length: a proper kilt comes just to the top of the knee-cap, and nothing looks worse than a kilt that is too long or one that looks like a miniskirt. Locate the person's waistline again, and measure the length from the person's waist to the top of the knee cap. Locating the top of a kneecap can be a challenge with a chubby or muscular person. To locate the top, place your thumb and forefinger on either side of the kneecap about midway down the knee, and slide your thumb and forefinger up the kneecap until they meet at the top. Measure down the thigh, rather than down the front, and keep the tape straight. Be sure that the person you are measuring is looking straight ahead while you measure. If the person is looking down watching your hands, the measurement that you make will be too short!!

Beginning a record sheet

Create a record sheet for your kilt, and lay it out as below, entering the measurements you took in the "inches" column. Leave the other spaces blank for now.

**If you are making a kilt for a larger man, and his waist measurement is larger than his hips, do not plan a kilt with smaller hips than waist. In the chart below, use the same measurement for the hips as you have for the waist.

Record Sheet

	inches	split	apron	pleats
waist				
hips				
length				
total finished length:				
total finished length + hem:				
length of fell: number of pleats:				
pleat size at waist: pleat size at hip:				

Tips & hints: So you're left handed. Well....ummmmmm...

The news isn't good for those of you who are left handed. Kilt construction by the instructions in this book is a right-handed process. At the time Elsie apprenticed at Gordon's as a young kiltmaker, in fact, labor laws were different, and left-handed people simply weren't hired as apprentices. The reasons are simple. Pleats in a kilt are asymmetric, and they are always folded toward the right hip and stitched from hip to waist. The direction of stitching can't easily be reversed (*i.e.*, it's difficult to sew a pleat from waist to hip), because the pleat must be shaped by stretching as you stitch, and it's difficult to hold a pleat when starting at the waist end. Furthermore, the kilt can't easily be rotated 90° for stitching, because it would mean stitching a blind stitch backwards with the fold facing you, rather than away from you.

So, what does all this mean? We don't have very satisfactory advice for lefties. All we can say is that, if you are left handed and bound and determined to make a kilt, you will have to work out a strategy for stitching the pleats that results in a job that is acceptable to you. Many of the other instructions in this book are "directional", and a left handed person will need to be creative to modify them as well.

Chapter 6

An overview of kilt construction

The directions for making a kilt occupy the bulk of the rest of this book. To help you gain a perspective on the process, we've outlined the major steps below so that you will have a general sense of where you're going before you plunge into actual construction of your kilt.

Laying out the kilt and marking the tartan (Chapter 7) involve the following steps:

- determining how the kilt will be tapered from the hips to waist in both aprons and pleats in order to accommodate the shape of the wearer
- ripping the fabric to the correct length for the kilt
- drawing the shape and size of the apron onto the tartan
- choosing between military pleating and pleating to the sett
- marking the locations of all pleats
- drawing the shape and size of the underapron onto the tartan.

Preparing to sew the kilt (Chapter 8) involves the following steps:

- determining the size of the pleats at the waist and the hips
- attaching a record sheet, and folding the tartan properly for work.

Sewing the kilt (Chapter 9) involves the following major steps :

- basting the edges of the apron to the right shape
- stitching and shaping all of the pleats
- finishing the lower edge of the kilt
- basting the pleats to hold them for pressing
- tailor basting to shape the apron and underapron between waist and hips
- cutting out the excess fabric from the pleats at the fell to reduce bulk
- stabilizing the pleats at waist and the bottom of the fell
- applying canvas interfacing to the kilt between the waist and the bottom of the fell
- folding a facing and finishing the free underapron edge
- folding a facing and making the fringe on the free apron edge
- attaching the top band
- pressing the kilt
- attaching the buckles and straps
- applying the lining.

Tips and Hints: How long will it take me to make a kilt?

How long it takes to make a kilt depends upon the size of the kilt and the number of pleats. A 5-yard kilt for a young dancer makes up faster than a man's kilt, and a hemmed kilt takes longer than one without a hem. It takes first-time kiltmakers at Elsie's kilt camp approximately 40 hours from lay-out to lining to make a 6 or 7-yard kilt with a hem. An experienced kiltmaker can make a kilt in under 20 hours.

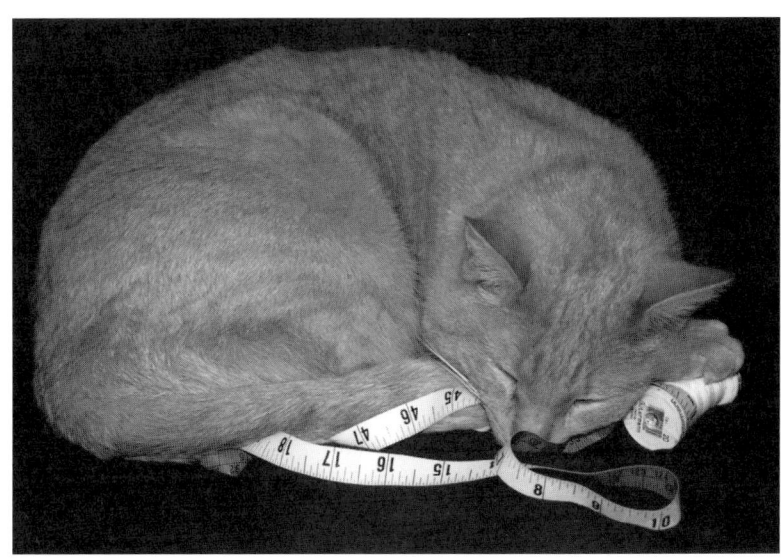

Ready? Well then, ask the cat to relinquish
the tape measure, and let's go!

Chapter 7

Laying out the kilt and marking the tartan

Instructions for the main part of kilt construction begin in this chapter. You will learn how to plan the shaping and pleating for your kilt and how to mark the tartan to get it ready for sewing. If you have not already begun a record sheet for your kilt, take a moment to go back to page 46 and prepare a record sheet. You will refer to it often!

Understanding shaping

Most people have hip measurements that are larger than their waists, and a kilt cannot be made as a simple cylinder. In order to nip the kilt in at the waist and flare it out at the hips and over the buttocks, a kilt must have shaping both in the apron, where the apron edges curve diagonally outward from waist to hips, and in the pleats, where the pleats flare at the hips to accommodate the buttocks.

Shaping in the apron

When viewed from the front, the apron of a kilt has a subtle A-line shape, with the apron being wider at the hips than at the waist.

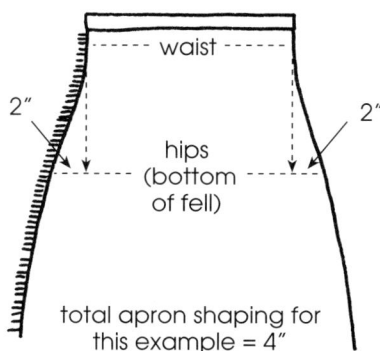

total apron shaping for
this example = 4"

All of the shaping in the apron is accommodated by folding the apron edges along diagonal curves at the apron edges. **Darts should never be placed in the apron of the kilt.**

- The amount of shaping in the apron is the difference between the width of the apron at the hips and the width of the apron at the waist. The total shaping is split evenly between the left and right sides of the apron.

- The illustration above shows a total apron shaping of 4", split evenly with 2" of shaping on each side of the apron.

Shaping in the pleats

When viewed from the back, a kilt also has a subtle "A" shape between waist and hips, with the pleats section being wider at the hips than at the waist.

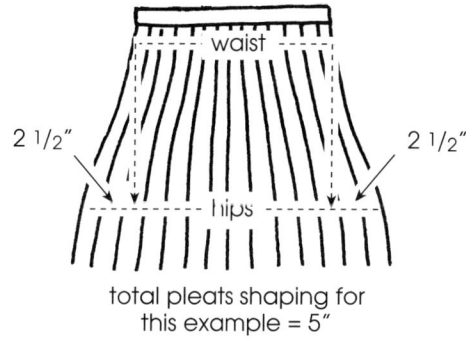

total pleats shaping for
this example = 5"

- The amount of shaping in the pleats is the difference between the distance across the pleats at the hips and the distance across the pleats at the waist. The total shaping is split evenly amongst all of the pleats.

- The illustration above shows a total shaping in the pleats of 5", split evenly over 15 pleats. Each pleat is $1/3$" smaller at the waist than at the hips.

When viewed from the side, the front of the kilt must hang absolutely flat and straight down, even on someone with a substantial tummy. By contrast, the back of the kilt above the hips does not hang straight down but rather snugs in to the small of

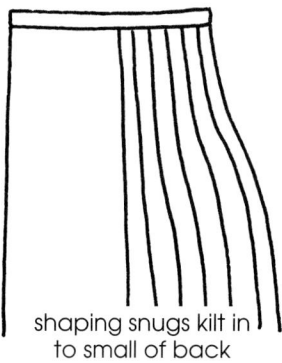

shaping snugs kilt in
to small of back

the back, flares out over the buttocks, and hangs straight from there to the bottom of the kilt.

Splitting measurements between apron and pleats

Now that you have taken waist and hip measurements for your kilt, you must decide how to shape the apron and pleats portion of your kilt. It might seem logical simply to divide the waist measurement in half, assigning half the distance to the apron and half to the pleats section and repeating the process with the hip measurement. Unfortunately, a half and half split will not produce the best-looking kilt. The following sections provides general guidelines for making splits so that your kilt will fit well.

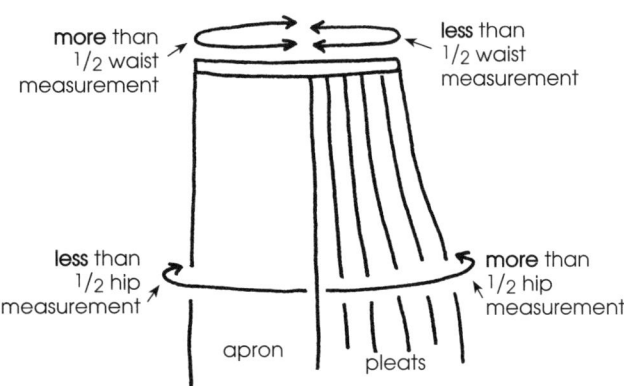

General guidelines for splits

- **at the waist:** assign *more* than half the waist measurement to the apron section and *less* than half to the pleats section. The difference can be as much as 2-3". This shapes the back of the kilt nicely by snugging the pleats in to the small of the back at the waist. Assigning more to the apron than the pleats at the waist also helps reduce the apron shaping problem in a kilt where the waist is much smaller than the hips, because it reduces the differential between the apron waist and hip widths.

- **at the hips:** assign *less* than half the hip measurement to the apron section and *more* than half to the pleats section. The difference is typically not more than 1". Because people's buttocks stick out in the back, a slightly unequal split at the hips makes a nicer-looking kilt. Make the difference more than 1" if the person has prominent buttocks and less than 1" if the person has a prominent tummy.

- **apron shaping:** a difference of 2-3" between the apron width at the waist and hips is easy to accommodate, with 1 to 1 $1/2$" of shaping on each side of the apron. The greater the difference be-

tween the width of the apron at the hip and the width at the waist, however, the more difficult it will be to shape the apron smoothly. More than 5" total (2 $1/2$" on each side) is a challenge to manage.

Here's what to do with the measurements you have:

1. Begin by realizing that there is no formula and no one right answer for splitting the measurements between apron and pleats. In fact, any two kiltmakers are likely to make the splits in somewhat different ways. This can be frustrating for beginning kiltmakers, for whom a rule is easier than being told "when you have more experience, you just *know*....". Well, let's bash on. A specific example appears in the box on the next page, and Appendix B shows many examples of measurements plus successful splits for those measurements.

2. Start by splitting the waist measurement and the hip measurement exactly in half and entering the splits on your record sheet in a splits #1 column for waist and hips.

3. For the waist:
   - Try several other splits, assigning *more* than half the waist measurement to the apron split and *less* than half the waist measurement to the pleats split. The difference can be as much as 2-3".

- Record the various splits in the waist splits column of your record sheet (the box on this page shows an example).
- Double-check to make sure that each of your splits does, in fact, add up to the actual waist measurement.

4 For the hips:

- Try several other splits, assigning *less* than half the hip measurement to the apron split and *more* than half the hip measurement to the pleats split.
- Record the various hip splits in the splits column of your record sheet (the box on this page shows an example).
- Double-check to make sure that each of your splits does, in fact, add up to the actual hip measurement.

5 Choose which waist split to select and which hips split to select using the following guidelines. The box on this page shows an example.

- Choose splits that will make the apron shaping manageable, preferably less than 3-4" difference between waist and hip width in the apron.

Example of Splits

Carolyn's Dress Wine Sutherland Kilt			7 yards		August 1998	
	inches	**split #1**	**split #2**	**split #3**	**apron**	**pleats**
waist	27 $\frac{1}{2}$"	apron 13 $\frac{3}{4}$" pleats 13 $\frac{3}{4}$"	apron 14 $\frac{1}{2}$" pleats 13"	apron 15" pleats 12 $\frac{1}{2}$"	15"	12 $\frac{1}{2}$"
hips	35"	apron 17 $\frac{1}{2}$" pleats 17 $\frac{1}{2}$"	apron 17" pleats 18"	apron 16 $\frac{1}{2}$" pleats 18 $\frac{1}{2}$"	17"	18"
length	20 $\frac{1}{2}$"					

Step #1: Start by splitting the waist and hip measurements evenly between apron and pleats (split #1 on the chart). While the difference between the waist and hip measurement of the apron is less than 4", which would not be difficult to construct (17 $\frac{1}{2}$ - 13 $\frac{3}{4}$ = 3 $\frac{3}{4}$"), the kilt would look better with more shaping in the pleats.

Step #2: Try a couple more splits, making sure that the numbers do, in fact, add up to the waist and hip measurements. Splits should be larger in the apron at the waist and larger in the pleats at the hips (splits #2 and #3 on the chart).

Step #3: Make a decision about which splits to select. Selecting split #3 for the waist and #2 for the hips will give 1" of shaping on each side of the apron (2" total difference between waist and hips in the apron, which is very manageable) and 5 $\frac{1}{2}$" of total shaping in the pleats (see below). Split #2 in the waist would also work but would not give as flattering shaping in the pleats. Split #1 in the hips would also work, although it would reduce the shaping in the pleats; split #3 in the hips has a difference that is a bit large.

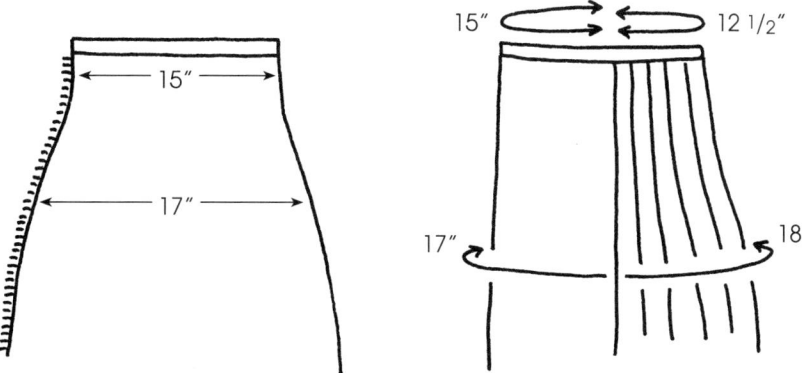

- Be sure that the apron width in the waist is *smaller* than the apron width in the hips!

- Choose a hips split that is not more than 1" bigger in the pleats section than in the apron section at the hips, unless the person has prominent buttocks.

- Compare your splits with those in the examples in Appendix B, if you want to be reassured that you have chosen reasonable splits.

- **Important!** Don't choose a half-and-half split even if you have a kilt with equal waist and hip measurements. Even in a kilt where hip and waist measurements are similar, shaping will produce a more attractive kilt. Assign a bit more than half the measurement to the pleats section at the hips and a bit less than half the measurement to the pleats section at the waist.

6 Be sure to indicate clearly on your record sheet which splits you've chosen, and enter the apron width at waist and hips in the apron waist and apron hips boxes and the distance across the pleats at the waist and hips in the waist pleats and hips pleats boxes. **Be absolutely certain that you have entered the numbers in the correct boxes.** You don't want to discover later that you have made the apron the size that the pleats should have been and vice versa.

7 And last, double-check to make sure that the apron box plus the pleats box does, in fact, add up to the waist measurement that you need. Do the same thing for the hips.

Determining and marking the right side of the fabric

For the next several steps, you will need a clean, flat table, the longer the better.

1 Start by laying out your piece of tartan on the table.

- **If you are working with double-width fabric,** lay the fabric folded on the table with the selvedges away from you.

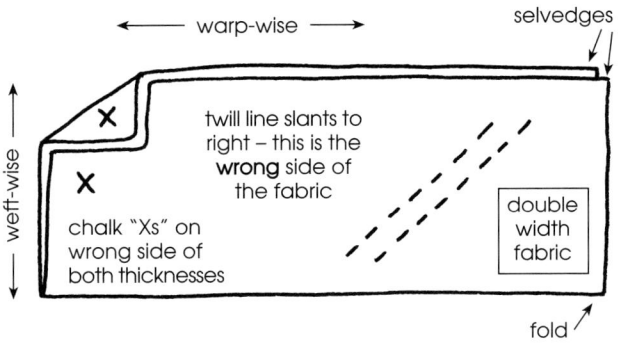

- **If you are working with single-width fabric,** check to see if the mill has marked the good (kilting) selvedge for you. If not, examine the fabric, and locate the best selvedge. Lay out the cloth with the good (kilting) selvedge away from you.

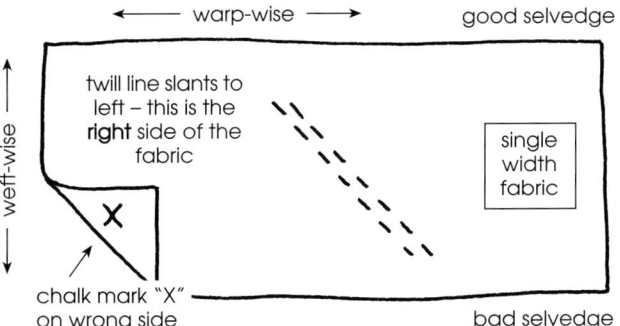

2 Tartan is woven as a twill weave, rather than as a plain weave, resulting in a weave pattern of subtle diagonal lines superimposed on the color pattern of intersecting stripes (see page 29). Examine your tartan, and find the diagonal weave pattern. Stand looking across the piece of fabric, with the double selvedge (or good selvedge) away from you.

- **If the diagonal lines slant from lower right to upper left** as you look across the tartan to the selvedge, your fabric is right side up.

- **If the diagonal lines slant from lower left to upper right** as you look across the tartan to the selvedge, your fabric is wrong side up.

3 Take your chalk (see tips and hints box on the previous page), and mark the *wrong* side of the fabric with a large "X". If you have double-width fabric, chalk an "X" on the wrong side of both the upper and lower thicknesses. 90% of the time, the inside is the right side in a folded double-width piece of fabric. The photograph at right illustrates a nicely-stitched kilt made from the wrong side of the tartan (notice that the twill lines slant up and to the right).

**If you have a double width of asymmetric tartan, go immediately to Appendix E for instructions before you proceed to mark and rip the tartan.

Marking the length of the kilt and ripping the tartan

If your kilt will not have a hem, go to Option A below. If your kilt will have a hem, go directly to Option B on the following page. For advice on whether or not to include a hem, see the tips and hints box on this page.

Option A: If your kilt *will not* have a hem:

1 Be sure that your fabric is laid out with the selvedge away from you and that you are working at the right hand end.

2 As illustrated in the kilt parts diagram on page 34, a kilt is made with a rise, which is an extension above the waistline. While kilts used to be made with a 2 $\frac{1}{2}$" or even a 3" rise, most kilts today are made with a 2" rise.

   The total length of a kilt is the length measurement from the waist to the top of the knee cap plus 2" for the rise.

3 Add 2" to the length measurement that you recorded. This is the total length of the kilt. Enter this on your record sheet.

4 Starting at the selvedge edge of your fabric, measure the total length of the kilt from the selvedge

the twill in this kilt runs the wrong way

edge along the right hand raw edge, and mark with a short chalk line at the edge of the fabric.

5 **Measure again**, and check to be sure that you have added a 2" rise to the original length measurement.

6 Take a pair of sharp scissors, and clip the edge of the fabric two threads above the chalk line to allow for fraying. If you have double-width cloth, clip *only* one layer!

Tips and Hints: To hem or not to hem?

A kilt is traditionally made without a hem, and the fabric selvedge serves as the bottom edge of the kilt. A kilt is hemmed only if the kilt owner is likely to grow or if the selvedge is so poor that the lower edge of the kilt would be unsightly if not hemmed.

For a child's or young adult's kilt, put as much into the hem as you can and still have a wide enough warp-wise piece to use for a top band. Try to put at least 2" into a hem, and preferably 3". For a dancer's kilt, avoid locating a prominent stripe at the bottom of the kilt if possible, because a narrow prominent stripe calls the judge's attention to the dancer's knees. Also, avoid white at the hem fold if possible, because the bottom edge of a young dancer's kilt is likely to get dirty, and a grimy line may show if the kilt is let down.

If you have been asked to make a kilt for a child or young adult in a pipe band, double-check to be sure that the pipe major wants you to put a hem in the kilt. A kilt with a hem has a bottom edge that looks different from a kilt without a hem and may not look right with the rest of the band kilts.

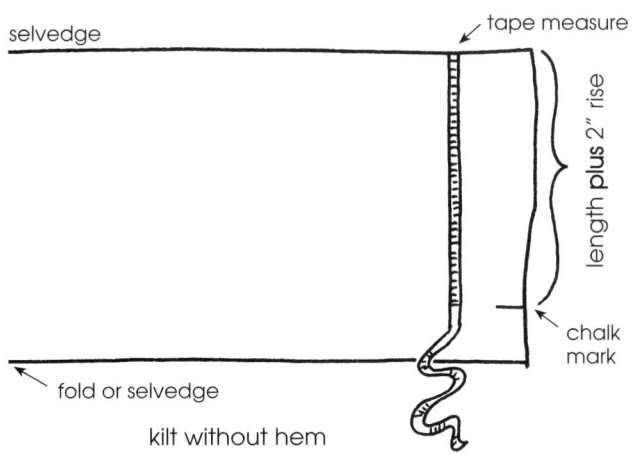

selvedge

tape measure

length **plus 2"** rise

chalk mark

fold or selvedge

kilt without hem

7 Measure again, and double check that you have added the rise. This is not the time to make a mistake! Once you rip the cloth, it's too late to remember that you forgot to add the rise or to discover that you measured wrong.

8 **Rip** the length of the cloth, rather than cutting. Ripping is preferable to cutting, because ripping will produce an absolutely straight edge.

9 If you have double-width cloth, lay the first piece on top of the remaining one, match the selvedges and stripes, and mark the same place for clipping and ripping. Double-check to be sure that you haven't made a mistake, clip the cloth, and rip off the extra.

10 **Be sure to save the ripped-off strip for the top band** (see tips and hints, this page). Breathe a sigh of relief, and congratulate yourself that you have survived this nerve-wracking step.

11 Pull the stray threads from the ripped edge. Once you've removed the few loose threads, the edge won't ravel anymore. Don't bother serging or zigzagging it.

12 Skip Option B, and go directly to Marking the top apron (page 55).

Option B: If your kilt *will* have a hem:

1 Be sure that your fabric is laid out with the selvedge away from you and that you are working at the right hand end.

2 As illustrated in the kilt parts diagram on page 34, a kilt is made with a rise, which is an extension above the waistline. While kilts used to be made with a 2 1/2" or even a 3" rise, most kilts today are made with a 2" rise.

   The total length of a kilt is the length measurement from the waist plus 2" for the rise.

3 Add 2" to the length measurement that you recorded. This is the total *finished* length of the kilt. Record this on your record sheet.

4 Decide how much hem you will put into the kilt. Use the guidelines in the tips and hints box (previous page), and remember that you must leave a strip a minimum of 1 1/2" wide and parallel to the long edge of the fabric from which to make the top band. You cannot use a weft-wise strip cut from the end of the fabric to make the top band (see tips and hints at right), so you **must** leave a strip along the top edge. Record the total finished length plus the hem on your record sheet.

5 Starting at the selvedge edge of your fabric, measure the total length of the kilt *plus the hem* from the selvedge edge along the right hand raw edge,

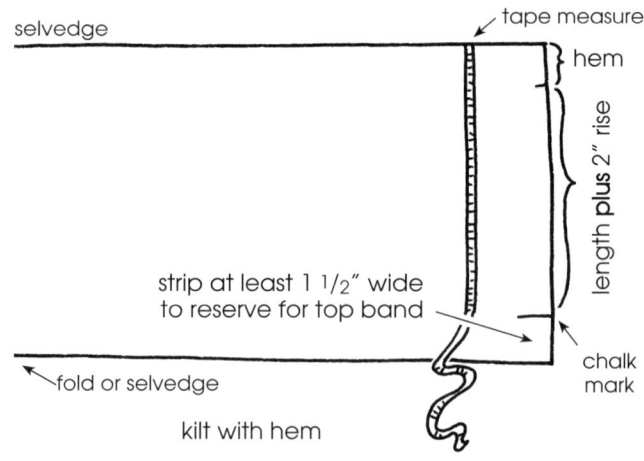

and mark with a short chalk line at the edge of the fabric.

6 Measure again, and check to be sure that you have added both the hem and a 2" rise to the original length measurement and that you have left enough material for the top band.

7 Take a pair of sharp scissors, and clip the edge of the fabric two threads above the chalk line to allow for fraying. If you are working with double-width fabric, mark and clip *only* the top layer. Do not clip both thicknesses!

8 **Measure again**, and double check that you have added the rise and the hem. This is not the time to make a mistake! Once you rip the cloth, it's too late to remember that you forgot to add the rise and hem or to discover that you measured wrong.

9 **Rip** the length of the cloth, rather than cutting. Ripping is preferable to cutting, because ripping will produce an absolutely straight edge.

Tips & Hints: Scraps for top band & fringe

Although tartan should be woven as a precise 45° weave, the distance between stripes in the warp is rarely identical to the distance between stripes in the weft. Any time that you need to match two pieces of tartan from the same piece of fabric, you must be sure to choose a weft-wise piece to match an edge parallel to the weft and a warp-wise piece to match an edge parallel to the warp. In practice, this means that the long, warp-wise scrap torn off to make the kilt the correct length will work for a top band piece, but it will not match the fringe edge, which is parallel to the weft. You must use a scrap cut parallel to the weft for the fringe.

10 If you have double-width cloth, lay the first piece on top of the remaining piece, match the selvedges and stripes, and mark the same place for clipping and ripping. Double-check to be sure that you haven't made a mistake, clip the cloth, and rip off the extra.

11 **Be sure to save the ripped-off strip for the top band** (see tips and hints on the previous page). Breathe a sigh of relief and congratulate yourself that you have survived this nerve-wracking step.

12 Pull the stray threads from the ripped edge. Once you've removed the few loose threads, the edge won't ravel anymore. Don't bother serging or zigzagging it.

Marking the top apron

1 **Laying out your cloth.** Locate the right side of your fabric (remember that you marked the wrong side with a chalk "X"), and lay the fabric out right side up on the table with the selvedge away from you. If you started with a double width of fabric, you can lay out just one piece for now. If you started with a single width of fabric, locate the middle of the length, and mark the middle with a chalk "X" at both selvedge and raw edge, then lay the fabric out flat. For the moment, you'll only need to work with the right hand end, as viewed with the selvedge away from you. Double check to make sure that the fabric is right side up and has the diagonal weave pattern slanting from lower right to upper left as you look across the fabric to the selvedge. Double-checking is always a good thing.

2 **Choosing and marking a center front stripe.** Choose the most prominent stripe in the tartan for the center front. For a dancer's kilt, avoid a dark stripe in the center front unless the velvet of the vest or jacket matches it perfectly. Consult your record sheet that lists how wide the apron will be at the hips. Divide that measure-

ment in half, and select a center stripe located at least that distance plus 7-9" from the fabric edge. This will leave enough cloth to make the fringe edge and self-facing at the right edge of the apron and still allow for alterations. Make a chalk mark at the center front along the raw edge.

3 **Erasing errant chalk marks.** Tailor's chalk without wax in it (see tips and hints page 52) can be easily "erased" from the fabric. Slap the fabric with your hand several times, and most of the mark will fade, or take a scrap of cloth and scrub the mark with it, and the mark will be gone.

4 **Calculating and marking the bottom of the fell.** The fell is the stitched portion of the pleats. To calculate the length of the fell, take the total *finished* length of the kilt (including the rise but not the hem), and divide by 3. Write the number of inches in the fell on your record sheet. Measure the length of the fell along the center front stripe from the top of the kilt, and make a chalk mark.

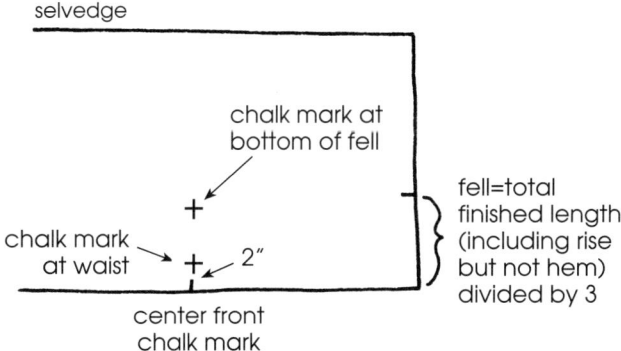

selvedge

chalk mark at bottom of fell

chalk mark at waist → + ← 2"

center front chalk mark

fell=total finished length (including rise but not hem) divided by 3

5 **Marking the apron edges.** At the center front stripe, measure 2" down from the top of the kilt, and put a chalk line to mark the waistline. **For the next marks, check to be sure that you are looking at the fabric with the selvedge away from you.**

– To mark the apron edges at the waistline, lay your tape measure along the waistline, and measure half the apron waist measurement to the left of the center front line. Make a chalk

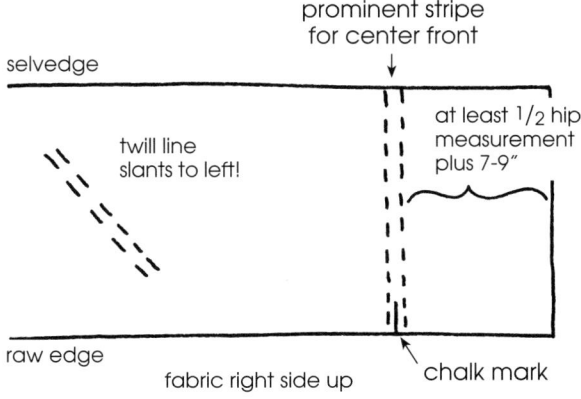

prominent stripe for center front

selvedge

twill line slants to left!

at least 1/2 hip measurement plus 7-9"

raw edge

fabric right side up

chalk mark

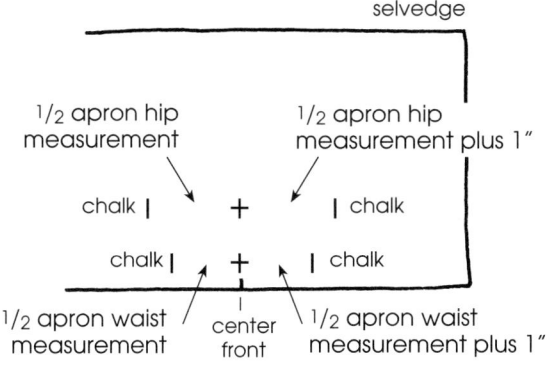

selvedge

1/2 apron hip measurement

1/2 apron hip measurement plus 1"

chalk | + | chalk

chalk | + | chalk

1/2 apron waist measurement

center front

1/2 apron waist measurement plus 1"

mark. Then, measure half the apron waist measurement *plus 1"* to the right of the center front line, and make a chalk mark.

– To mark the apron edges at the bottom of the fell, lay your tape measure along a line at the level of the bottom of the fell, and measure half the apron hip measurement to the left of the center front line. Make a chalk mark. Then, measure half the apron hip measurement plus 1" to the right of the center front line, and make a chalk mark. The extra inch insures that the fringe edge completely covers the underapron.

– Starting at the top of the kilt, draw a chalk line at the right apron edge from the top of the kilt *parallel to the tartan stripes* as far as the waistline chalk mark. **Make absolutely certain that the apron edge does not taper between the waistline and the top of the kilt.** From the waistline chalkmark, draw a smoothly-curving chalk line connecting the waist and hip marks at the right apron edge. Continue the chalk line down to the bottom of the kilt in a subtly-flaring A-line shape. Repeat for the left edge of the apron. Except on a very small kilt, don't make the flare less than $1\,^1/_2$" on each side. Without enough flare below the hip mark, the apron edge tends to open out when a person wears the kilt.

Locating the center back stripe

1 If you have two pieces of fabric, slide the piece you've been working on over until you locate the edge at the opposite end from the apron you just marked. If you have a single piece, locate the chalk mark "X" that you made earlier at the approximate center back.

2 The center back stripe should be the same as the center front stripe. If you are working with two pieces of cloth, be sure that the stripe you pick is at least $2\,^1/_2$" away from the raw edge to allow the join between the two pieces to be hidden within the pleat.

In a pinch, if you are working with a bare minimum of cloth, you can pick a stripe for the center back that is different from the center front (after all, no one can see the front and back of your kilt at the same time!).

3 Mark the center back stripe with an "X" along the raw edge.

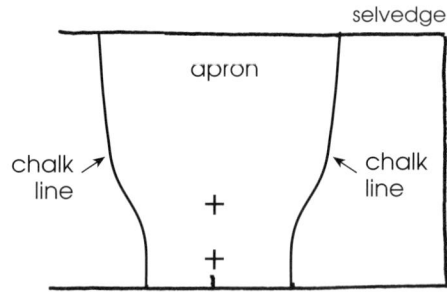

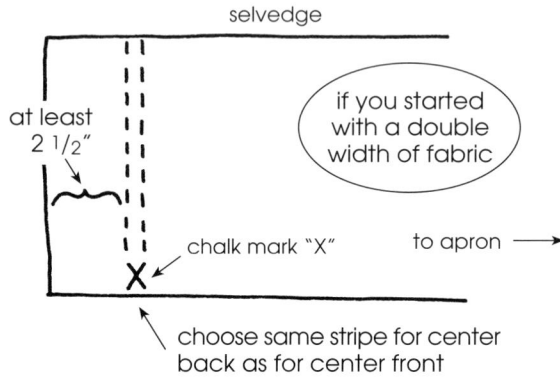

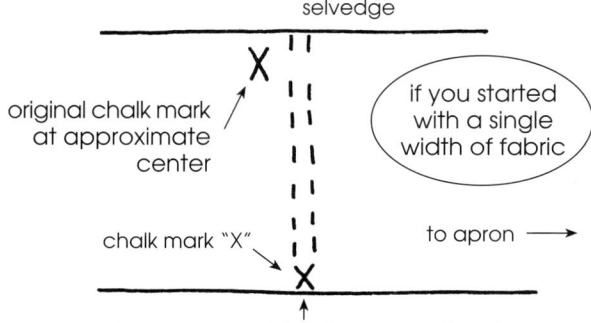

Choosing between pleating to the sett and pleating to the stripe

Before you can mark the pleats, you must decide whether you will pleat your kilt to the sett or to the stripe. Use the Color Figures and the descriptions below to help you make the choice.

Pleating to the sett

In a kilt pleated to the sett, each pleat is folded in a different place with respect to the tartan sett so that the overall tartan is replicated in the pleated back of the kilt. A kilt pleated to the sett looks much the same from the back and from the front, as shown by the Ancient Duncan kilt in Color Figure 2. Color Figures 34 and 35 show close-ups of both the Wallace and Dress Royal Menzies tartan and kilt backs pleated to the sett. While individual color blocks and stripes are not quite the same size in the pleated back of the kilt as they are in the tartan itself, all of the elements of blocks and stripes are there. Most dancer's kilts are pleated to the sett.

Pleating to the stripe (military pleating)

In a kilt that has been pleated to the stripe, each pleat is folded in exactly the same place with respect to the tartan set, with the same stripe running the length of each pleat. A kilt pleated to the stripe looks significantly different when viewed from the back than when viewed from the front, as shown by the Weathered Ferguson kilt in Color Figure 3. The apron shows the full tartan, while the pleats are decidedly stripey. Military pleating has a nice slimming effect for larger individuals, and many tartans make up particularly smartly when military pleated.

The back of a kilt pleated to the stripe may have a predominant color that is quite different from the predominant color of the apron. The Weathered Ferguson kilt in Color Figure 3, for example, has a strong red cast in the pleats but not in the apron, because each pleat has a red stripe down the center. In Color Figure 36, a close-up of the Black Stewart tartan and a kilt pleated to the stripe shows another example, where the kilt front is dominantly black, while the kilt back is dominantly reddish-purple.

If a tartan has two strong colors, and one color appears on the top of a pleat and the other is hidden inside the pleat, a kilt can have a surprising and pleasing flash of colors when the pleats open up as the wearer walks. Color Figure 37 shows a close-up of the Hunting Ross tartan pleated with a dark stripe in each pleat and a bright green stripe inside. When the wearer is standing still, the kilt will look very dark from the back. When the wearer walks, the pleats will open and flash the bright green beneath.

Which stripe is chosen for pleating to the stripe can have a profound influence on the look of a kilt. Color Figures 34c and d show two examples of the Wallace tartan pleated to the stripe, the first with the black stripe in red centered in each pleat and the second with the yellow stripe in black centered in each pleat. One kilt looks very red from the back, while the other looks very dark. They hardly look as if they've been pleated from the same tartan! For comparison, look at Color Figure 34b, which shows the Wallace tartan pleated to the sett. Yet another look!

Another consideration in choosing pleating to the stripe as opposed to the sett is the fact that a length of tartan will give more pleats if pleated to the stripe than if pleated to the sett. This can be a significant factor in a tartan with a very large sett, which may not give enough pleats if pleated to the sett. You may be able to gain an extra two to three pleats by making a choice of pleating to the stripe.

If you plan to pleat your kilt to the sett, go directly to Option A below. If you plan to pleat your kilt to the stripe (military pleating), skip Option A and go to Option B on page 62.

Option A: Marking pleats for pleating to the sett

The aim of pleating to the sett is to reproduce the overall pattern of the tartan in the pleated portion of the kilt, and because each tartan is different, no formula exists for how to pleat a kilt to the sett. This can be frustrating for beginning kiltmakers. The overall philosophy boils down to selecting sections of the tartan to appear in the pleats so that adjacent pleats display adjacent prominent elements of the tartan. Two different examples will illustrate the philosophy. **Take the time to work through both examples before tackling your own tartan. Then, use the instructions accompanying the examples to plan the pleating for your own tartan.**

Marking simple tartans with large color blocks and few narrow stripes

Simple tartans include those such as Barclay, Cunningham, Duncan, Erskine, Ferguson, Galloway, Hamilton, Kincaid, Lennox, Oliphant, Ramsay, Rob Roy, Rose, Ruthven, Sinclair, Strathclyde, and Wallace.

In a simple tartan, each pleat can be folded to show a solid color, a color boundary, or a stripe centered in each pleat, as shown Color Figure 34b.

Studying the sett

1 Begin with the assumption that the pleats in your kilt will probably be somewhere between about ⁵/₈" and 1" wide at the hips.

2 Study a full repeat of your tartan, and identify the prominent elements of the tartan that are between about ⁵/₈" and 1" wide. Each prominent element will be represented in one pleat. Here is an example:

> In the Wallace tartan at right, brackets show the prominent adjacent elements of the tartan. If successive pleats are folded to show adjacent prominent elements of the tartan, the overall effect will be a color pattern across the pleats that looks like the color pattern in the tartan.
>
> Notice that some of the tartan elements in the Wallace tartan at right consist of one solid color (elements B, D, F, and H). Other elements have a prominent stripe down the middle (elements A and E). Others have a color block boundary down the middle (elements C and G). The pleats will show the same patterns. Some will be solid color pleats (such as pleats B, D, F, and H). Others will have a stripe up the *center* of the pleat (pleats A and E). The remaining ones will have a color block boundary down the middle (pleats C and G).

Marking the pleats to the right of the center back

1 Once you have studied the overall structure of the sett and chosen the elements to reproduce in the pleats, go back to your piece of tartan that is laid out on the table. **Be sure that you are working at the top edge of the kilt and that the selvedge is away from you.**

2 Go to the center back, and mark the center back pleat with three parallel chalk lines each about 2 inches long, one for the center of the pleat and one on either side of the center mark (the distance from the center line doesn't matter - ³/₈" to ¹/₂" is fine). Note what element of the tartan forms the center back pleat. Here is an example:

> In the Wallace tartan, the center back stripe is tartan element E, a striped element . The center back pleat will have the stripe up the center of the pleat.

3 Starting at the center back pleat, *go one full repeat of the tartan* to the right, and put your finger on the tartan. Your finger should now be pointing to an element identical to that in the center back pleat. The center of the *next pleat over from the center back pleat* will lie in the center of the

tartan elements for Wallace tartan

| A | B | C | D | E | F | G | H | A | B |

A B C D E F G H A B
↓ ↓ ↓ ↓ ↓ ↓ ↓ ↓ ↓ ↓

elements repeated in Wallace kilt pleated to the sett

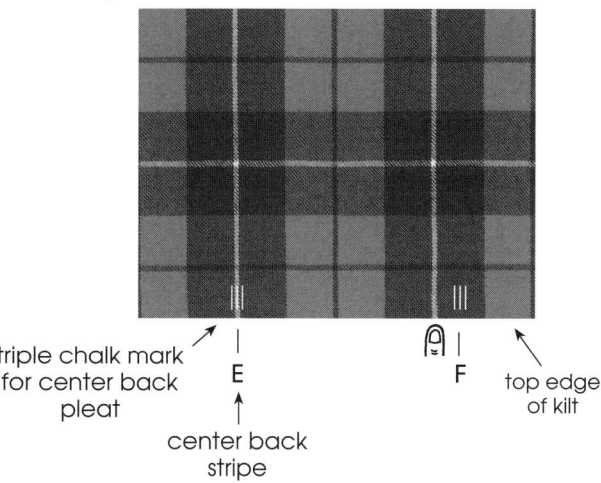

triple chalk mark for center back pleat

center back stripe

E   F

top edge of kilt

next tartan element immediately to the right of your finger. Locate the center of the pleat, and mark it with a chalk line. Draw a parallel line on each side of the center line. *The centers of adjacent pleats must be **more** than one full pattern repeat apart.* Here is an example:

In the Wallace tartan, going over one full repeat to the right will bring your finger to tartan element E again (previous page). The next tartan element to the right of E is tartan element F, a solid color element. The center of the second pleat that you mark will lie in the center of the color block, slightly more than one full tartan repeat to the right of the center back pleat.

4   Go one full repeat to the right of the pleat you have just marked, and put your finger on the tartan, which should show the same tartan element as the second pleat you marked. Locate the next tartan element immediately to the right of your finger, and mark the line in the center of the element. Add the parallel lines. Again, you should have moved over more than one full tartan repeat from the 2nd pleat. Here is an example:

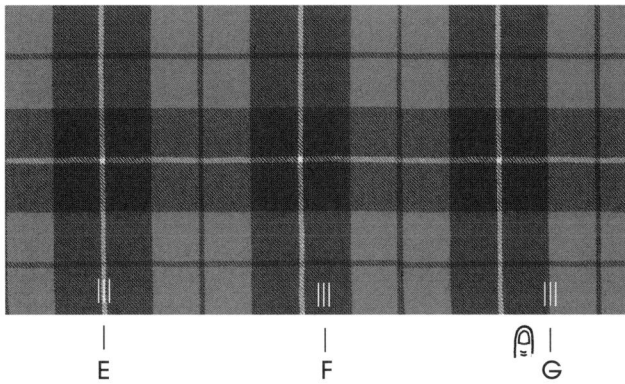

In the Wallace tartan, going over one full repeat to the right from the second pleat you marked will bring your finger to tartan element F again. The next tartan element to the right of F is tartan element G, a color-boundary element (illustration above). The center of the third pleat that you mark will lie at the boundary between the color blocks.

5   Continue to work your way across the fabric, picking up successive elements of the tartan and marking as you go. Make sure that each pleat

that you mark is *more than* one full tartan repeat to the right of the previous one.

6   The last pleat before the apron chalk line should be about 9" over from the bottom left edge of the apron. The apron is underlain by a deep pleat to help the kilt hang well and to accommodate the turned out knees of a dancer. Placing the last pleat too close to the apron edge will not allow enough fabric for the deep pleat.

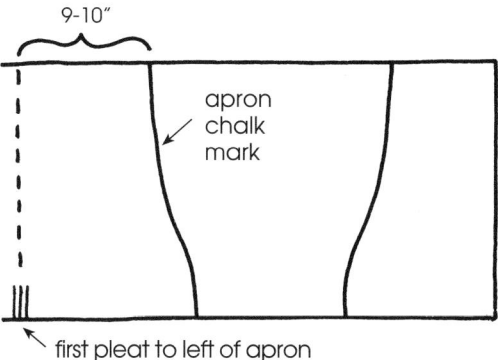

7   **If you wish to include a hidden pleat at the edge of the underapron for added weight or for growth, see Appendix C for instructions on placement and marking. You must mark the hidden pleat at this point – it cannot be added later.**

Marking more complex tartans

Quite frankly, most tartans fall into the "more complex" category, because they have smaller color blocks, more stripes than those described in the previous section, and many stripes that are not centered in the color blocks. Just a few examples include any of the Black Watch-based tartans (*e.g.,* Campbell, Gordon, MacKenzie, Murray of Atholl, MacLachlan, and dozens of others), MacBeth, MacBean, MacLeod, MacPherson, Menzies, Scott, Stewart, Sutherland – the list goes on and on!

In a kilt with many stripes, not all can be centered in pleats, as is the case with a simple tartan. Some of the stripes will form the edges of pleats, as shown in the Dress Royal Menzies kilt in Color Figure 35b and on page 60. Notice that all of the pleats have stripes lined up with the edges of the pleats with the exception of the single pleat in the center of the dark block, which has a centered stripe. **Notice that, as each edge-stripe pleat tapers toward the top of**

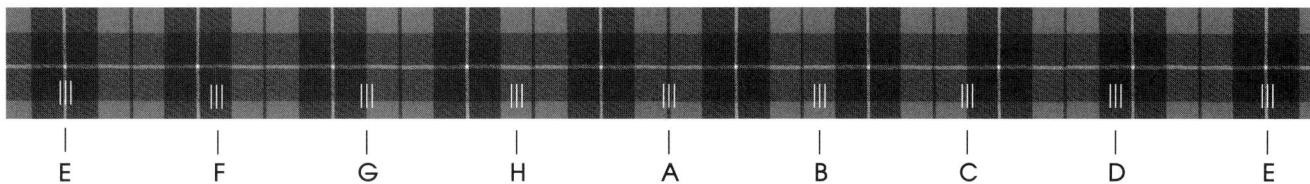

the kilt, the taper is accommodated in the solid color next to the stripe, while the stripe remains along the edge of the pleat.

Studying the sett

1 Be sure that you understand the example of marking pleats in simple color-block tartans, as illustrated with the Wallace tartan in the previous section.

2 Study a full repeat of your tartan, and identify the prominent elements of the tartan that are between about $5/8$" and 1" wide. Each prominent element will be represented in one pleat. Here is an example:

> In the Dress Royal Menzies shown at right, brackets show the prominent elements of the tartan that should be picked up in the pleats. Notice that element A has a prominent stripe down the middle, as did two of the elements in the Wallace example. The remaining elements have a prominent stripe or stripes that are not centered in the element (B through G).
>
> Creating a pleat from element A is straightforward, because the white stripe can be centered in the pleat.
>
> Tartan elements B through G have one or more stripes lying at the edge of a tartan block. Rather than centering any one of those stripes in the pleat, run the stripes straight up the inside or outside edge of a pleat, with any taper being accommodated in the solid color adjacent to the stripes. A pleat showing elements B through G will therefore be edge-stripe pleats, rather than centered-stripe pleats.

3 Identifying tartan elements that are the right size for the pleats in a tartan with many small stripes can be a real challenge and may take some time. Don't forget that pleats typically taper from hips to waist. Choose elements in such a way that tapering the pleat won't eliminate important stripes in the elements (see, for example, Color Figure 17 for a good choice and a poor choice of pleating elements with prominent stripes). Use chalk on the wrong side of the fabric to test some possibilities. Keep in mind that you will likely have a mix of solid-color elements, color-boundary elements, centered-stripe elements, and edge-stripe elements.

Marking pleats to the right of the center back

Once you have identified the elements in your tartan, the only difference in marking a complex tartan occurs for pleats with stripes that need to be

tartan elements for Dress Royal Menzies tartan

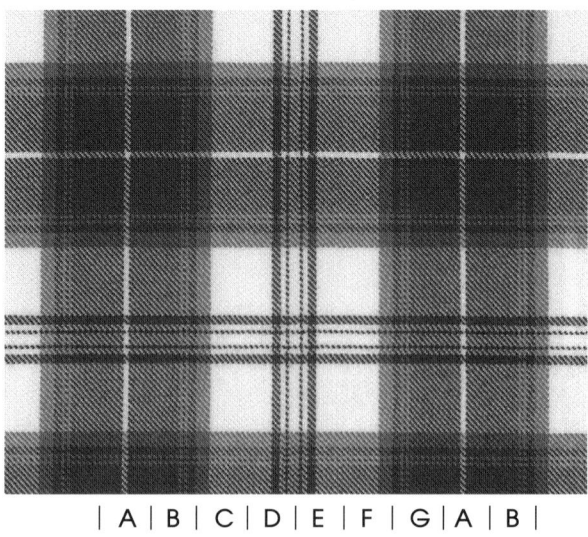

| A | B | C | D | E | F | G | A | B |

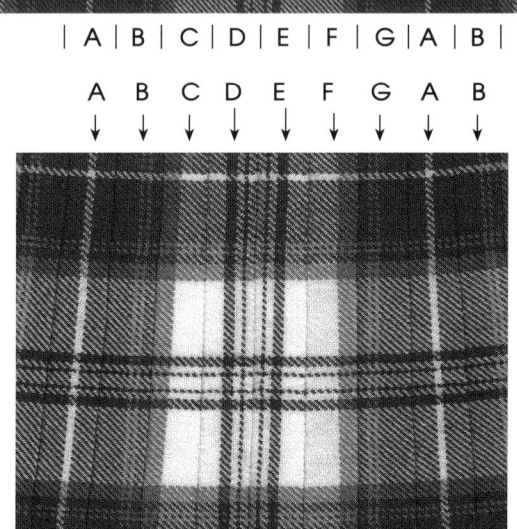

elements repeated in Dress Royal Menzies pleated to the sett

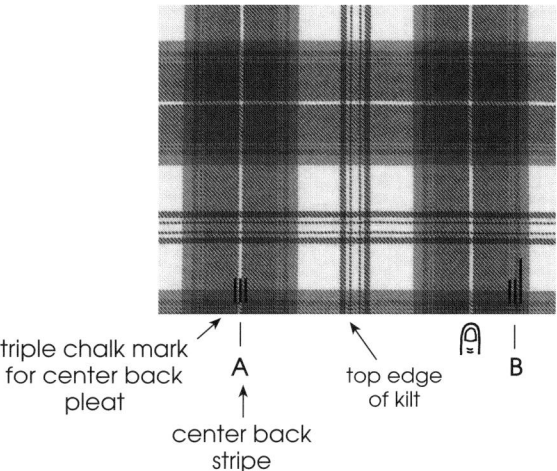

triple chalk mark for center back pleat — A — center back stripe — top edge of kilt — B

held straight along one edge. For such pleats, mark the approximate center of each edge-stripe pleat as usual, then mark a line on each side of the center. Use a long mark (approximately 4" long) directly down the stripe that must be held straight along the edge to remind you which stripe to hold straight and on which edge of the pleat the stripe should lie. Here is an example:

In the Dress Royal Menzies kilt shown at left, the center back stripe is tartan element A, a centered-striped element. The center back pleat will have a white stripe up the center of the pleat. It would be marked with 3 lines of equal length.

Going over one full repeat to the right will bring your finger to tartan element A again. The next tartan element to the right of A is tartan element B, an edge-stripe element with a double light blue stripe and a single dark blue stripe along the right edge of the element. The dark blue stripe will lie straight along the right hand edge of the pleats as viewed with the selvedge away from you. This pleat would be marked with a short chalk line at the *approximate* center of the pleat (although the exact location of the center will depend upon the width of the pleat). Make a long chalk line to the right down the dark blue stripe, and a short chalk line to the left of the first. This marking will tell you to hold the dark blue stripe straight along the right hand edge of the pleat.

Going over one full repeat to the right from the second pleat you marked will bring your finger to tartan element B again. The

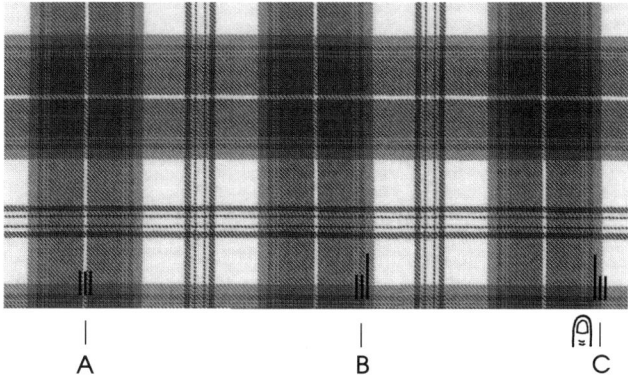

next tartan element to the right of B is tartan element C, an edge-stripe element with a light blue stripe on the left hand side. The light blue stripe will lie straight along the left hand edge of the pleat as viewed with

the selvedge away from you. Mark it with a short line in the approximate center of the pleat, a long line along the light blue stripe, and a short line to the right of the first. This marking will tell you to hold the light blue stripe straight along the left hand edge of the pleat.

Going over one full repeat to the right from the third pleat you marked will bring your finger to tartan element C again. The next tartan element to the right of C is tartan element D, an edge-stripe element whose right hand edge lies directly down the center of the group of four dark blue stripes on white in the middle of the large white undercheck. Pleats D and E will split the center of the group of stripes, and the right hand edge of D and the left hand edge of E will lie in the exact center of the white stripe in the middle of the group. This way, the long straight quadruple stripe will be preserved in the pleated back of the kilt (see the pleated kilt on the previous page and in Color Figure 35b). To mark pleat D, make a short chalk mark at the approximate center of the pleat, a long chalk mark to the right down the center white of the group of stripes, and a short chalk mark to the left of the first. The long line will remind you to keep half of the central white stripe straight down the right hand side of the pleat.

Going over one full repeat to the right from the fourth pleat you marked will bring your finger to tartan element D again. The next tartan element to the right of D is tartan element E, the other half of the group of stripes described above. Mark it with a short chalk mark at the approximate center of the pleat, a long chalk mark to the left down the center white of the group of stripes, and a short chalk mark to the right of the first. The long line will remind you to keep half of the central white stripe straight down the left hand side of the pleat.

The next pleat, F, will be a mirror image of pleat C and will be marked with short lines in the center and on the left and a long line down the light blue stripe on the right.

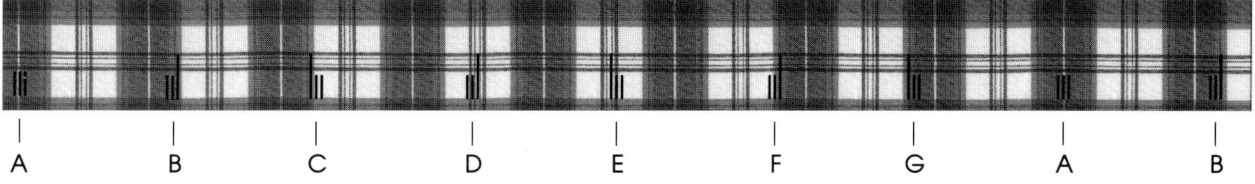

When you are ready to mark your kilt:

1 **Be sure that you are working at the top edge of the kilt and that the selvedge is away from you.** Mark the center back pleat, and continue to mark the remaining pleats, remembering that, in most tartans, you will have a mix of various types of elements. When you encounter an edge-stripe pleat, use the marking technique described on pages 60 and 61, and be sure that the long mark is on the correct side of the center mark.

2 Continue to work your way across the fabric, picking up successive elements of the tartan and marking as you go. Make sure that each pleat that you mark is *more than* one full tartan repeat to the right of the previous one.

3 The last pleat before the apron chalk line should be about 9" over from the bottom left edge of the apron. The apron is underlain by a deep pleat to help the kilt hang well and to accommodate the turned out knees of a dancer. Placing the last pleat too close to the apron edge will not allow enough fabric for the deep pleat.

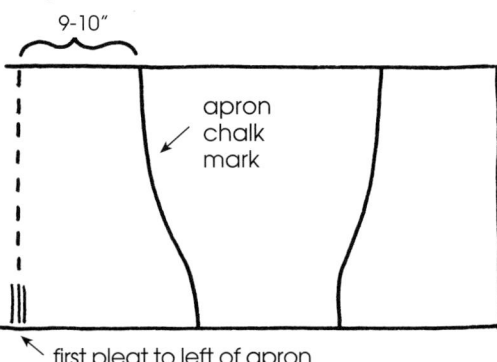

4 **If you wish to include a hidden pleat at the edge of the underapron for added weight or for growth, see Appendix C for instructions on placement and marking. You must mark the hidden pleat at this point – it cannot be added later.**

5 Skip Option B, and proceed to Determining the Number of Pleats on page 63.

Option B: Marking pleats for pleating to the stripe (military pleating)

**Skip this section, if your kilt is pleated to the sett, and go directly to Determining the Number of Pleats on page 63.

Studying the sett

Marking pleats for pleating to the stripe is easy, because each pleat will have exactly the same stripe down the center. The only choice you need to make is which prominent stripe to choose. Different choices for the same tartan typically give entirely different looks, as shown in Color Figures 34, 35, and 36. Experiment with various pleatings, and do a test pinning of several possible combinations to decide which you like the best.

Marking the pleats to the right of the center back

1 Once you have chosen the stripe to feature, go back to your piece of tartan that is laid out on the table. **Be sure that you are working at the top edge of the kilt and that the selvedge is away from you.**

2 Go to the center back, and mark the center back pleat with three parallel chalk lines each about 2" long, one for the center of the pleat directly down the stripe and one on either side of the center mark (the distance from the center line doesn't matter - $3/8$" to $1/2$" is fine).

3 Starting at the center back pleat, *go one full repeat of the tartan to the right*, locate the stripe, and mark it with a chalk line. Draw a parallel line on each side of the center line. Here is an example from the Wallace tartan:

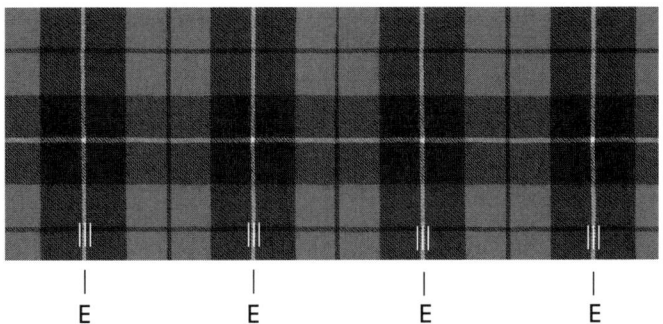

4 Continue to work your way across the fabric, marking an identical stripe for each pleat, until the last pleat that you mark is about 9" from the bottom left edge of the apron. The apron is underlain by a deep pleat to help the kilt hang well and to accommodate the turned out knees of a dancer. Placing the last pleat too close to the

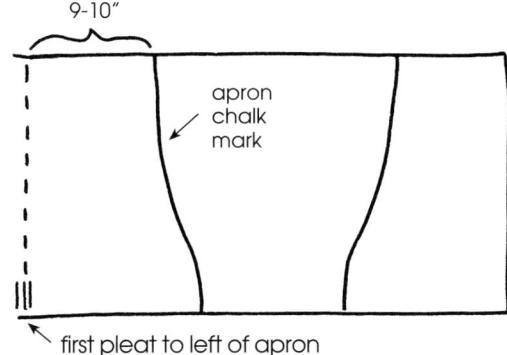

apron edge will not allow enough fabric for the deep pleat.

5 **If you wish to include a hidden pleat at the edge of the underapron for added weight or for growth, see Appendix C for instructions on placement and marking. You must mark the hidden pleat at this point – it cannot be added later.**

Determining the number of pleats, and marking the remaining pleats

You have already marked half the pleats plus the center back pleat. When pleating to the sett, the total number of pleats in the kilt will almost always be an odd number of pleats, because the center pleat must have an equal number of pleats on each side.[1] Count the number of pleats you have marked so far (including the center back pleat), subtract one, and add that number to the number you've already marked to give the total number of pleats in your kilt. For example, if you have already marked 12 pleats including the center back pleat, subtract 1 to give 11. You must mark an additional 11 pleats. Add 12 + 11 to give a total of 23 pleats. Enter this number on your record sheet.

With military pleating, a kilt can have either an even number of pleats or an odd number of pleats. Start by marking an odd number of pleats as described in the previous paragraph. You can always add an additional pleat if you have room before marking the underapron.

What you do next will depend on whether you started with a double or single width of fabric. If you started with double-width fabric, continue on to Option A below. If you started with single-width fabric, skip Option A and continue on to Option B on this page.

Option A: If you started with double-width fabric and have two pieces to be joined

1 Be sure that the selvedge of the fabric is away from you. Slide your marked piece of fabric to the right to make room to lay out the second piece of fabric. Be sure that the center back pleat is still handy on the right-hand piece of fabric.

2 Be sure that the second piece is oriented so that the ripped edge and selvedge matches with the first piece, and be sure that the second piece is right side up (check for both the chalk mark and the diagonal twill line). Double check this! Later on, you will sew these two pieces together. For

now, all you are concerned with is marking the pleats to the left of the center back stripe.

3 Begin at the center back stripe on the right hand piece of cloth. Mark pleats to the left of the center stripe on the *second* piece of fabric, using the same technique that you used to mark the right hand piece but working progressively to the left. Be sure to start the first pleat on the second piece of fabric *at least one full repeat to the left of the raw edge* in order to have enough fabric to make a full-sized pleat and successfully sew the join (illustration below).

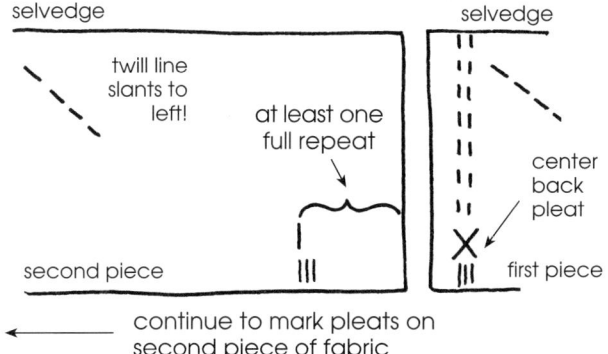

continue to mark pleats on second piece of fabric

4 Continue to work your way across the fabric, marking as you go, until you have marked the total number of pleats. Double-check to make sure that you have the correct number of pleats, and triple check that the pleats are marked in the correct places. It's easier to fix mistakes now than after you've sewn a bunch of pleats!

Option B: If you started with single-width fabric

1 Begin at the center back stripe (which you marked with an "X"). Mark pleats to the left of the center stripe using the same technique that you used to mark the right hand piece. Continue to work your way across the fabric, marking as you go, until you have marked the total number of pleats.

2 Double-check to make sure that you have the correct number of pleats, and triple check that

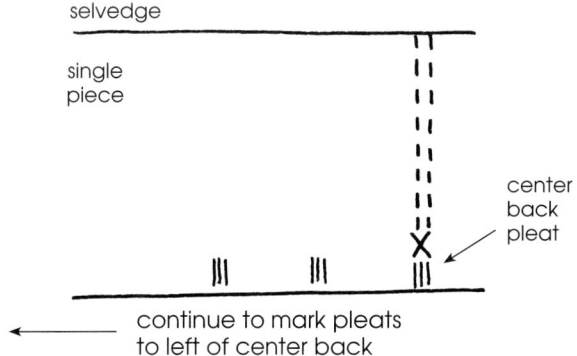

continue to mark pleats to left of center back

---

[1] A kilt will have an *even* number of pleats if you have located the center back line *between* pleats by splitting the center back element in two, as illustrated with elements D and E on pages 60 and 61, rather than by placing the center back down the middle of a pleat.

the pleats are marked in the correct places. It's easier to fix mistakes now than after you've sewn a bunch of pleats!

If you are pleating to the sett, here's a good way to check the work you've done. The first pleat next to the apron and the last pleat next to the underapron *must* be mirror images of one another. If they are not, you have made a marking or counting error. Remember also that most kilts will have an odd number of pleats, with the same number of pleats on each side of the center back pleat.

Marking the underapron

Choose and mark a center front stripe for the underapron

1 Consult your record sheet that lists the apron split in the hips. Divide that measurement in half, and select a center stripe located at least that distance plus 15-17" from the lower edge of the last pleat. This will leave enough cloth to make the inverted pleat at the right hand edge of the underapron and still allow for alterations.

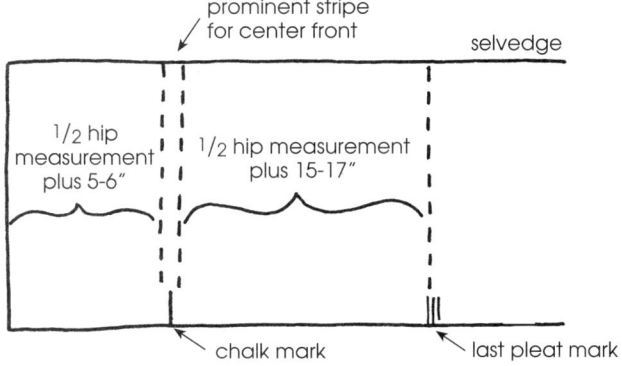

2 Make a chalk mark at the underapron center front along the raw edge. Measure the other half of the apron hip measurement to the left of the marked center stripe, and make sure that the lower left edge of the underapron will fall at least 6" from the raw edge of the fabric in order to leave enough cloth for self-facing and alterations. If the left underapron edge will be too far to the left, move the center stripe to the right, and make the inverted pleat shallower. The center stripe for the underapron does not have to be the same as the center stripe for the top apron. Because the underapron never shows, it doesn't really matter.

Marking the bottom of the fell and the underapron edges

1 As you did for the top apron, mark the bottom of the fell and the waistline with chalk along the center front stripe of the underapron.

2 For the next marks, check to be sure that you are looking at the fabric with the selvedge away from you. To mark the underapron edges at the waistline, lay your tape measure along the waistline, and measure half the apron waist measurement to the left of the center front line. Make a chalk mark (illustration below). Then, measure half the apron waist measurement *plus* $1/2$" to the right of the center front line, and make a chalk mark. Making the underapron slightly smaller than the top apron at the waist insures that the underapron can be buckled snugly so that the top apron can lie flat over it.

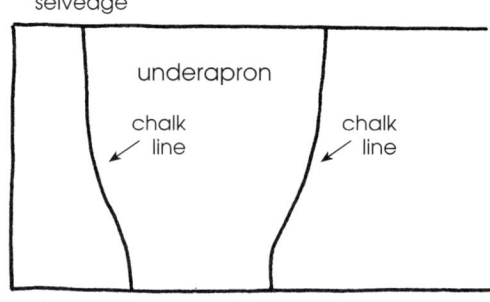

3 To mark the underapron edges at the hips, lay your tape measure along the mark at the bottom of the fell, and measure half the apron hip measurement to the left of the center front line (illustration above). Make a chalk mark. Then, measure half the apron hip measurement *plus 1*" to the right of the center front line, and make a chalk mark. If the kilt already has a huge amount of shaping, you can cut the extra inch down to an extra half inch to make the underapron edge easier to shape.

4 Starting at the top of the kilt, draw a chalk line parallel to the tartan stripes as far as the waistline chalk mark and then a smoothly-curving chalk line connecting the waist and hip marks at the right underapron edge. Continue the chalk line down to the bottom of the kilt in a subtly-flaring A-line shape as you did for the apron. Repeat for the left edge of the underapron.

Do not cut it off any extra fabric until the kilt is pleated! If you have made a marking error, you cannot to fix it if you have already cut the fabric.

Chapter 8

Preparing to sew the kilt

N ow that you have marked your tartan and determined the number of pleats, you need to determine how big each pleat will be before you can start sewing your kilt. This chapter teaches you how to determine pleat size and do the final preparation for actually sewing your kilt.

Determining the size of the pleats

The size of each pleat at the hip and waist determines both the size of the back of the kilt and the shaping from buttocks to waist. The "size" of a pleat refers to the *width of the portion of the pleat that shows in the back*, not the depth of the pleat. Pleats are typically no less than $1/2$" at the waist and no more than $1\,1/4$" at the hips.

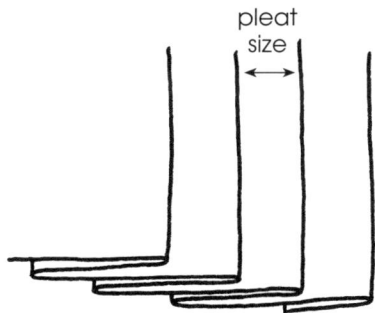

The traditional way of determining the size of pleats involves only a tape measure, a knowledge of the number of pleats in the kilt, and the measurements of the back waist and hip. Pleat size can also be determined using a calculator, if you are feeling less than traditional or want to use the metric system (see hints and tips box on the next page).

The following steps outline the traditional method for determining pleat size. Two illustrative examples appear in this section on pages 67 and 68.

The traditional method

1 On a piece of paper, write down the back hip measurement in inches and the number of pleats in the kilt.

2 Compare the back hip measurement and the number of pleats. It is very likely that the back hip measurement in inches will be smaller than the number of pleats (*e.g.*, 14 $1/2$", 23 pleats). **If this is so**, proceed to step 3. If, on the other hand, the back hip measurement is *larger* than the number of pleats (*e.g.*, 24", 19 pleats) which happens only if the sett and the person are large or if you

haven't bought enough tartan), proceed to step 2a below.

   a **Start here only in the unlikely event that the back hip measurement in inches is larger than the number of pleats.** Take your tape measure, and count over 1" for each pleat in the kilt, starting at the zero end of the tape measure, and note the number of inches.

   b Then, count over an additional $1/2$" for each pleat in the kilt, starting where you left off after counting the inches. Note the number of inches on the tape.

   c Proceed to step 4.

3 Start here if the back measurement in inches is smaller than the number of pleats. Take your tape measure, and count over $1/2$" for each pleat in the kilt, starting at the zero end of the tape measure. Note the number of inches on the tape (which will be the same as half the number of pleats).

4 Compare the number of inches on the tape with the needed back hip measurement.

   – If the number of inches equals, or is very close to, the back hip measurement, go to step 8.

   – If the number of inches is *smaller* than the back hip measurement, count over an additional $1/4$" for each pleat in the kilt, starting where you left off after counting the half inches. Note the number of inches on the tape.

   – If the number of inches on the tape is *larger* than the back hip measurement, go back to the measurement that you had before adding the half inches (*i.e.*, take away the half inches that you counted), and count over an additional $1/4$" for each pleat in the kilt. Note the number of inches on the tape.

5 Again, compare the number of inches on the tape with the needed back hip measurement.

   – If the number of inches equals, or is very close to, the back hip measurement, go to step 8.

- If the number of inches is still *smaller* than the back hip measurement, count over an additional $1/8$" for each pleat in the kilt, starting where you left off after counting the quarter inches. Note the number of inches on the tape.
- If the number of inches on the tape is *larger* than the back hip measurement, go back to the measurement that you had before adding the quarter inches (*i.e.*, take away the quarter inches that you counted), and count over an additional $1/8$" for each pleat in the kilt. Note the number of inches on the tape.

6 Again, compare the number of inches on the tape with the needed back hip measurement.

- If the number of inches equals, or is very close to, the back hip measurement, go to step 8.
- If the number of inches is still *smaller* than the back hip measurement, count over an additional $1/16$" for each pleat in the kilt, starting where you left off after counting the eighth inches. Note the number of inches on the tape.
- If the number of inches on the tape is *larger* than the back hip measurement, go back to the previous measurement (*i.e.*, take away the eighth inches that you counted), and count over an additional $1/16$" for each pleat in the kilt. Note the number of inches on the tape.

7 Again, compare the number of inches on the tape with the needed back hip measurement.

- If the number of inches equals, or is very close to, the back hip measurement, go to step 8.
- If the number of inches is still *smaller* than the back hip measurement, count over an additional $1/32$" for each pleat in the kilt, starting where you left off after counting the sixteenth inches. Note the number of inches.
- If the number of inches on the tape is *larger* than the back hip measurement, go back to the previous measurement (*i.e.*, take away the sixteenth inches that you counted), and count over an additional $1/32$" for each pleat in the kilt. Note the number of inches on the tape.

8 Once you have counted to as close as you can to the back hip measurement (see tips and hints box at right), add up the fractions of an inch that you have counted. If you have, for example, counted halves, quarters, and thirty-seconds of an inch, each pleat will be $1/2 + 1/4 + 1/32$ of an inch, or $25/32$" of an inch. If you have counted halves, quarters, and sixteenths of an inch, each pleat will be $1/2 + 1/4 + 1/16$ of an inch, or $13/16$". If you have counted inches, eighths, and sixteenths, each pleat will be $1\,3/16$".

9 Repeat the process to determine the size of each pleat at the waist.

Tips & hints: A mathematical alternative for determining pleat size

Of course, you can also use a calculator to determine pleat size. The method is easy and straightforward, although it doesn't have the "*je ne sais quoi*" of the traditional method. Here's what to do:

- determine the number of pleats in the kilt (*e.g.*, 21)
- determine the back waist measurement (*e.g.*, 12.5")
- divide the back waist measurement by the number of pleats ($12.5 \div 21 = .59$"), giving inches per pleat
- each pleat will be .59" at the waist
- repeat for the hip size of each pleat

The only thing remaining to do is to acquire a ruler divided into hundredths of an inch or to convert the decimal pleat size to the nearest $1/32$ of an inch.

Using a calculator to check the pleat size quickly is a simple and easy double-check on pleat size determined by the traditional method.

Another solution to determining the pleat size is to use the metric system. Take your measurements in centimeters and millimeters, use a calculator to determine pleat size, and use a metric ruler with millimeters for sizing your pleats. No worries about fractions!

Tips & Hints: What do I do when the counting method doesn't come out even?

It is highly unlikely that you will count to the exact back waist or hip measurement on the dot. Far more likely is the situation where one pleat size repeated will make the back too small and a pleat size only $1/32$" bigger will make the back too big. You can deal with this in one of two ways:

Option 1: Choose the pleat size that will make the finished back size as close as possible to the required back measurement.

– Hip pleat size: err on the larger side; avoid a pleat size that will make the back too small at the hips.

– Waist pleats: it's fine to choose a pleat size that would make the back slightly too small at the waist. Pleats at the waist typically turn out bigger than you expect them to anyway, unless you are absolutely meticulous. This effect is caused by the fact that the pleats taper from hip to waist. Each pleat would prefer to be straight, rather than tapered, and a pleat tends to expand unexpectedly as you stitch it down.

Option 2: Choose the pleat size that will make the finished back size as close as possible to the required back measurement, and increase or decrease every other pleat (or every third pleat, or every fourth pleat) by $1/32$" to make the back come out exactly the right size.

Determing pleat size, example 1

Step 1   back hip measurement = $20\,1/4$"

          number of pleats = 25

Step 2   The back hip measurement is smaller than the number of pleats, so we will skip step 2.

Step 3   Count 25 half inches from the zero end of the tape (diagram below). This will bring you to $12\,1/2$" on the tape.

Step 4 $12\,1/2$" is clearly smaller than $20\,1/4$". If you were to make each pleat in the kilt $1/2$" in size, the back of the kilt would be only $12\,1/2$" across. You obviously need to make each pleat bigger than $1/2$". So, starting at $12\,1/2$" on the tape, count 25 one quarter inches on the tape (diagram below). This will bring you to $18\,3/4$" on the tape.

Step 5 $18\,3/4$" is still smaller than $20\,1/4$", so making each pleat $1/2$" + $1/4$" (or $3/4$" in size) would still make the kilt too small across the back. So, starting at $18\,3/4$" on the tape, count 25 one eighth inches on the tape. This will bring you to $21\,7/8$" on the tape.

Step 6 $21\,7/8$" is clearly larger than $20\,1/4$", so making each pleat $1/2$" + $1/4$" + $1/8$" (or $7/8$" in size) would make the kilt too big across the back. So, go back to the measurement on the tape from Step 5 ($18\,3/4$") and count 25 one sixteenths on the tape. This will bring you to $20\,5/16$". This is plenty close enough!

Step 7   Skip.

Step 8   Each pleat at the hip will be $1/2$" + $1/4$" + $1/16$" = $13/16$" (or $6\,1/2$ eighths).

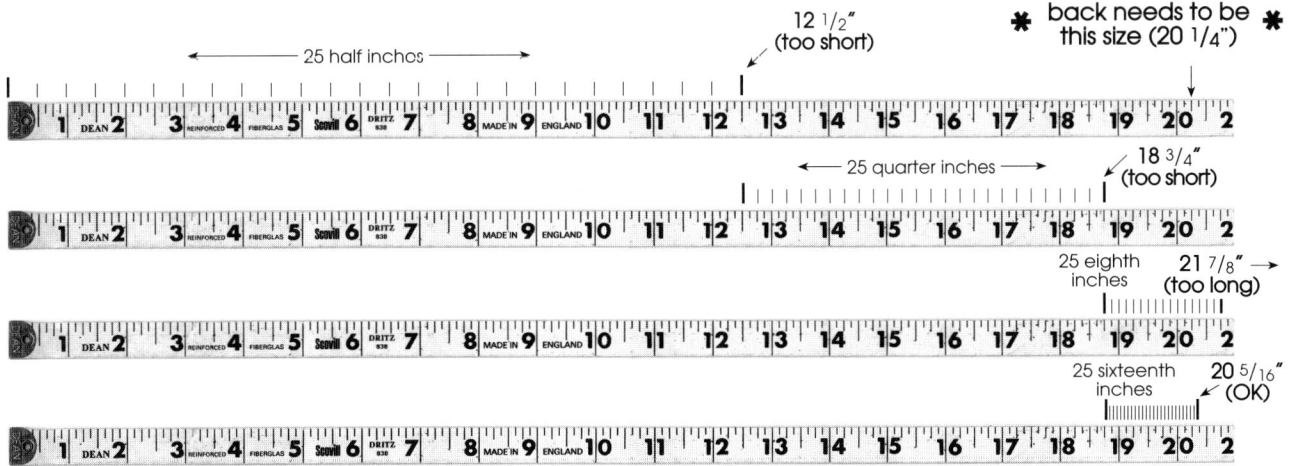

Determining pleat size, example 2

Step 1: back hip measurement = 16 $^1/_2$"

number of pleats = 23

Step 2: The back hip measurement is smaller than the number of pleats, so we will skip step 2.

Step 3: Count 23 half inches from the zero end of the tape (diagram below). This will bring you to 11 $^1/_2$" on the tape.

Step 4 11 $^1/_2$" is clearly smaller than 16 $^1/_2$". If you were to make each pleat in the kilt $^1/_2$" in size, the back of the kilt would be only 11 $^1/_2$" across. You obviously need to make each pleat bigger than $^1/_2$". So, starting at 11 $^1/_2$" on the tape, count 23 one quarter inches on the tape (diagram below). This will bring you to 17 $^1/_4$" on the tape.

Step 5: 17 $^1/_4$" is larger than 16 $^1/_2$", so making each pleat $^1/_2$" + $^1/_4$" (or $^3/_4$" in size) would make the kilt too big across the back. So, take away the one quarter inches you've counted, and go back to 11 $^1/_2$" on the tape. Count 23 one eighth inches on the tape. This will bring you to 14 $^3/_8$" on the tape.

Step 6: 14 $^3/_8$" is clearly smaller than 16 $^1/_2$", so making each pleat $^1/_2$" + $^1/_8$" (or $^5/_8$" in size) would make the kilt too small across the back. So, starting at 14 $^3/_8$" on the tape, count 23 one sixteenth inches on the tape (diagram below). This will bring you to 15 $^{13}/_{16}$" on the tape.

Step 7: 15 $^{13}/_{16}$" is still smaller than 16 $^1/_2$", so making each pleat $^1/_2$" + $^1/_8$" + $^1/_{16}$" (or $^{13}/_{16}$" in size) would still make the kilt too small across the back. So, starting at 15 $^{13}/_{16}$" on the tape, count 23 one thirty second inches on the tape (diagram below). This will bring you to 16 $^{17}/_{32}$" on the tape. This is clearly as close as you can get!

Step 8: Each pleat at the hip will be $^1/_2$" + $^1/_8$" + $^1/_{16}$" + $^1/_{32}$ = $^{23}/_{32}$" (or 5 $^3/_4$ eighths).

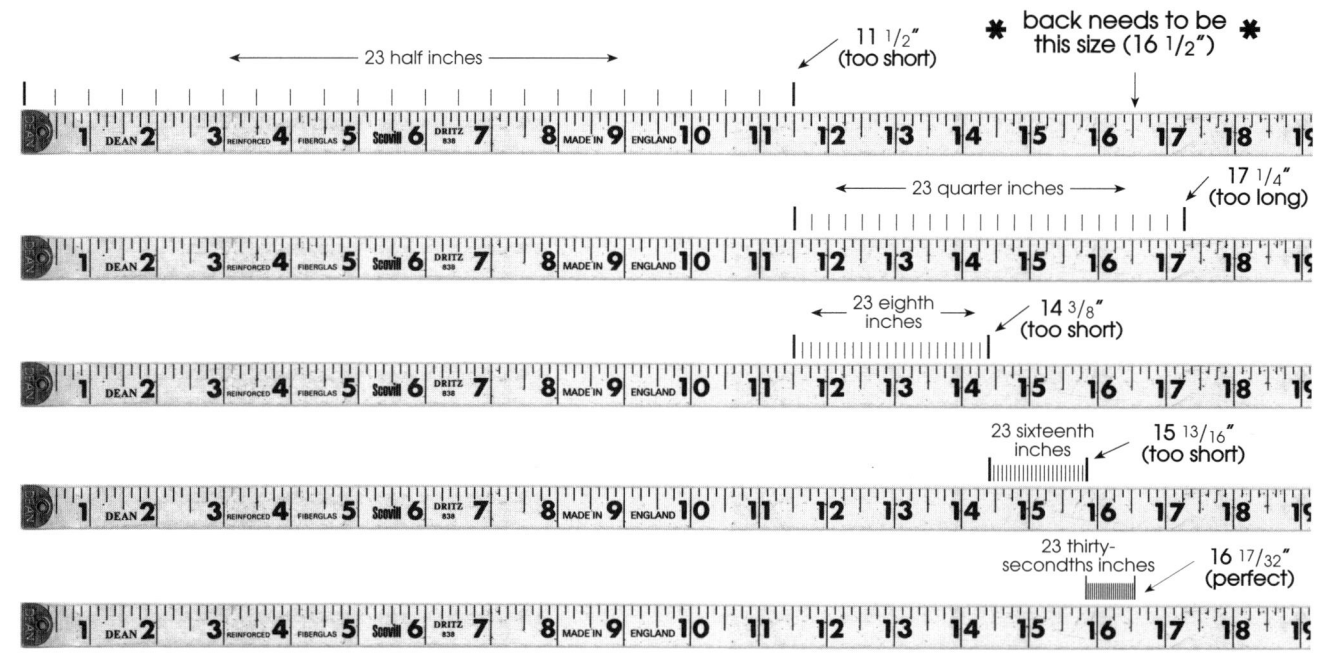

Just as an aside, traditional kiltmakers refer to pleat sizes in terms of eighths of an inch. A pleat $^1/_2$" in size would be referred to as being 4 eighths in size. A pleat $^{13}/_{16}$" in size would be referred to as being 6 $^1/_2$ eighths. A pleat $^{25}/_{32}$" in size would be called a pleat that is 6+ eighths in size (with the "+" referring to the additional $^1/_{32}$").

Tips & hints: Intrigued about why the traditional pleat-sizing method works? Read on!

The traditional method of determining the sizes of pleats seems arcane and baffling, and it's not clear to most people why the method even works. The explanation is actually quite simple and boils down to determining the size of a pleat by successive approximations. Here's what you're really doing when you use the method:

- The first step of the approximation involves counting $1/2$" times the number of pleats in the kilt. Once you have done this, you have determined simply how big the back of the kilt would be if you made each pleat $1/2$" in size. For some kilts, this is a pretty close approximation (*e.g.*, a back measurement of $11 \, 1/2$" with 23 pleats would count to exactly $11 \, 1/2$" with $1/2$" pleats). For other kilts, this is a lousy approximation (*e.g.*, if you made $1/2$" pleats for a kilt with 23 pleats but you needed the back to be 20" across, you would be off by nearly 8". You clearly need to make a closer approximation than $1/2$" pleats).

- The remaining steps of the process simply allow you to make a closer approximation to the needed size for each pleat. By counting an additional $1/4$" times the number of pleats in the kilt, for example, you will arrive at a measurement on the tape that is exactly the same as you would have had you counted $3/4$" times the number of pleats from the zero end of the tape. Mathematically speaking, $(1/2 \times 23) + (1/4 \times 23) = 3/4 \times 23$.

Why did this somewhat arcane technique develop? Why didn't kiltmakers originally just divide the number of inches by the number of pleats and come up with pleat size? The answer is probably that the tape measure method requires no skill in arithmetic. Kilts have been made the same way for over 100 years, and, particularly in the 19th century, one might not have been able to expect much in the way of math skills among young apprentices!

Making a record sheet to attach to your kilt

You will need to refer to kilt measurements and pleat sizes repeatedly during kilt construction, and traditional kiltmakers prepare a small square of paper with the pertinent data on it and stitch it directly to the apron of the kilt so that it can't be lost. Here's one format for your record sheet:

```
Jessie's Dress Nova Scotia kilt         8/00
6 yards;  6½" sett

                     apron splits   pleats splits
waist    25½            13½             12
hip      31¾            15½             16¼
length  20½+ 2" = 22½"  plus 4" hem
fell  7½"

  19 pleats
    waist: ½+⅛ (5/8")
    hips: ½+¼+1/16+1/32 (1/32 less than 7/8")
              (add 1/32 every third pleat)
no hidden pleat
```

Once you have filled out your record sheet, take basting thread and a needle, and baste the paper to the center bottom of the apron with several stitches in each corner. If you plan to hem the kilt, sew the paper to the center of the apron so that you won't have to remove it and re-stitch it when you turn up the hem.

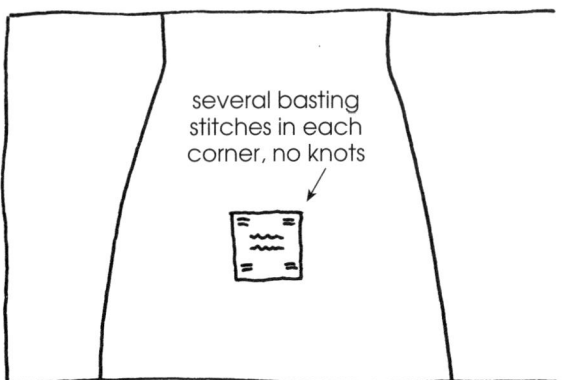

several basting stitches in each corner, no knots

Folding tartan to prepare for stitching

Once you have marked the kilt, fold the tartan accordion style starting right side up at the underapron edge and ending with the apron edge on the top of the stack. Keep the fabric stacked in this fashion, and unfold only the section on which you will be working. If you avoid moving the fabric around a lot, the chalk marks will be less likely to rub off.

Tips & Hints: Your Work Place

Be sure that your work place is well lit, and use a directional lamp shining on your tartan as you work. You don't want bright sunlight later on to reveal a badly-done stitch that you didn't see while you were sewing! Appendix F lists a source for good work lights.

You will work with the kilt in your lap most of the time, with your right leg crossed over your left one. Unless you have very long legs, a small riser 3-4" high under your left foot (*e.g.*, a very short stool or a thick piece of wood) can help take the strain off your back and neck by raising your knee up a little.

Chapter 9

Sewing the kilt

Well, here goes! You're finally ready to start sewing your kilt! By the end of this chapter, you will have a finished kilt. So, collect your needle, thread, thimble, scissors, work light, and let's go!

Basting the apron edges

Place the accordion stack of tartan on a table in front of you, with the top edge of the kilt to the left and the selvedge to the right. Sit in front of the table. Unfold the apron portion, and pull it into your lap, allowing the tartan to drape in front of your knees.

The right hand apron edge

1 Put basting thread in your needle, and do not knot the thread. **Do not wax the basting thread,** because the wax can leave a mark on your fabric when the basting is pulled out.

2 Fold the right apron edge to the back along the chalk line, and baste from the back side in a line about $1/4$" from the edge. Start your stitching with a double stitch, and begin stitching at the bottom of the kilt unless the kilt will have a hem. If the kilt will have a hem, start 6-7" up from the bottom so that you will not have to undo the basting when it comes time to stitch the hem. As you stitch, skew and stretch the cloth a little to keep the stripes straight and parallel both front and back. You can check to make sure that the stripes are straight by poking your needle through from back to front. The needle should go into and emerge from the same stripe.

3 Stop stitching when you reach the start of the shaping at the bottom of the fell. Open up the apron edge, and do a running stitch along the chalk line so that you won't lose your shaping line. The apron will have canvas interfacing above the bottom of the fell, and you will not want to baste the apron edge together until later, when the canvas is inserted.

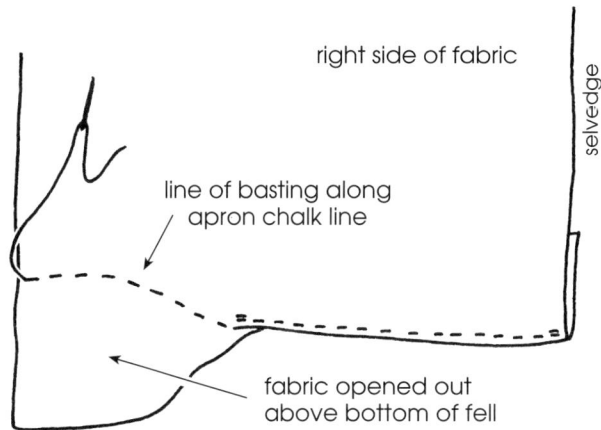

right side of fabric

selvedge

line of basting along
apron chalk line

fabric opened out
above bottom of fell

The left hand apron edge

1 Fold the left apron edge to the back along the chalk line, and baste from the right side in a line about $1/4$" from the edge. Start either at the bottom or 6" up depending on whether the kilt will have a hem. As you stitch, skew and stretch the cloth a little to keep stripes straight.

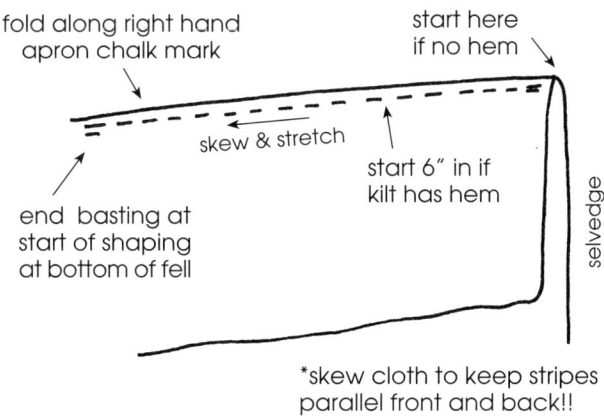

fold along right hand
apron chalk mark

start here
if no hem

skew & stretch

start 6" in if
kilt has hem

end basting at
start of shaping
at bottom of fell

selvedge

*skew cloth to keep stripes
parallel front and back!!

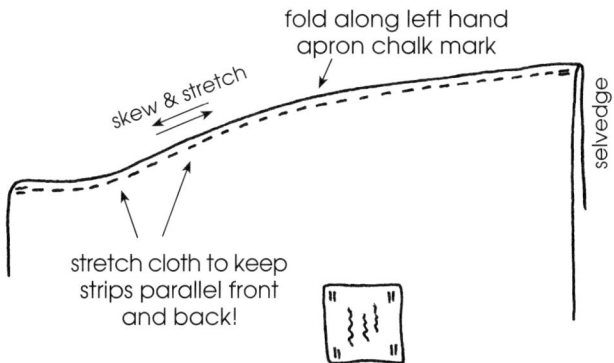

fold along left hand
apron chalk mark

skew & stretch

stretch cloth to keep
strips parallel front
and back!

selvedge

Why are our instructions are different?

If you have made a kilt before, or if you have read other materials on kiltmaking, you may find as you work through our instructions that our methods differ from those that you have previously used or encountered. The method for making kilts that we present in this book is the one that Elsie learned 50 years ago as an apprentice and kiltmaker with the renowned firm Thomas Gordon's of Glasgow. Our instructions include a superior method for stitching pleats, details for achieving a superb fit, and steps for all of the interior construction necessary for making a kilt that will hold its shape for a lifetime.

One of the most pronounced differences between our intructions and those of others is the method we teach for stitching the pleats. Many people make kilts by pinning or pinning and basting all the pleats before stitching any of them. Our instructions, on the other hand, teach you to fold and stitch one pleat at a time. Stitching one pleat at a time keeps all of the extra material out of the way, allows you to work both hands along the pleat edge as you stitch without bunching up a handful of material, and gives you maximum control over shaping each pleat from hip to waist so that the finished kilt fits perfectly. Even if you have made a kilt the other way, try it our way as you work through these instructions! We virtually guarantee that you will find it easier to fold and stitch each pleat permanently *before* the next one is folded and stitched.

2   Continue basting all the way to the top of the kilt. At the shaping, you will find it more difficult to keep the stripes straight and parallel both front and back. Use smaller stitches, work a few inches at a time, and skew and stretch as you go. Be very careful to keep the stripes parallel on both front and back – it's crucially important to shaping the kilt properly. Baste along a line parallel to the tartan stripes between the waist and the top of the kilt. **Do not taper the edge above the waist.** End your basting with a few double stitches, rather than a knot (which can be a real pain when it comes time to remove the basting).

3   If you have planned a hidden pleat, see Appendix C for how to baste the hidden pleat before starting to stitch the pleats.

Stitching the pleats

Stitching the pleats in a kilt is the most time-consuming part of making a kilt and the most crucial in terms of fit and appearance. If pleats aren't truly accurate in size, the kilt won't fit properly, and small errors in each pleat compound alarmingly over a couple dozen pleats. Good-looking pleats are important, too. Kilts are precise and tailored garments, and nothing looks worse than irregular, wiggly stripes or stitching that shows. The finest compliment for your beautifully hand-made kilt is the astonishment of someone who can't believe that all the stitching was done by hand from the right side of the pleats, because the stitching is so fine that it doesn't show!

Each pleat is folded, sized, and stitched before the next one is folded and stitched, and all of the shaping of the back of the kilt from hip to waist is accomplished during folding and stitching.

The overall strategy for stitching a pleat is illustrated below. The edge of a previous pleat is stitched down to the next pleat, which is already folded *before* stitching. The *sizing* of a pleat is accomplished when you fold a pleat and stitch the previous pleat to it, and each pleat is stitched through the edge of the pleat itself and the two thicknesses of fabric from the next folded pleat.

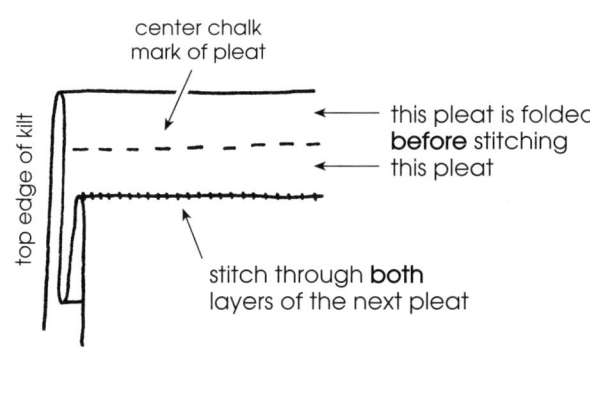

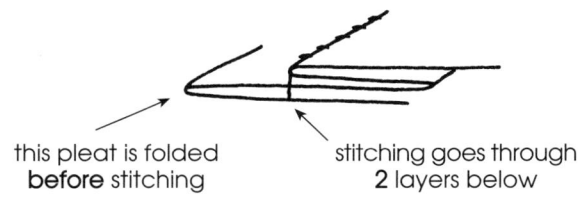

end-on view of pleats

Stitching down the apron edge and making pleat #1

1   Start with the accordion stack of fabric in front of you on the table, with the top edge of the kilt to the left. Sit straight in front of the table in a chair without arms, and pull the apron into your lap. Pull another yard or so off the table, and drape it in front of you.

2 Get ready to stitch before you fold the first pleat.

- Select a thread that will match the color of the left hand apron edge between the bottom of the fell and the top of the kilt. Thread your needle with just enough thread to sew an 8" seam (putting a lot of extra thread into your needle wastes time and invites tangling), wax the thread by pulling it through your beeswax three times, and knot the end of the thread securely. Set the needle aside where you can easily reach it. Once you have folded a pleat and are ready to stitch, you don't want to have to drop the fabric to get your needle and thread ready!

- Select one common pin, and have it ready as well.

- Take your tape measure, and drape it around your neck. Not only will it make you look like the real thing, but you won't be groping for your tape measure while you are trying to get a pleat set.

- Put your thimble within easy reach. You will be making thousands of stitches before you reach the end of the pleats, and your finger will take a terrible beating without a thimble!

- Cross your right leg over your left leg. No kidding. This is actually a crucial part of the process.

3 Locate the mark for the first pleat adjacent to the apron. Fold the fabric under in the general vicinity of the chalk marks, and leave a good foot of ease in your lap tucked up against your tummy before draping the extra fabric back down your leg again. If your first pleat is a solid-block or centered-stripe pleat (true for certain pleats in kilts pleated to the sett and true for all pleats in kilts with military pleating), go to Option A on the next page. If your first pleat is an edge-stripe pleat (true for certain pleats in kilts pleated to the sett), go to either Option B on page 75 or Option C on page 75.

Tips & Hints: A word about basting

Most people who make a kilt for the first time have successfully avoided basting all their lives. Well, maybe not entirely, but most sewing projects don't require much, if any, basting. Basting can't be avoided when making a kilt, however. Some of the basting is done to hold a portion for permanent stitching, but much of the basting is done to hold the kilt in shape for pressing. You'll be amazed at how much thread you use for basting! Here are some tips:

- Don't skip the basting. When the directions tell you to baste, there's a good reason for it.

- Do not wax your basting thread. Wax can leave marks on your kilt when you remove the basting.

- Use stitches of moderate size. Huge stitches won't hold properly, and teeny stitches are not only a waste of time but are a pain to remove.

- When you finish a section of basting, take a couple of large stitches in the same place to anchor the thread. Don't cast off by knotting or stitching teeny stitches. You'll eventually need to remove any basting that shows, and you don't want to spend hours picking out little knotted bits.

Tips & hints: Selecting thread

Basting thread: Cheap white thread is fine for basting, because strength isn't needed. Never baste a kilt with colored thread, particularly a kilt made from a dress tartan. Colored thread can leave marks on light-colored portions of the tartan.

Sewing thread: Select high quality 100% polyester thread in matching colors for the permanent stitching such as pleats, hem, and fringe edge. Gütermann and Mölnlycke make excellent thread. Do not use cotton (Mercerized) or silk thread. If you have trouble matching a color, select a shade slightly darker, rather than slightly lighter than the tartan.

Heavy thread: Use carpet (button) thread in either white or black where heavy thread is called for in the instructions (e.g., for steeking, canvas, top band, etc.). Do not simply double regular sewing thread. If the kilt will be lined in white or off-white, consider using white, rather than black, carpet thread, because black stitching in the canvas interfacing beneath the lining commonly shows through as unattractive black lines unless the lining is unusually opaque.

Option A: If the pleat is a solid-block pleat, or if it will have a color boundary or stripe down the center of the pleat

– The pleat should have three chalk marks of equal length, and the pleat should be a solid color pleat, or a pleat with either a stripe or a color boundary directly in the center of the pleat. If the pleat has *unequal* chalk marks for a stripe along the edge of the pleat, go to Option B or C.

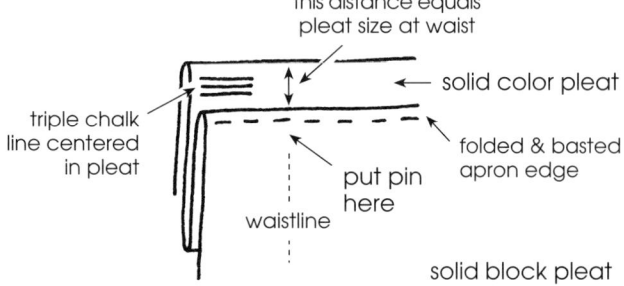

triple chalk line centered in pleat

this distance equals pleat size at waist

solid color pleat

put pin here

folded & basted apron edge

waistline

solid block pleat

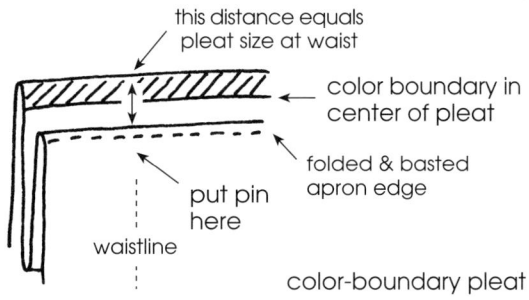

this distance equals pleat size at waist

color boundary in center of pleat

put pin here

folded & basted apron edge

waistline

color-boundary pleat

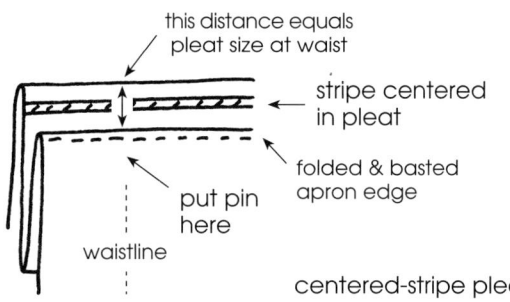

this distance equals pleat size at waist

stripe centered in pleat

put pin here

folded & basted apron edge

waistline

centered-stripe pleat

– Consult the record sheet sewn to the front of the kilt, and determine how big the pleat should be at the waist. Pick up the first pleat, and fold it so that the center line of the pleat will lie exactly half way across the pleat. If the pleat will be a $1/2$" pleat at the waist, for example, the center of the stripe should be exactly $1/4$" from the edge of the fold.

– Locate the waistline, which is 2" down from the edge of the kilt. Take the apron edge, and lap it onto the folded pleat at the waistline, making the distance from the apron edge to the folded

edge of the pleat *exactly* equal to the measurement of the pleat needed at the waist. Put a single pin in at the waistline to hold the top edge of the pleat.

– Consult the record sheet sewn to the front of the kilt, and determine how big the pleat should be at the hip. Move down to the bottom of the fell, and fold the pleat so that the center line of the pleat will lie exactly half way across the pleat. If the pleat will be a $3/4$" pleat at the hip, for example, the center of the stripe should be exactly $3/8$" from the edge of the fold.

– Lap the apron edge onto the folded pleat at the bottom of the fell, making the distance from the apron edge to the folded edge of the pleat *exactly* equal to the measurement of the pleat needed at the hip. Pinch the apron tightly to the pleat with your left thumb and fingers just above the bottom of the fell.

– Proceed to step 4 on page 76.

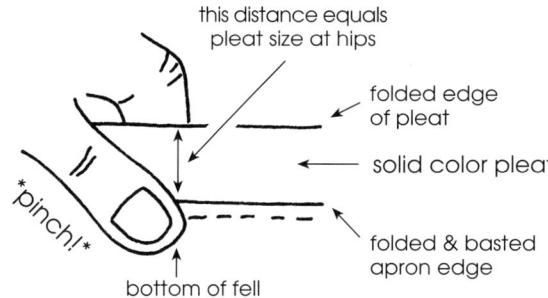

this distance equals pleat size at hips

folded edge of pleat

solid color pleat

pinch!

folded & basted apron edge

bottom of fell

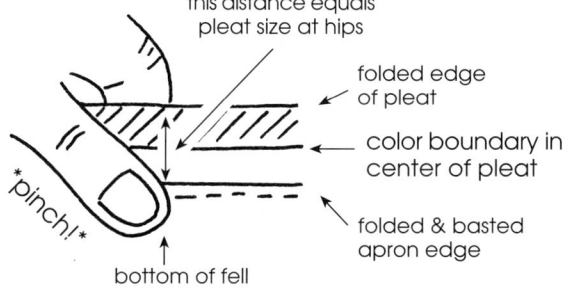

this distance equals pleat size at hips

folded edge of pleat

color boundary in center of pleat

pinch!

folded & basted apron edge

bottom of fell

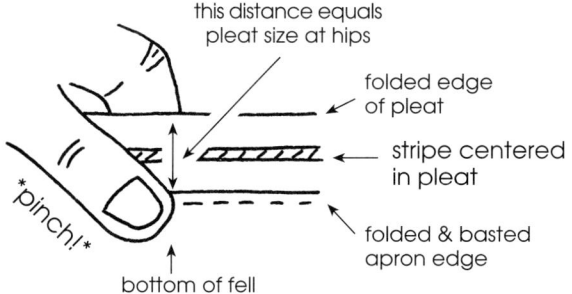

this distance equals pleat size at hips

folded edge of pleat

stripe centered in pleat

pinch!

folded & basted apron edge

bottom of fell

Option B: If the pleat will have a straight stripe down the *edge* of the pleat *away from* the apron

– The pleat should have 2 short chalk marks and 1 long chalk mark on the side *away from* the apron.

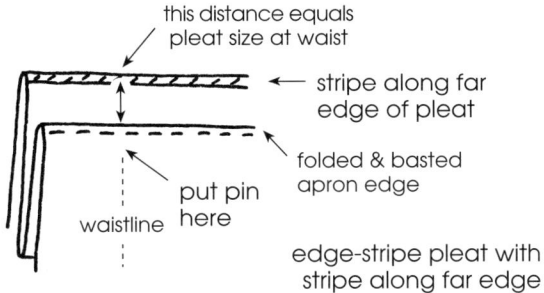

this distance equals pleat size at waist

stripe along far edge of pleat

folded & basted apron edge

put pin here

waistline

edge-stripe pleat with stripe along far edge

– Consult the record sheet sewn to the front of the kilt, and determine how big the pleat should be at the waist. Pick up the first pleat, and fold it so that the far edge of the stripe lies exactly on the fold of the pleat.

– Locate the waistline, which is 2" down from the edge of the kilt. Take the apron edge, and lap it onto the folded pleat at the waistline, making the distance from the apron edge to the folded edge of the pleat *exactly* equal to the measurement of the pleat needed at the waist. Put a single pin in at the waistline to hold the top edge of the pleat.

– Consult the record sheet sewn to the front of the kilt, and determine how big the pleat should be at the hip. Move down to the bottom of the fell, and fold the pleat so that the far edge of the stripe lies exactly on the fold of the pleat.

– Lap the apron edge onto the folded pleat at the bottom of the fell, making the distance from the apron edge to the folded edge of the pleat *exactly* equal to the measurement of the pleat needed at the hip. Pinch the apron tightly to the pleat with your left thumb and fingers just above the bottom of the fell.

– Proceed to step 4 on page 76.

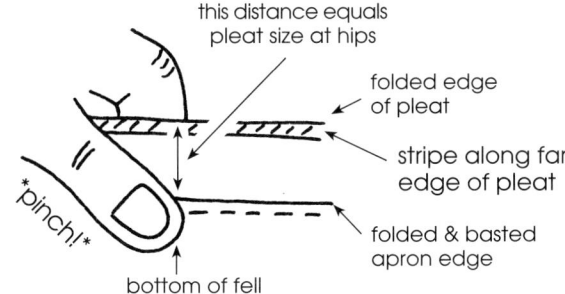

this distance equals pleat size at hips

folded edge of pleat

stripe along far edge of pleat

folded & basted apron edge

pinch!

bottom of fell

Option C: If the pleat will have a straight stripe down the edge of the pleat *nearest* the apron

– This pleat should have 2 short chalk marks and 1 long chalk mark on the side *toward* the apron.

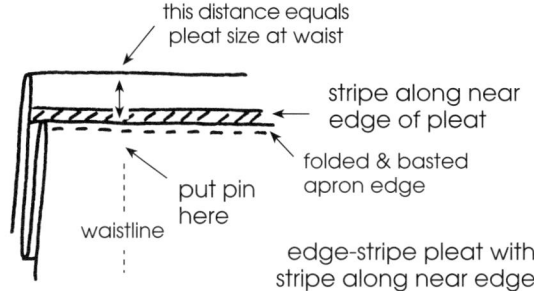

this distance equals pleat size at waist

stripe along near edge of pleat

folded & basted apron edge

put pin here

waistline

edge-stripe pleat with stripe along near edge

– Consult the record sheet sewn to the front of the kilt, and determine how big the pleat should be at the waist. Pick up the first pleat, and fold it over so that the near edge of the stripe will lie at a distance from the fold exactly equal to the measurement of the pleat needed at the waist.

– Locate the waistline, which is 2" down from the edge of the kilt. Take the apron edge, and lap it onto the folded pleat at the waistline, lining up the apron edge with the near edge of the stripe, checking to be sure that the width of the pleat is *exactly* equal to the measurement needed at the waist. Put a single pin in at the waistline to hold the top edge of the pleat.

– Consult the record sheet sewn to the front of the kilt, and determine how big the pleat should be at the hip. Move down to the bottom of the fell, and fold the pleat so that the near edge of the stripe will lie at a distance from the fold *exactly* equal to the measurement of the pleat needed at the hip.

– Lap the apron edge onto the folded pleat at the bottom of the fell, lining up the apron edge precisely with the near edge of the stripe, checking to be sure that the width of the pleat is exactly equal to the measurement needed at the hip.

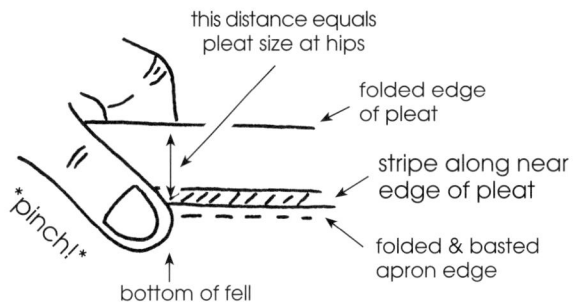

this distance equals pleat size at hips

folded edge of pleat

stripe along near edge of pleat

folded & basted apron edge

pinch!

bottom of fell

Pinch the apron tightly to the pleat with your left thumb and fingers just above the bottom of the fell.

4 Keep your left thumb and fingers pinching the pleat just above the bottom of the fell, and double-check the measurement. Bring the needle through from the back side of the first pleat, just catching the edge of the apron exactly at the bottom of the fell.

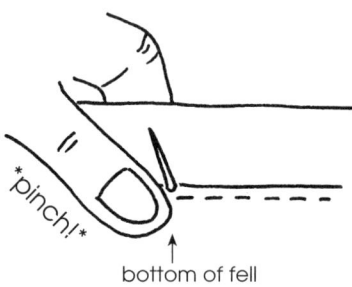

bottom of fell

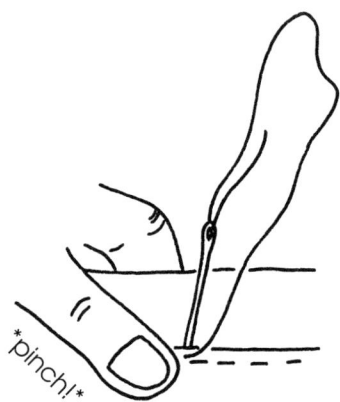

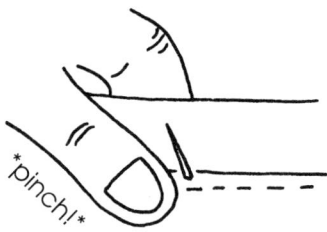

Pull the needle up through the cloth, poke it straight down through the two thicknesses of the pleat, and pull the needle through to the bottom.

Bring the needle up through the edge of the apron at the bottom of the fell again, and pull the thread taut. This provides a bit of reinforcement for the first stitch. Continue to pinch the pleat with your left thumb and fingers.

5 A pleat cannot be properly stitched unless the fabric itself is held taut. In order to hold the fabric taut, you will pull it with your left hand while you anchor it on the right underneath your right leg. Here's how to do it. The position may seem

awkward at first, but it's worth working at. There is really no other way to hold the kilt and make a properly shaped and stitched pleat. You'll feel comfortable with it after the first few pleats, so don't cheat!

– Be sure that your right knee is crossed over your left one.

– Place the stack of fabric on a table in front of you.

– Place the pleat to be stitched across your thigh just behind the top of your kneecap, with the top of the kilt to the left and the bottom of the fell directly over your thigh. Check to be sure that you have left plenty of fabric in your lap so that the yardage draped down your leg won't be pulling on the pleat you have just folded.

– Lift your right leg slightly off your left thigh, and use your right hand to tuck the middle portion of the kilt firmly around your right thigh. Drop your right thigh, and clamp the fabric between your right thigh above and your left thigh below. See? Crossing your legs right over left *is* important.

– You should be able to tug on the top edge of the kilt at the pleat and not have the kilt slip out from under your leg. You do not need to put the *entire* kilt in a huge wad under your right leg – just tuck enough of the middle portion that you can get a good grip.

6 Pleats in virtually all kilts taper from hips to waist. The secret to producing a perfect pleat is to pull the kilt taut with the left hand while stitching with the right. If you do not pull it taut, the pleat will not taper perfectly from hips to waist, and the stripes will tend to wiggle and wander.

7 Start by tugging on the pleat from the waistline in order to straighten the pleat.

Pull the pleat down across your thigh to the left to anchor the shape and size temporarily while you move your left hand, shifting your left hand to within a few inches of where you will begin stitching at the bottom of the fell. Pinch the pleat tightly between the thumb and fingers of your left hand, and rest the knuckles of your left hand on your knee (see color photo on the back cover).

Begin stitching from the bottom of the fell toward the top of the kilt. Use a very fine edge stitch (see Appendix A), and be sure to draw each stitch tight by pulling the thread *to the right*, rather than straight up or to the left. Your stitches should be made in the very edge of the apron and should be completely invisible.

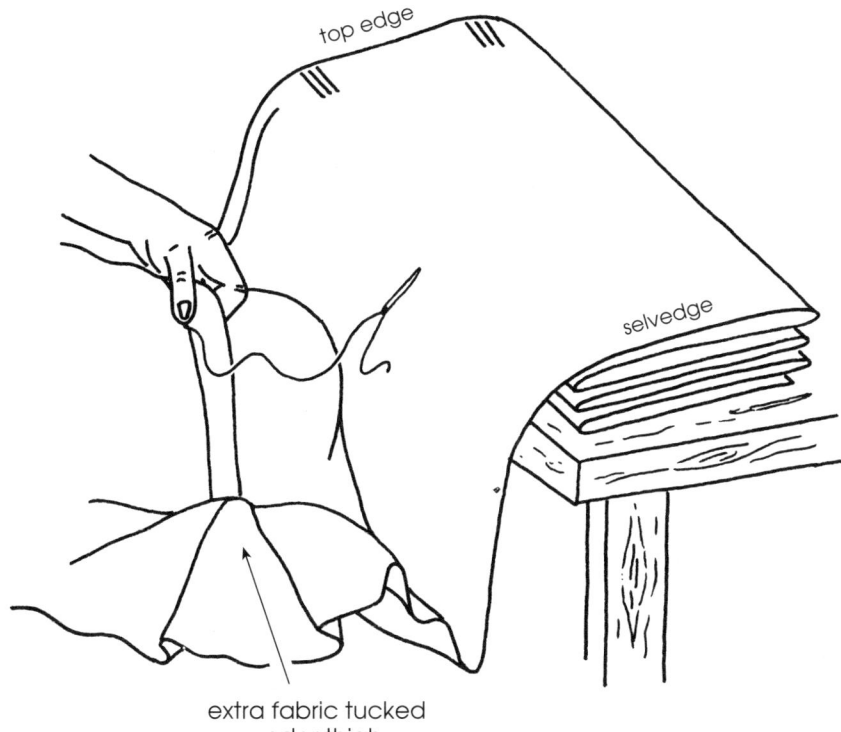

top edge

selvedge

extra fabric tucked
under thigh

8 Stitch the pleat from right to left, keeping the pleat taut as you stitch. Move your left hand along the pleat as necessary, and adjust the part tucked under your left leg so that you are always stitching directly over your thigh.

9 When you reach the waistline, remove the pin. Continue stitching to the top of the kilt, but be sure to maintain a constant pleat size above the waistline. **Do not taper the pleat from the waistline to the top of the kilt!** End your stitching about $1/4$" from the top of the kilt, and make many stitches on top of one another to anchor the top of the pleat. Do not knot the thread.

Congratulations! You have just folded pleat #1 and stitched the apron edge down.

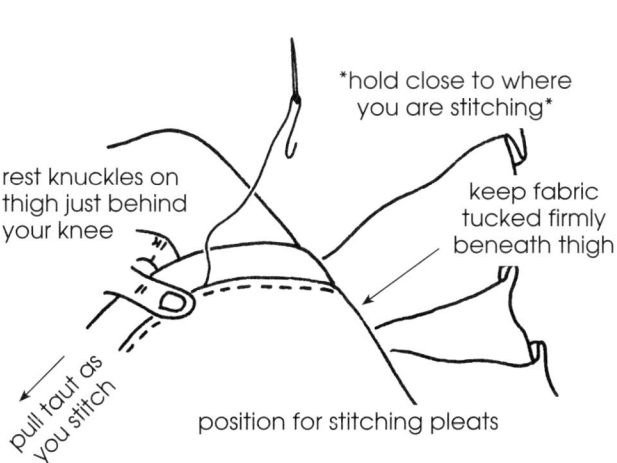

your knee
under the kilt

folded
edge of
pleat

extra fabric
tucked under
your thigh

basted
apron edge

bottom of fell

pin at
waistline

pleat to be stitched is draped over knee and straightened by tugging

tug with
left hand

*hold close to where
you are stitching*

rest knuckles on
thigh just behind
your knee

keep fabric
tucked firmly
beneath thigh

pull taut as
you stitch

position for stitching pleats

Inserting reinforcement for the buttonhole and stitching down pleat #1

1 Cut a small piece of hair canvas about 2" square. Fold the piece in half, and set it within easy reach. Thread your needle with thread to match the edge of the first pleat, and wax the thread. Be sure that you are holding the kilt correctly in your lap.

2 Locate the chalk marks for pleat #2, and fold the pleat at the waistline using the technique described on pages 74 or 75, depending upon the type of pleat.

3 Open up pleat #2 from below, and insert the piece of folded canvas, centered on the waistline. This piece of interfacing will reinforce the buttonhole that will convey the underapron strap through the kilt to the buckle at the waistline.

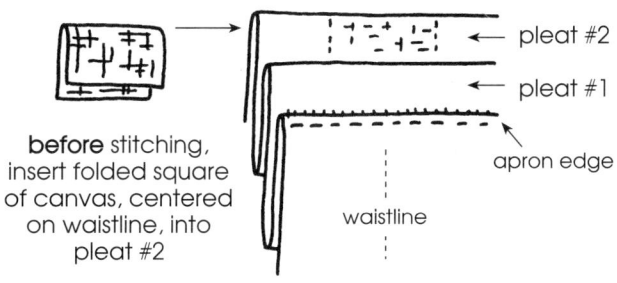

before stitching,
insert folded square
of canvas, centered
on waistline, into
pleat #2

pleat #2

pleat #1

apron edge

waistline

4 Refold the pleat, check the measurement at the waist, and pin the pleat at the waistline.

5 Go to the bottom of the fell, measure pleat #2 at the hip, and stitch down pleat #1 in the same manner as you stitched down the apron edge. **Be sure that you have folded pleat #2 before stitching and that you stitch through both thicknesses of pleat #2 as you stitch the edge of pleat #1.** Be sure to use the technique for holding the pleat taut during stitching.

Tips & Hints: The importance of pleating accurately

$^1/_{32}$" doesn't sound like much, does it? After all, it's about the width of one thread in the kilt fabric. Suppose, however, that you are making a kilt with 25 pleats. If each pleat is too large by only $^1/_{32}$", the kilt will be too big by 25 pleats times an extra $^1/_{32}$", or over $^3/_4$" too big!

Making the buttonhole and stitching down pleat #2

1 Thread your needle with thread to match the edge of pleat #2, and wax the thread.

2 Measure down 2" along the folded edge of pleat, and put a chalk mark at the waistline. Choose one of the following:

– **If your kilt will have 1" straps** (see tips and hints on page 105), measure $^5/_8$" along the folded edge of pleat #2 on each side of the waistline mark. Make a chalk mark at each point.

– **If your kilt will have 1 $^1/_4$" straps** (see tips and hints on page 105), measure $^3/_4$" along the folded edge of pleat #2 on each side of the waistline mark. Make a chalk mark at each point.

3 Locate and fold pleat #3, check the measurement at the waist, and pin the pleat at the waistline. Align the pleat at the bottom of the fell, and stitch

the pleat only as far as the first chalk mark below the waistline. **Be sure that you have folded pleat #3 before stitching and that you stitch through both thicknesses of pleat #3 as you stitch the edge of pleat #2.**

4 You will leave a gap in the stitching between the chalk marks on each side of the waistline in order to form the buttonhole for the underapron kilt strap. To do this, stop stitching at the chalk mark below the waistline, but do not cut your thread. Insert your needle into the fold of pleat #2, and run the thread through the fold. Bring the needle back out through the folded edge of pleat #2 at the chalk mark above the waistline, and continue stitching the pleat to the top of the kilt.

Stitching the remaining pleats

Fold and stitch the remaining pleats. For each solid-color, color boundary, or centered-stripe pleat, follow the directions in Option A on page 74. For each edge-stripe pleat, follow the directions in Options B or C on page 75. The only difference is that you will be stitching down a pleat edge rather than the apron edge. Read the following section and accompanying tips and hints boxes for advice on how to make better pleats.

First and foremost, if you find yourself stitching a pleat without first folding the next pleat, you have made a mistake. In practice, it's actually hard to make this mistake, because the unfolded fabric gets in the way and reminds you to fold the next pleat first before stitching.

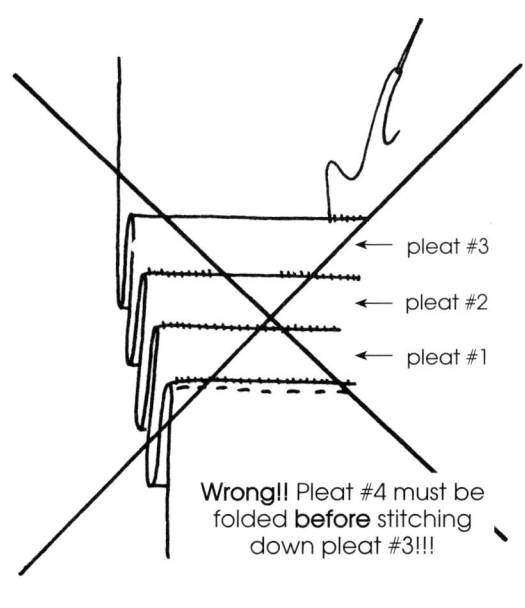

Wrong!! Pleat #4 must be folded **before** stitching down pleat #3!!!

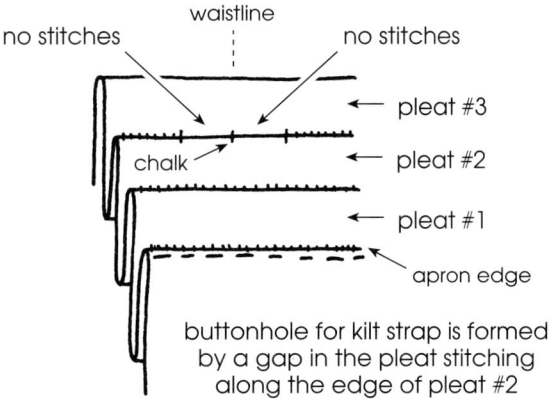

buttonhole for kilt strap is formed by a gap in the pleat stitching along the edge of pleat #2

A Trick for Making Perfectly Matched Pleats

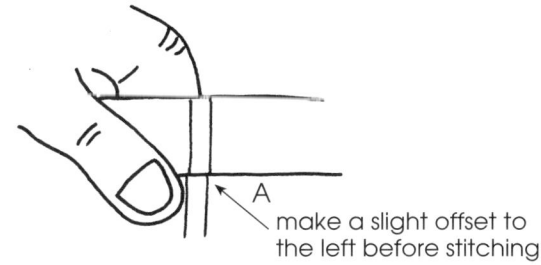

make a slight offset to the left before stitching

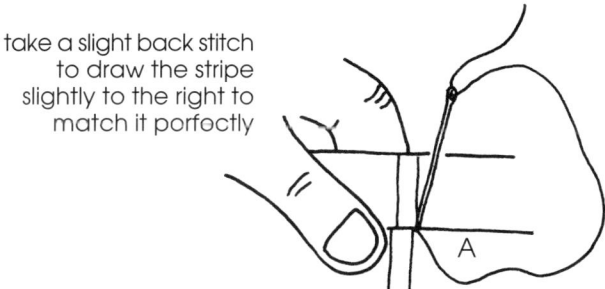

take a slight back stitch to draw the stripe slightly to the right to match it porfectly

We all want our pleats to look like the photo above on the right, not like the one on the left. Unfortunately, this is easier said than done. If you find this hard to believe, take a close look (surreptitiously, of course!) at kilts being worn at the next Highland gathering you attend. You'll see a remarkable number with badly matched stripes. As a kiltmaker, you, too, will experience the frustration of trying to align the stripes perfectly before completing a stitch, only to watch those very stripes skew a little as you pull the stitch tight. Once stitched tightly, the stripes make stair steps, rather than continuing smoothly straight across the kilt.

The solution? Mismatch the stripes before stitching by skewing pleat A just a little to the left (diagram above left). As you stitch a slight back stitch, pleat A will skew a little to the right (diagram above right). With a little bit of practice, you'll be able to judge the amount of offset necessary to pull the stripe perfectly into place as you stitch down the pleat. Then, you can be smug at the next Highland gathering when you see kilts with stair steps in the stripes.

Advice on Pleating

- Be sure to sit properly, hold the pleat taut, pinch the pleat close to where you are stitching, and pull the thread tight and *to the right* as you stitch. Holding the pleat properly as you stitch will help you avoid many of the blunders illustrated in the Color Figures.

- Make small, nearly invisible stitches that are close together. You don't want your stitches to show (Color Figure 12b)! Also, make each stitch a very slight back stitch.

- "Stair-step stripes" (Color Figure 13b and 14) are a glaring error in pleating. If you have trouble matching stripes perfectly, try the strategy suggested in the tips and hints box on page 79.

- Work hard to taper pleats evenly from hips to waist (2" below the kilt top). Pleats that narrow, widen, and narrow again are unsightly (Color figure 15b). Holding the kilt taut helps you to make a pleat that tapers smoothly. **Be absolutely certain, however, that each pleat is stitched with a constant width between the waist and the top of the kilt!**

- Be sure to keep any stripe or color boundary straight and either centered in the pleat or straight along the pleat edge. Wiggly stripes look unsightly (Color Figure 15c), as do stripes that are supposed to be centered and aren't (Color Figure 18c). If you are making a kilt with military pleating, don't blunder and place the prominent stripe off-center (Color Figure 18b).

- *Be accurate in pleat size*, or the kilt will not fit. After you have done several pleats, measure at the waist and hip, and compare this measurement to what you ought to have (simply multiply the number of pleats that you have stitched by the size of each pleat). If the measurement is a little long or a little short, you have plenty of pleats left that can be increased or decreased by 1/32" (which won't be noticeable) so that the final size at waist and hips is correct.

- If you find that the waist pleats are consistently a bit too big, don't be surprised. This is a common problem that stems from the taper of pleats from the bottom of the fell to waist. Each pleat would rather be straight, and the pleats tend to want to slide straight and to expand at the waist as you stitch them. Pinning the pleat at the waist *slightly* smaller (try $^1/_{32}$") than you need it to be can help solve the problem.

- If you make a crummy pleat, take the time to rip it out. Poor workmanship isn't obvious in many other parts of a kilt, but it stands out like a sore thumb in the pleats.

Stitching the Inverted Pleat

1 Once you have stitched the last pleat, thread your needle with thread that matches the edge of the last pleat, wax the thread, and knot it firmly. Take the folded edge of the last pleat, and line it up at the waistline with the chalk line along the right underapron (which will be a diagonal line).

2 Put a pin at the waistline. Fold back the edge of the last pleat at the bottom of the fell, and start

the thread with several stitches in the fabric on the back of the pleat about half an inch from the edge of the pleat.

3 Fold the pleat back down, and line the folded pleat edge up with the chalk line at the fell, matching the stripes. **Do not fold the underapron.** Pull the thread straight from the anchor point, but don't pull it so tightly that the

chalk mark at right underapron

← folded edge of last pleat

lap folded edge of last pleat to chalk mark at right edge of underapron

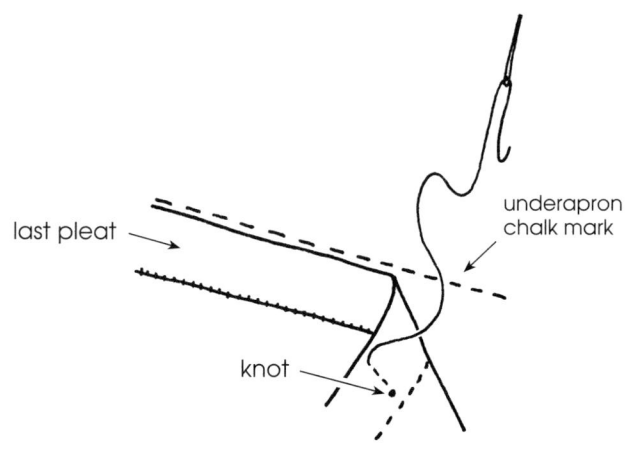

last pleat →

underapron chalk mark

knot

More Advice on Pleating

- Be sure to measure the kilt at waist and hip when you have completed the center back pleat. The distance from the apron edge to the *center* of the center back pleat (not the edge) should be equal to half the waist and hip measurements. If the actual measurement is significantly off, now is the time to track the problem down, when you have sewn only half the pleats, rather than discovering it when all of the pleats are done.

- Be very careful not to skip a pleat. With a good deal of extra fabric in your lap for easement, it's easy to miss a set of chalk marks and to skip a pleat. Get into the habit of checking the back of your work as you fold each pleat. The folds on the inside of the kilt should all be approximately the same depth. A skipped pleat will show up as an extra large fold that is very obvious, if you take the time to look for it.

- You should be in the habit of scrutinizing the color pattern that emerges as you pleat the kilt. If the pattern does not look like the tartan or is not symmetrical (Color Figure 16 b & c) (*e.g.*, if one side of a block has a red stripe but the other doesn't), one of three things has likely happened:

    - Chances are very good that you've missed one of the pleats that you marked. You'll need to rip out pleats until you get to the one you missed. If you don't, not only won't the kilt look right, but it won't fit properly, because the kilt will be too small by the size of the missing pleat.

    - You may have folded a pleat in the wrong place and inadvertently repeated or omitted a portion of the tartan (Color Figure 16b). You'll need to rip out pleats until you can refold the one that's folded improperly. If you don't take the time to do this, the back of the kilt will never look right, although the kilt will fit fine.

    - You may have marked the kilt wrong. If this appears to be the case, you should stop *immediately*, and locate the problem. If you have, indeed, marked the kilt wrong, you will certainly need to re-mark the kilt before proceeding, and it is very likely that you will need to take out all the pleats you have stitched as well. That's why it makes good sense to double and triple check your markings.

---

fabric puckers. Stitch the last pleat to the underapron along the chalk line *through only one thickness* from the bottom of the fell to the waist. Match the stripes, and ease the bias, stretching as necessary. Stitch the pleat to the underapron along a line parallel to the tartan stripes between the waist and the top of the kilt. **Do not taper the underapron edge above the waist!**

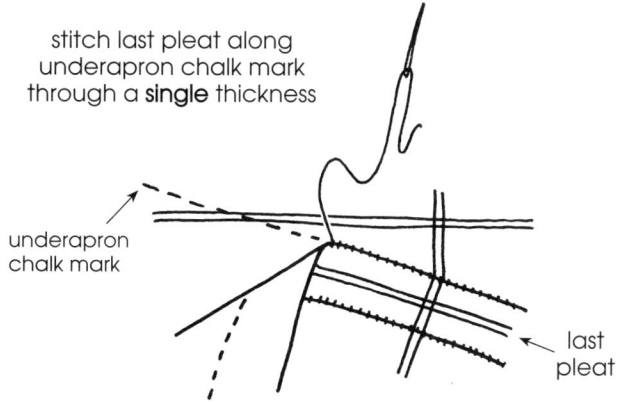

stitch last pleat along
underapron chalk mark
through a **single** thickness

underapron
chalk mark

last
pleat

4 Stitching the last pleat to the underapron chalk line will produce a very deep fold. Don't worry that you've made a mistake! The depth of this pleat will be split in half, with half folded to the back and half to the front in a box pleat shape. This is the inverted pleat, and, once the pleat is finished, it should be 3-4" deep both front and back, rather than 8" deep one way!

Phew! Congratulations! You're done with the trickiest and most crucial part of the kilt! If you stitched the pleats accurately, and if you measured correctly to draw the apron chalk lines, you can now be sure that the kilt will fit! The rest of the work to finish the kilt is considerably less nerve wracking.

Aren't you amazed that all that cloth that you started with is now stitched into such a compact package??

Stitching the join

**You can skip this section if you started with a piece of single-width fabric and go directly to Finishing the Bottom edge on page 83).

The two pieces of fabric in the middle of the kilt back should be sewn together so that the seam is inconspicuous. This means matching the tartan as closely as possible and hiding the seam on the inside of the pleat where the fabric folds back so that the seam won't show when the pleat opens up as the wearer walks.

1   Turn the kilt over, and work from the wrong side, with the top edge of the kilt to your right, for a change. All of the pleats should have their folds toward you.

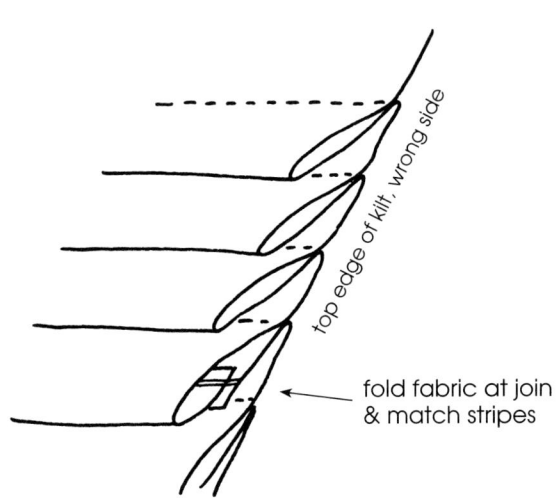

fold fabric at join
& match stripes

2   Locate the two raw edges at the join. One will be on top of the other. Take the top edge, and fold it under and away from you to make a pleat. Adjust the fold so that the tartan on the upper piece matches the tartan on the lower piece.

3   Pick a prominent line in the tartan about midway along the underneath side of the pleat. Clip the upper piece of fabric about $^5/_8$" toward the raw edge from this prominent stripe. Clip the lower piece of fabric about $^1/_4$" toward the raw edge from this prominent stripe. Rip off the excess from each raw edge. If the pieces are at least 2" wide, save them – one can be used for the fringe.

4   Holding the kilt with the top side to the right, open up the raw edges at the join, and fold both back away from you. Align the closer piece so that it is offset toward you from the other piece by about $^1/_4$".

5   Stitch the join seam with matching waxed thread along a line about $^1/_4$" in from the raw edge of the closer piece, starting about 1" above the bottom of the fell and ending at the bottom of the kilt. Stitch with small running stitches, using a back stitch (see Appendix A) every 2 or 3 stitches. Anchor the end of the seam with several stitches.

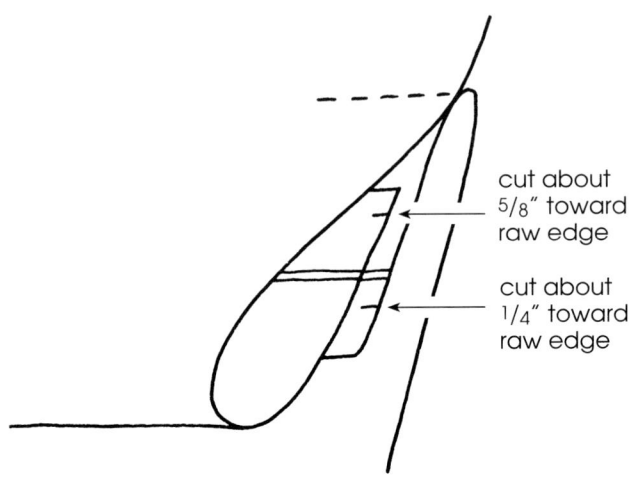

cut about
$^5/_8$" toward
raw edge

cut about
$^1/_4$" toward
raw edge

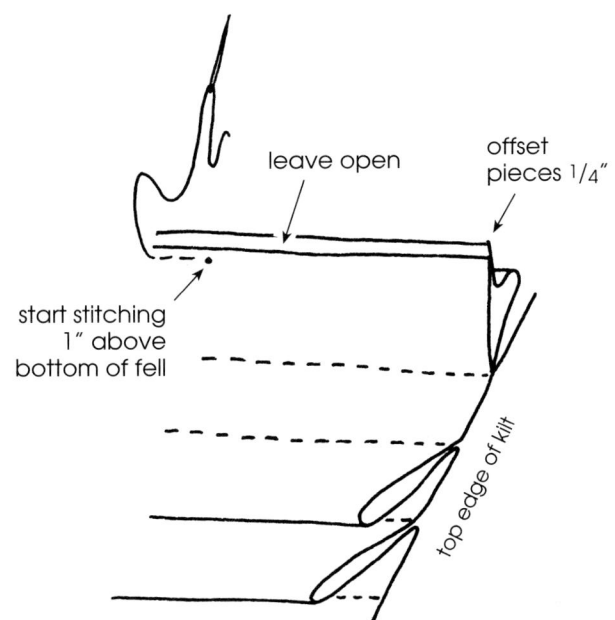

leave open

offset
pieces $^1/_4$"

start stitching
1" above
bottom of fell

6 Turn the kilt around, with the top edge of the kilt to the left. Spread the fabric at the bottom edge of the kilt, and open the join seam so that the fabric lies flat.

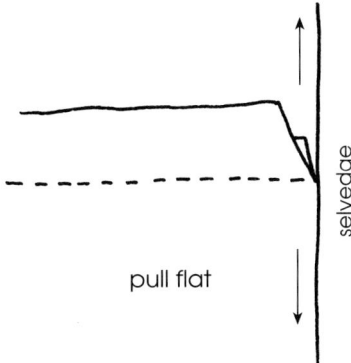

pull flat

7 Stitch the join seam as a flat-felled seam. To do this, fold the seam allowance away from you, and turn under the longer raw edge, enclosing the shorter raw edge. Stitch the folded edge down to the fabric underneath, making sure that the join seam is flat and that the stripes match. Use a small blind stitch and matching, waxed thread. Stitch from the bottom of the kilt to about 1" above the bottom of the fell.

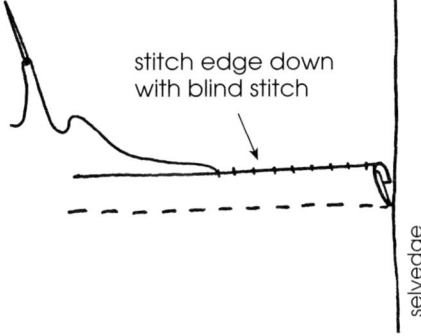

stitch edge down with blind stitch

selvedge

Finishing the bottom edge

If your kilt will have no bottom hem, go to Option A below. If your kilt will have a hem, skip Option A and go directly to Option B on page 84. If your kilt has a hidden pleat, go to Appendix C.

Option A: If your kilt will *not* have a hem

Even if your kilt will not have a hem, you need to make a few modifications to the bottom edge of the kilt in order to keep portions of the underapron and deep pleat from sagging below the top apron and giving the kilt an unsightly appearance from the front.

1 Start by trimming the excess fabric from the left *underapron* edge. Don't blunder and trim the wrong edge! If you are holding the kilt right side up with the top to the left, the underapron edge is the farthest away from you. Clip the underapron edge about 6" from the chalk mark at the bottom edge of the kilt, and rip off the excess. Save the scrap for fringe or buckles.

2 Measure about 9" from the chalk mark at the left underapron edge toward the center of the underapron, and make a small chalk mark. Fold the lower edge of the kilt to the inside on the diagonal, tapering from about $^7/_8$" at the raw edge to nothing at the chalk mark you just made. Knot a basting thread, and baste about an inch back from the selvedge edge. This taper keeps the underapron edge from sagging below the top apron at the left corner and looking unsightly.

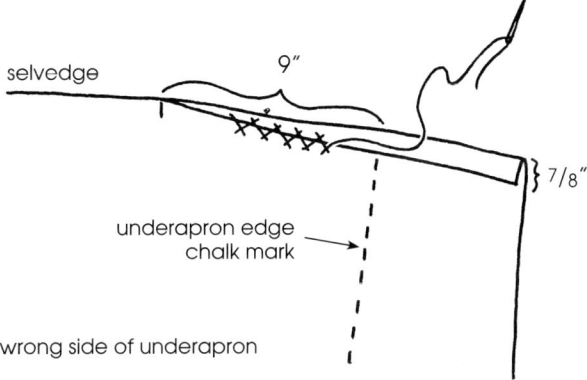

selvedge   9"

underapron edge chalk mark

$^7/_8$"

wrong side of underapron

3 On the inside, stitch the edge with a herringbone stitch (see Appendix A) using waxed, matching thread .

4 Turn the kilt to the front, and go to the left edge of the top apron. Bring the apron at the lower edge of the kilt to the lap line on the first pleat (which will be straight down the tartan from the bottom of the fell). Pinch and hold the apron at the lap line, and locate the middle of the deep pleat behind the apron edge. Mark both the lap line and the midpoint of the deep pleat with pins or chalk.

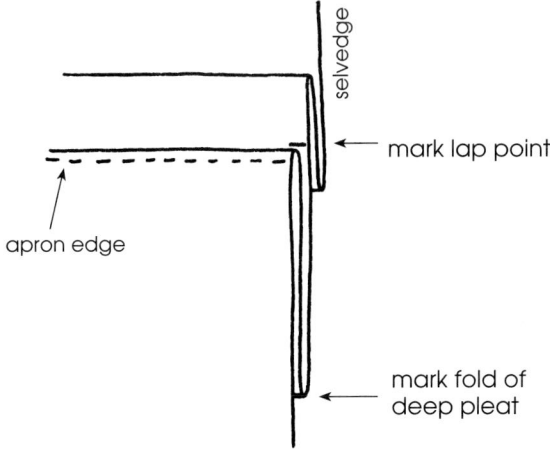

selvedge

mark lap point

apron edge

mark fold of deep pleat

5   Turn the kilt to the wrong side, and open up the deep pleat. Fold a dip in the bottom of the kilt to the inside that tapers from nothing just past the apron edge to about $^3/_8$" at the midpoint of the deep pleat, to nothing again at the lap line for the apron. Baste, and then stitch with a herringbone stitch. The "dip" keeps the point of the deep pleat from sagging below the top apron.

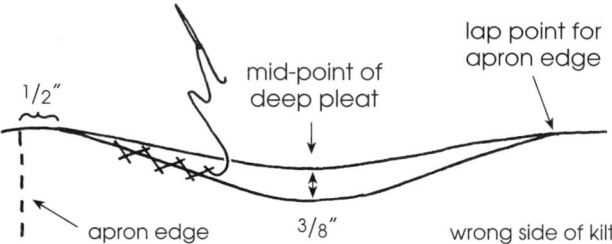

6   Skip Option B, and go directly to Completing the Inverted Pleat on page 85.

Option B: If your kilt will have a hem

A kilt hem is not turned up evenly everywhere. Some portions are turned up slightly more than others in order to keep the corners of the underapron and deep pleat from sagging below the top apron and giving the kilt an unsightly appearance from the front.

1   Start by trimming the excess fabric from the left *underapron* edge. Don't blunder and trim the wrong edge! If you are holding the kilt with the top to the left, the underapron edge is the farthest away from you. Clip the underapron edge about 6" from the chalk mark at the bottom edge of the kilt, and rip off the excess. Save the scrap for fringe or buckles.

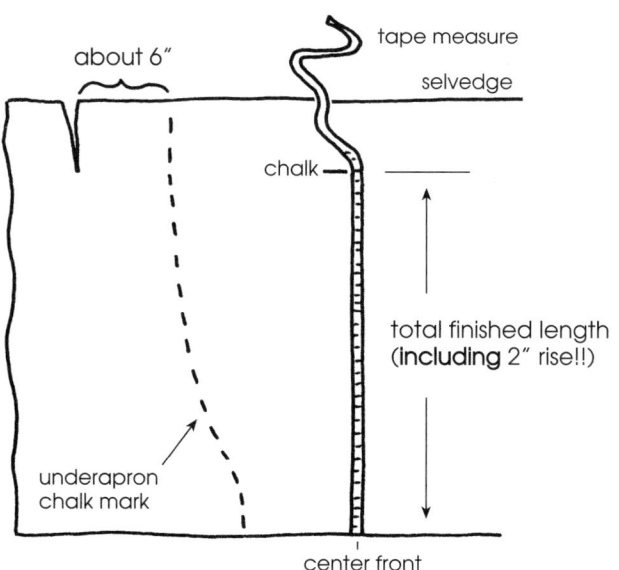

2   Check your record sheet to determine the total final length of the kilt (which includes the 2" rise, remember). Turn the kilt to the right side of the *underapron*, and measure the total final length down from the top of the kilt edge roughly in the center of the underapron. Determine where the kilt will be turned up, and mark this with a pin or chalk mark on the right side of the underapron. Double and triple check the measurement. You don't want to have to take the hem out.

3   Measure about 9" from the chalk mark at the left underapron edge toward the center of the underapron, and make a small chalk mark . Fold the lower edge of the kilt to the inside on a diagonal, tapering from the actual hem length at the chalk mark to a hem allowance with an extra $^7/_8$" at the raw left edge of the underapron. This taper keeps the underapron edge from sagging below the top apron at the left corner and looking unsightly.

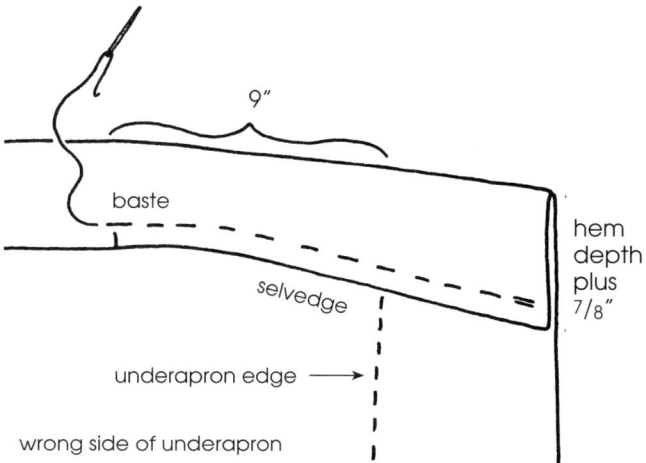

4   Hold the kilt with the hem facing away from you. Knot a basting thread, and baste from right to left about an inch back from the selvedge edge, starting with the tapered portion. Stretch the fabric a little to keep the stripes even. When you reach the normal part of the hem, continue folding up the hem and basting until you are within an inch or two of the first pleat (remember that the first pleat you stitched lies at the *apron* edge, so you will baste across nearly the entire back of the kilt before stopping). Be sure to turn the hem up along a line exactly parallel to one of the tartan stripes, rather than turning up a measured hem allowance from the inside. Selvedges in some tartans are a bit wavy, and what's important is the line at the bottom of the kilt as viewed from the outside, not the depth of the hem allowance as viewed from the inside.

5 When you are within a few inches of the first pleat, turn the kilt to the front, and go to the left edge of the top apron. Bring the apron at the lower edge of the kilt to the lap line on the first pleat (which will be straight down the tartan from the bottom of the fell). Pinch and hold the apron at the lap line, and locate the middle of the deep pleat behind the apron edge. Mark both the lap line and the midpoint of the deep pleat with pins.

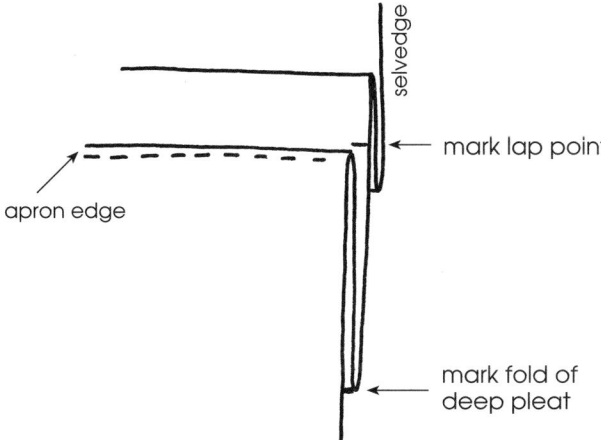

selvedge

← mark lap point

apron edge

← mark fold of deep pleat

6 Turn the kilt to the wrong side, and open up the deep pleat. Turn up the hem with an extra $3/8$" at the middle of the deep pleat. Taper to the regular hem allowance at the apron lap line and just outside the chalk mark at the edge of the apron. The "dip" keeps the point of the deep pleat from sagging below the top apron.

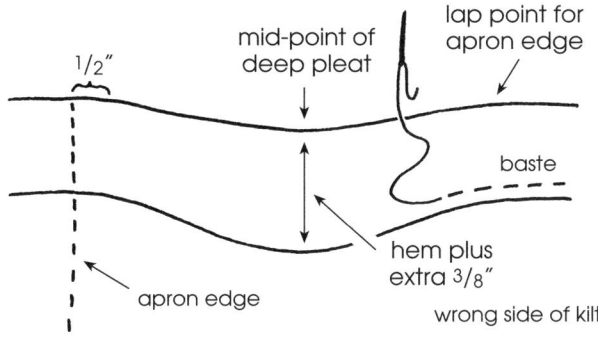

1/2"

mid-point of deep pleat

lap point for apron edge

baste

hem plus extra 3/8"

apron edge

wrong side of kilt

7 Continue basting across the dip, and baste the remaining hem at the exact hem length. The right edge of the apron hem is *not* basted on a taper. Before basting the last of the hem, pull a $1/2$" fringe on the apron edge. Be sure not to pull more than $1/2$", because a longer fringe quickly becomes ratty.

8 On the inside, stitch the hem edge with a herringbone stitch (see Appendix A) using waxed, matching thread. **Do not use a blind stitch.** Start at the *fringe* edge and work to the *right*.

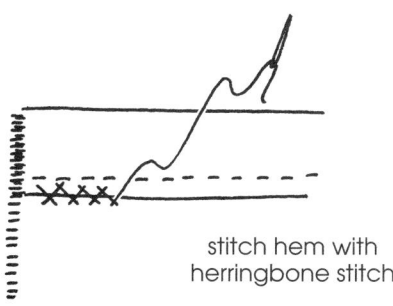

stitch hem with herringbone stitch

9 Baste the right and left edges of the top apron, which you had left open in order to do the hem. Be sure to skew and stretch to keep the stripes straight and even.

Completing the inverted pleat

1 Turn the kilt to the wrong side, with the top edge to the left. Fold the inverted pleat away from you.

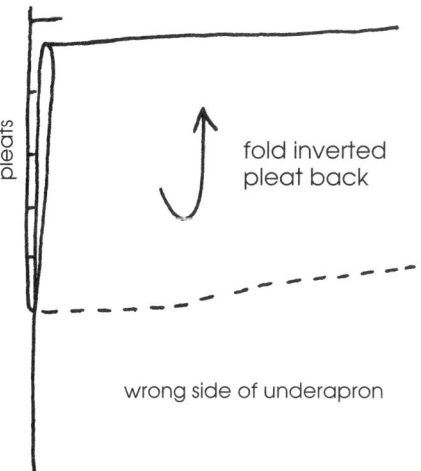

pleats

fold inverted pleat back

wrong side of underapron

2 Make a small dart $1/2$"-$5/8$" in depth in the inverted pleat at the top edge of the kilt, tapering to nothing about 1" above the bottom of the fell. This dart will help shape the inverted pleat beneath the underapron. Make the dart close to the

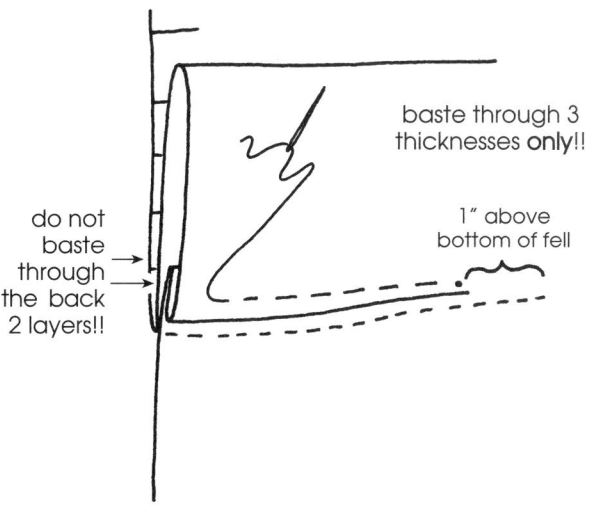

baste through 3 thicknesses **only**!!

do not baste through the back 2 layers!!

1" above bottom of fell

last pleat stitching, but be sure to hold the folded edge of the dart back from the pleat stitching a bit, otherwise you will have an unsightly bulge when you fold the inverted pleat back down against the underapron.

3 Slide your left hand inside the inverted pleat when you baste the dart, and be sure to stitch through *only 3 thicknesses* of fabric. Do not catch in the other side of the inverted pleat.

4 Open out the inverted pleat, and swing the dart toward the underapron. If the dart does not lie flat, you have probably stitched through too many thicknesses. If this happens, remove the basting, and baste again.

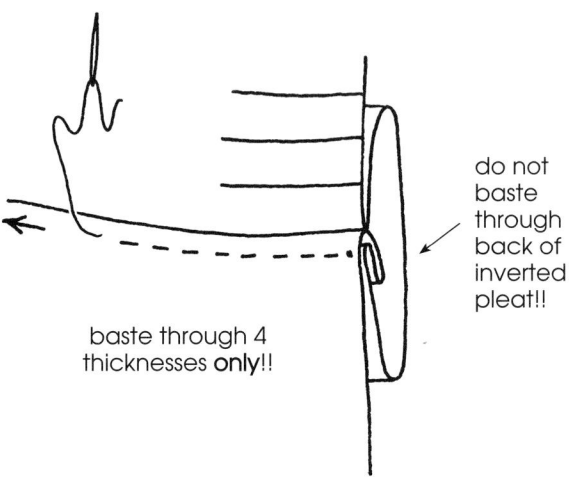

do not baste through back of inverted pleat!!

baste through 4 thicknesses **only**!!

5 Turn the kilt over to the right side, with the top edge to the right this time. Slide your left hand inside the inverted pleat from the end at the bottom of the fell. Starting at the top of the kilt, baste the underapron edge to the first layer of the inverted pleat along a line about $1/4$" in from the last pleat stitching. Baste through the dart, but do not catch in the back of the inverted pleat. Skew to keep the stripes straight, and baste down to the bottom of the fell.

6 Fold the edge of the underapron along the chalk line, and continue basting along the underapron edge to the bottom of the kilt. Stretch and skew the fabric to keep the stripes straight, even, and parallel front and back. If your kilt has a hidden pleat, stop here and go to Appendix C, Finishing the Edge of the Hidden Pleat.

Basting the pleats

Pleat basting keeps the free edges of the pleats folded in the right places for pressing. Pleat basting also tames a somewhat unruly pile of eight yards of fabric and makes it easier to work on as you finish the kilt. Basting goes quickly and is very satisfying – once the basting is done, your kilt will suddenly look more like a kilt!

When a kilt is basted for pressing, the pleats must never be splayed. If the pleats are splayed during pressing, the lower edge of the kilt will be wider than the pleats at the hips, and the bottom will ripple and wave, instead of holding a nice straight line (see page 115). This commonly happens when a kilt is taken to a dry cleaning establishment for pressing. If you have to press a kilt, baste it with straight pleats, not splayed ones, and press it yourself according to our instructions!

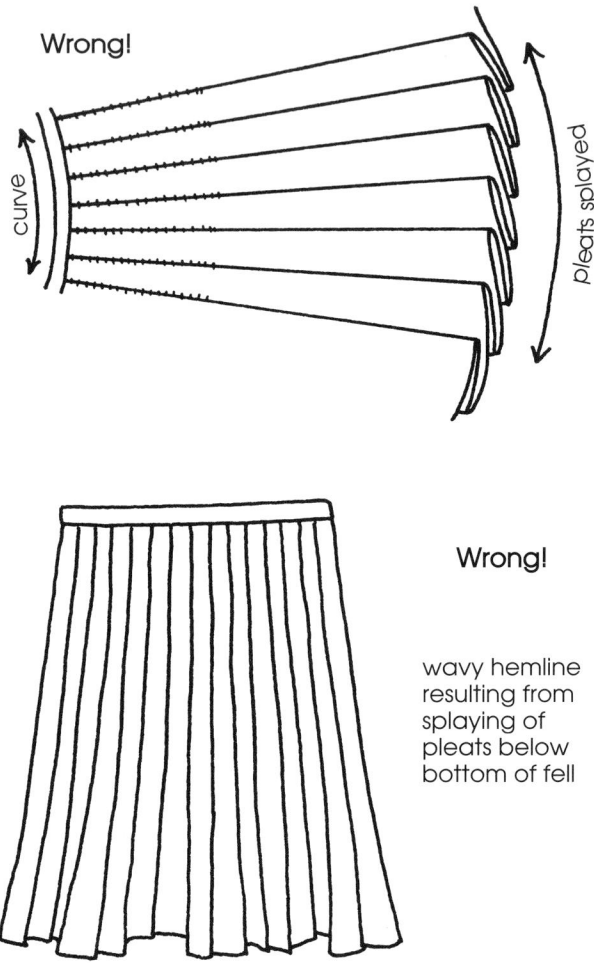

Wrong!

curve

pleats splayed

Wrong!

wavy hemline resulting from splaying of pleats below bottom of fell

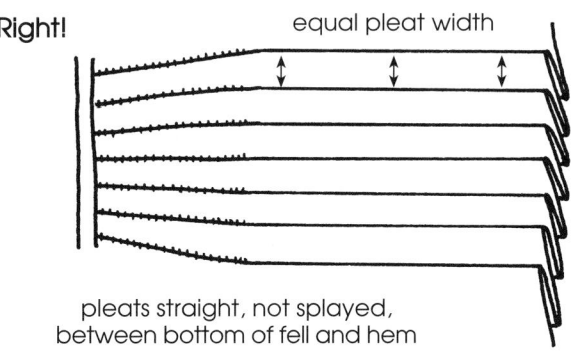

Right!

equal pleat width

pleats straight, not splayed, between bottom of fell and hem

1 As you baste the pleats, remember that pleats in a kilt are absolutely straight from the bottom of the fell to the hem and have the same width from bottom of the fell to hem. The only taper occurs in the portions of the pleats that you have already stitched.

2 Hold the kilt flat in your lap, right side up, with the top of the kilt hanging off to the left. Spread your knees apart a bit so that as much of the kilt can lie flat in your lap as possible.

3 Thread a needle with basting thread. Start with the lower left corner of the top apron, and stitch several anchoring stitches. Reach for pleat #1, and fold the bottom edge *along the same line that the pleat is folded on at the bottom of the fell.* Lap the top apron onto pleat #1, keeping the pleat width the same as at the bottom of the fell. Make several basting stitches through the top apron and pleat #1.

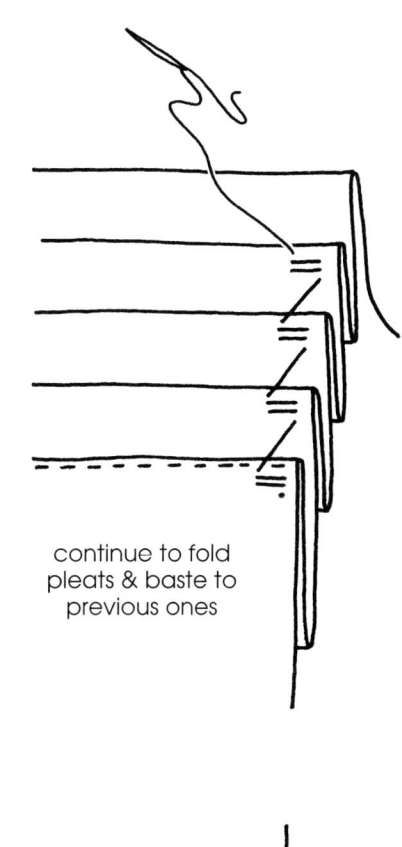

continue to fold pleats & baste to previous ones

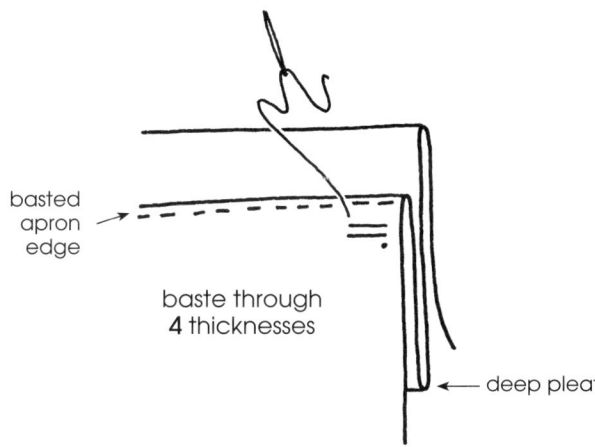

basted apron edge →

baste through **4** thicknesses

← deep pleat

4 Reach for the second pleat, and fold it along the proper line. Lap pleat #1 onto pleat #2, keeping the proper pleat width, and make several basting stitches through pleats #1 and #2.

Continue across the entire kilt. **Remember that each pleat must look the same in both width and pattern at the bottom of the kilt as it does at the bottom of the fell.**

5 When you reach the inverted pleat, butt the last pleat up against the underapron edge, and fold the inverted pleat evenly with half to the front under the underapron and half to the back with the regular pleats. Baste both the last pleat and the underapron edge to the inverted pleat.

6 Go back to the apron edge, and do a second identical line of basting roughly 2-3 fingers down from the bottom of the fell.

7 Add two or three more rows of basting between the top and bottom rows, making sure that the rows are no more than 4" apart. Be sure that all

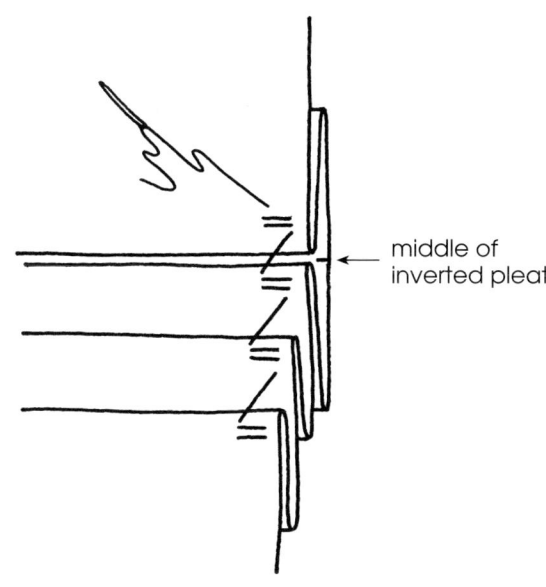

← middle of inverted pleat

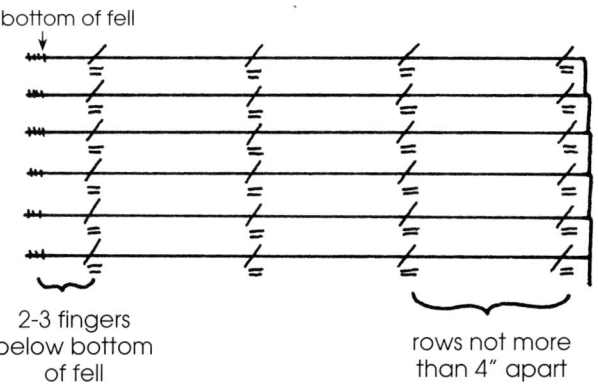

bottom of fell

2-3 fingers below bottom of fell

rows not more than 4" apart

pleats are identical in width and are folded straight from the bottom of the fell.

8 Turn the kilt over, and baste one more time from the wrong side along the bottom of the kilt, starting at the end with the inverted pleat. When you reach the dip in the hem at the deep pleat, be sure that you *don't* align the dip with the bottom of the kilt – remember that the point of the deep pleat is about $^3/_8$" shorter than the rest of the kilt.

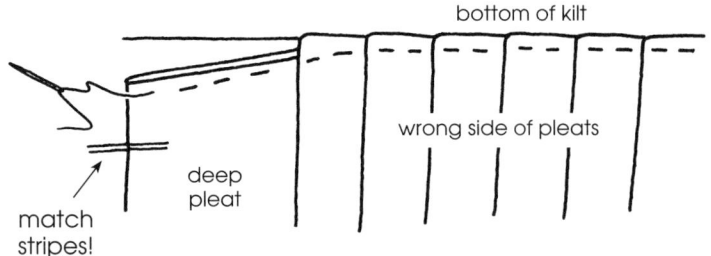

Shaping the right underapron

1 Turn the kilt over to the wrong side, and go to the inverted pleat. Hold the kilt in your lap with the top to the left.

2 Permanently tack the inverted pleat from 1" above the bottom of the fell to the top of the kilt. Use good thread and a short running stitch (see Appendix A). Be sure that the stitches do not show through to the right side of the kilt or create dimples in the right side.

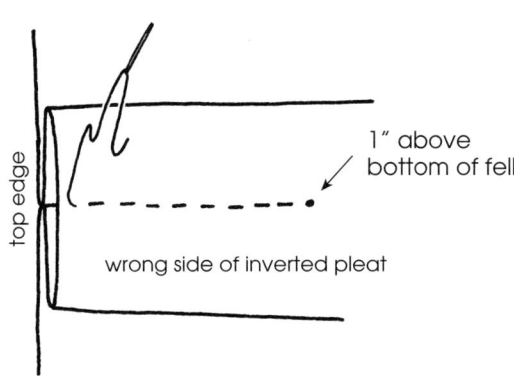

3 Lay the kilt smoothly across your knees with the wrong side up, with the underapron edge of the inverted pleat across your lap. To shape the right side of the underapron, baste the edge of the inverted pleat to the wrong side of the underapron from the level of the bottom of the fell to the top of the kilt. **Be sure to match the stripes at the front edge of the inverted pleat as you baste.** If the kilt has much shaping, this will require skewing the inverted pleat and smoothing and stretching the underapron as you stitch. Be sure

that the underapron is as smooth as possible while you baste the edge of the inverted pleat.

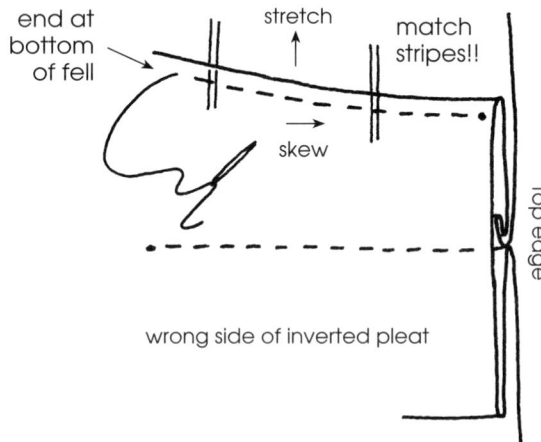

4 If you now turn the kilt over, you'll see that the right underapron looks wrinkled or even bubbly, particularly if the kilt has a lot of shaping. Wool is remarkable stuff, however, that can be molded into all kinds of shapes with heat, pressure, and a little moisture. When it comes time to press your kilt, you will be amazed to discover that all of that wrinkling and bubbling can be pressed and shaped away. To avoid unsightly creases during pressing and to spread out the shape changes evenly, though, you will need to tailor stitch the area to hold it in place during pressing.

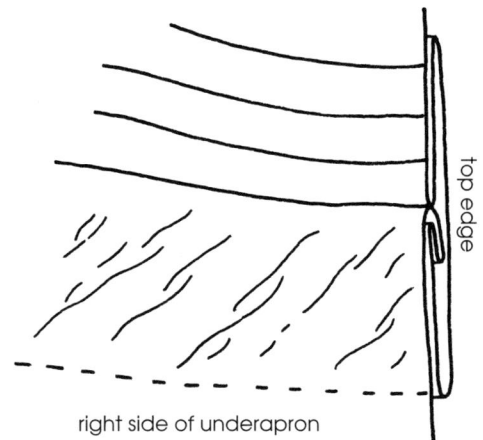

5 Turn the kilt back to the wrong side with the top at the left. Using basting thread, make several rows of tailor stitching (see Appendix A) from the wrong side, starting at the bottom of the fell and stitching toward you. Lay the fingers of your left hand flat underneath the underapron to hold the area as smooth and as flat as possible during basting. Stretch a little if necessary. Do several running stitches along the front edge of the inverted pleat, and run a second row of tailor stitching away from you as far as the center of

the inverted pleat, keeping your left hand flat underneath. Do several running stitches to the left, and stitch a third row of tailor stitching toward you. Stitch several more rows, and hold the last row of basting about 3/4" down from the top of the kilt so that the basting stitches won't be caught in the top band seam, where they will be hard to remove.

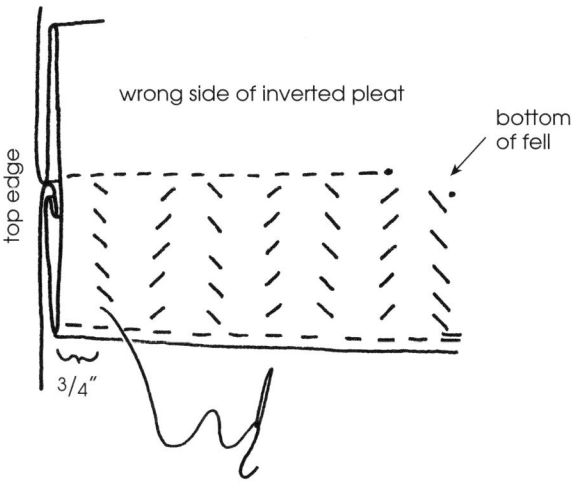

6   Turn the kilt over. Despite the fact that the right underapron will still look a little bubbly, you should not have folds or major wrinkles. If you do, remove all the basting including the basting along the edge of the inverted pleat, and try again, stretching and smoothing a bit more this time.

Shaping the left apron

If you have included a hidden pleat in your kilt as described in Appendix C, skip to step 5 below. Otherwise, start with step 1.

1   Take out the basting stitches on the side of the apron next to the pleats. Turn the kilt over to the

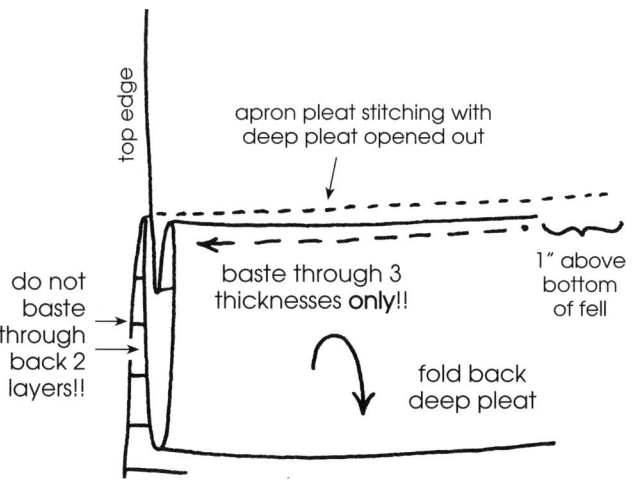

wrong side, with the top edge to the left. Fold the deep pleat back toward you.

2   Make a small dart $1/2$"-$5/8$" in depth in the deep pleat at the top edge of the kilt, tapering to nothing about 1" above the bottom of the fell. This dart will help shape the deep pleat beneath the apron. Make the dart close to the apron pleat stitching, but be sure to hold the folded edge of the dart back from the stitching a bit, otherwise you will have an unsightly bulge when you fold the deep pleat back down against the apron.

3   Slide your left hand inside the deep pleat from the top of the kilt when you baste the dart, and be sure to stitch *through only 3 thicknesses* of fabric. Do not catch in the other side of the deep pleat.

4   Fold the deep pleat back down against the apron. If the dart does not lie flat, you have probably stitched through too many thicknesses. If this happens, remove the basting, and baste again.

5   Lay the kilt smoothly across your knees with the wrong side up, the apron edge of the deep pleat across your lap, and the top of the kilt to the left. To shape the left side of the apron, baste the edge of the deep pleat to the apron from the bottom of the fell to the top of the kilt. **Be sure to match the stripes at the front edge of the deep pleat as you baste.** If the kilt has much shaping, this

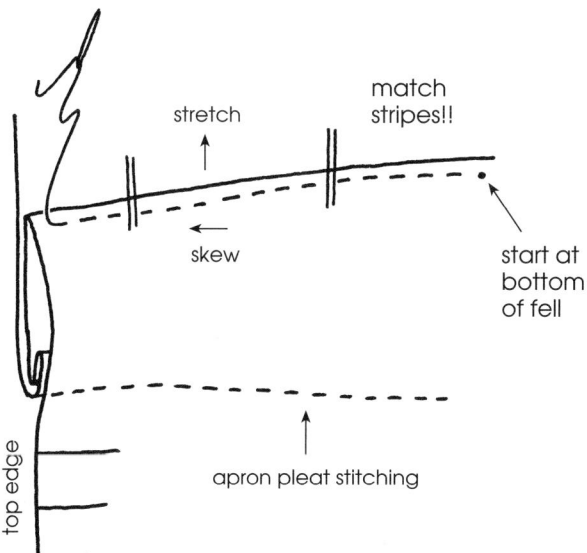

will require skewing the deep pleat and smoothing and stretching the apron as you did for the underapron and the inverted pleat. Be sure that the apron is as smooth as possible while you baste the edge of the deep pleat. If the kilt has a great deal of shaping, you may find it difficult to align the stripes without a great deal of skewing. If the deep pleat is too cock-eyed, you can add another dart parallel to the first one as described in steps 2 and 3 above.

6   Turn the kilt to the right side, with the top of the kilt to the left. Tailor baste the left side of the apron from the bottom of the fell to the top of the kilt along several rows starting at the bottom of the fell, as you did for the underapron. **Be sure that the stripes on the front side remain horizontal as you baste**, and be sure to use flat fingers underneath the deep pleat as you baste. Stretch a little as you go, if the kilt has a lot of shaping. Hold the last row of basting about $3/4$" down from the top of the kilt so that the basting stitches won't be caught in the top band seam, where they will be hard to remove.

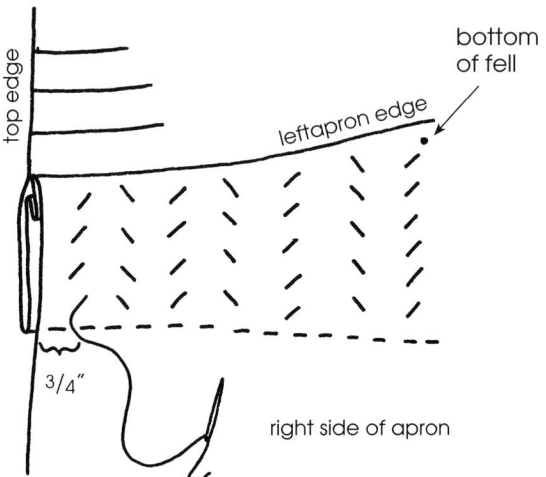

Cutting the pleats

Take a deep breath – you are about to cut your beloved kilt!

To remove some of the bulk from the back of the kilt, you will trim away a portion of each pleat between the bottom of the fell and the top of the kilt. This will leave ragged edges that will be covered later by canvas and lining. Just to be on the safe side, read steps 1 through 5 below, and study the diagrams *before* you bring scissors close to your kilt! Be sure that you understand *before you cut* what you will do, where and why. Nothing can replace the fabric along a misplaced cut.

1   Turn the kilt over to the wrong side, with the top of the kilt *toward* you, rather than to the right or left. Find the inverted pleat, and fold it to the right out of the way. **Do not cut the inverted pleat.** If you cut the inverted pleat, you will have no material available for altering the underapron.

2   Start with the pleat adjacent to the inverted pleat. Locate the pleat stitching on the right hand side

of the pleat. With a pair of sharp scissors, make a curved cut about $1/2$" to the left of the pleat stitching *through only one thickness*, starting at the top of the kilt and curving out to the edge of the pleat on the left at a point about 1" above the bottom of the fell. **Do not cut out the pleats as far down as the bottom of the fell, and be sure to cut through only one thickness of cloth in the pleat.**

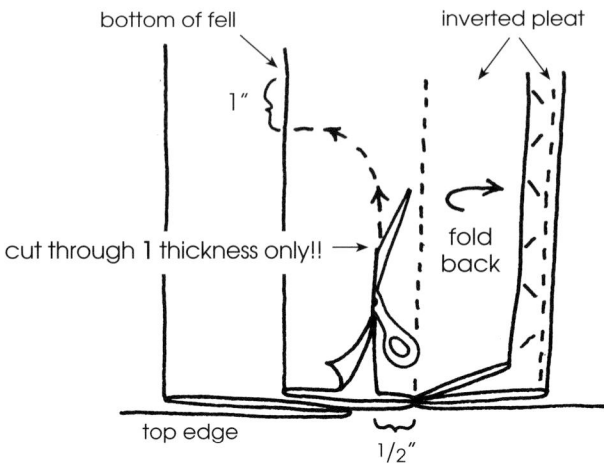

3   Open out the cut portion, and locate the stitching line on the lower part of the pleat. Make a second curved cut about $1/2$" to the left of this stitching through only one thickness, curving outward to the edge of the pleat on the left at a point about 1" above the bottom of the fell. You will have removed a piece the shape of an arched window.

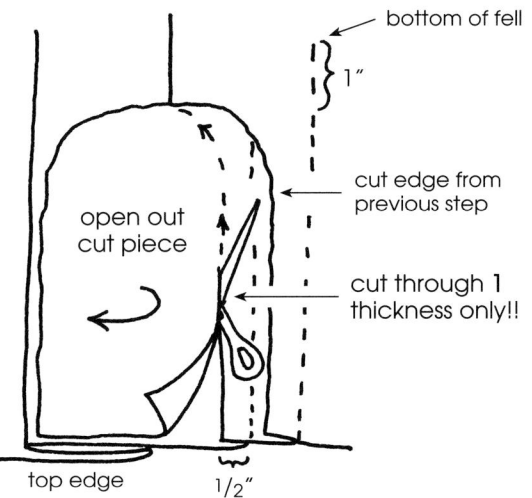

4   Notice that the upper part of each pleat is stitched along a different line from the lower part of the same pleat, with the lower portion stitched farther to the left than the upper portion. That's why it's crucial to cut only one thickness of the pleat at a time. If you were to cut both thicknesses at once, the lower part of the pleat would

be cut out too close to the stitching, which could ruin the kilt.

5 Proceed to the left from the pleat that you finished cutting in step 3, carefully cutting each layer of each pleat separately. Cut all but the last two pleats.

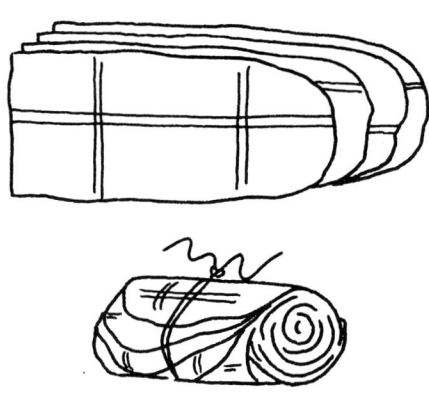

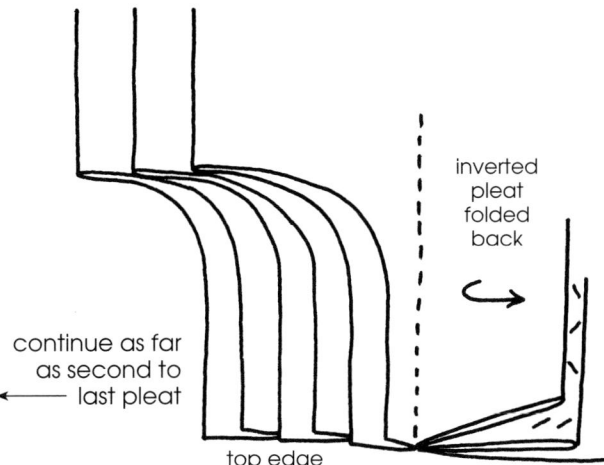

6 The only pleat that will be cut differently from the first pleat is the buttonhole pleat, which must be cut along lines $1\,^1/_4$" from the stitching, rather than $^1/_2$" from the stitching. You can be sure that you've found the buttonhole pleat by sticking your finger through the buttonhole from the right side of the kilt – your finger will lie inside the buttonhole pleat. Trim both portions of the buttonhole pleat $1\,^1/_4$" from the stitching, curving back to the folded pleat edge about 1" above the bottom of the fell, as for the other pleats.

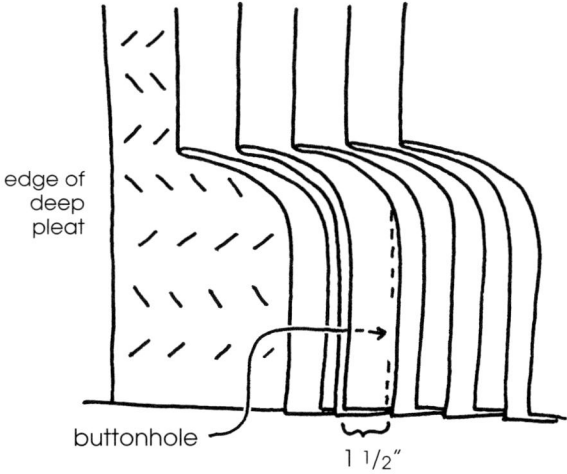

7 Cut the remaining pleat $^1/_2$" from the pleat stitching. Wrap your scraps neatly, and save them for the kilt buckles.

Doing the steeking

The pleats need to be stabilized just above the bottom of the fell, and a set of stitches called "steeking" accomplishes this. Steeking is done from the wrong side of the kilt, and stitches must not be visible from the right side of the pleats.

1 Turn the kilt over to the wrong side, with the top edge *away* from you, rather than to the right or to the left. Cross your right leg over your left, and allow the stitched pleats to hang over your knee somewhat, with the bottom of the fell roughly at the top of your kneecap. Thread a needle with carpet thread. Wax and knot the thread, and put the needle where you can reach it easily.

2 Steeking is worked from right to left, along a line about half way between the bottom of the fell and the cut line for the pleats. Start at the right with pleat #1, the first pleat to the left of the deep pleat. Fold all of the other pleats to the left, revealing the entire width of the first pleat. Smooth the pleat, and straighten the stripes. Place your left hand under the kilt with flat fingers, and give the kilt a little tug with your right hand to make sure that the kilt at the bottom of the fell is smooth and extended but not stretched. Let the

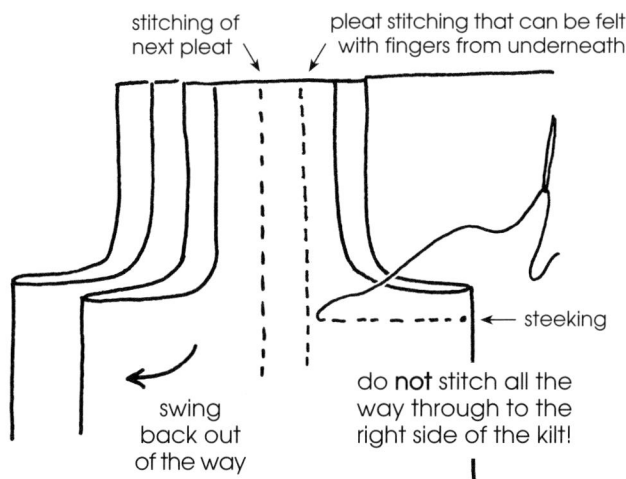

kilt curve over your knee at the bottom of the fell.

3 Starting at the right hand edge of the first pleat, make a stitch through the pleat along a line half way between the bottom of the fell and the cut edge of the pleat and through as many layers as possible without catching the layer on the right side of the kilt.

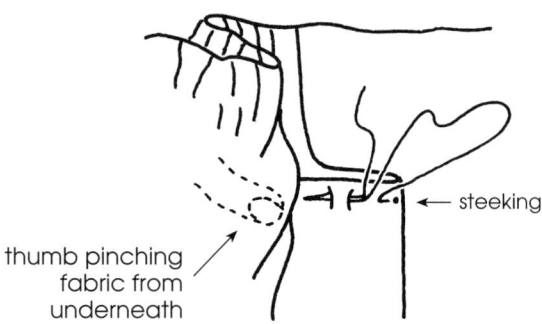

thumb pinching fabric from underneath

← steeking

4 Continue stitching using a medium running stitch with a back stitch every 2 to 3 stitches, keeping your left fingers flat underneath the kilt. Stitch the first pleat from right to left as far as the pleat stitching that you can feel from underneath with your flat left fingers. Do not stitch all the way to the left edge of the pleat, because the kilt is too thin toward the left edge. When you finish the steeking for the first pleat, you do not need to anchor the thread.

5 **Be absolutely sure that your stitches are not visible from the right side of the kilt.** Even if the thread itself is not visible, a stitch that catches just a wee bit of the right side of the kilt will pull the right side into a dimple when you tighten the stitch. No amount of pressing will disguise this! Check often for dimples or visible stitches. If you find one, pull out the offending stitches and re-do them.

6 Once you have done the steeking for one pleat, fold the next pleat back down to the right, leaving all of the others folded to the left out of the way.

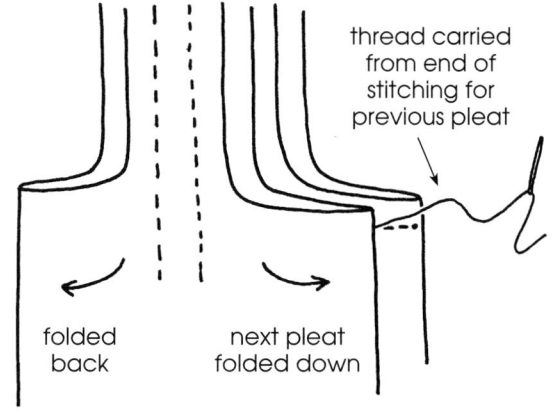

thread carried from end of stitching for previous pleat

folded back

next pleat folded down

Smooth the pleat, and make sure that the kilt at the bottom of the fell is smooth and extended. Gently pull your sewing thread to the right so that it lies on a straight line underneath pleat #2, but do not pull it taut. Make a stitch near the edge of the second pleat using the same thread, and make sure not to pull the first stitch so tight that it puckers the edge of the pleat.

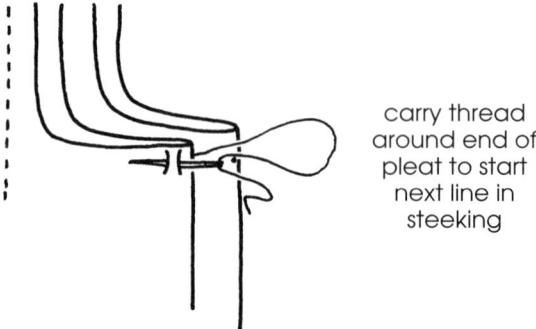

carry thread around end of pleat to start next line in steeking

Don't worry about anchoring the thread — just carry the thread from the steeking of one pleat to another. Stitch as for the first pleat along a line about half way between the bottom of the fell and the cut edge of the pleat, with a back stitch every 2 to 3 stitches.

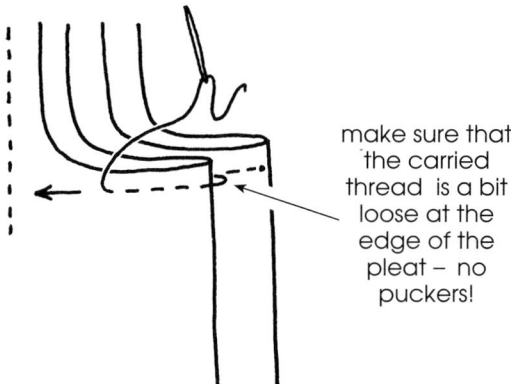

make sure that the carried thread is a bit loose at the edge of the pleat – no puckers!

7 Sew the steeking for each pleat in turn, folding each down to the right as you go and checking for dimples and visible stitches. Stop at the center of the inverted pleat, and anchor the thread.

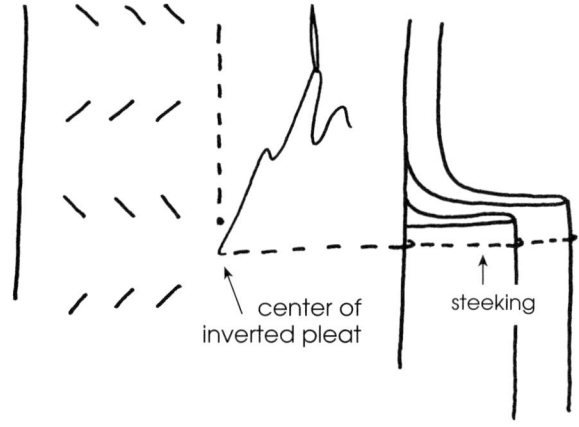

center of inverted pleat

steeking

Opening the buttonhole

Turn the kilt over to the wrong side, with the top edge to the left. Locate the buttonhole pleat, and clip the upper buttonhole seam allowance about 1 1/4" below the buttonhole and as far as the pleat stitching. Fold the upper seam allowance toward you to open the buttonhole, trimming the underlying seam allowances if they are in the way. Use carpet thread and a running stitch to anchor the buttonhole seam allowance along a line about 3/4" toward the center back from the buttonhole. Be sure that the stitching does not show through on the right side of the kilt.

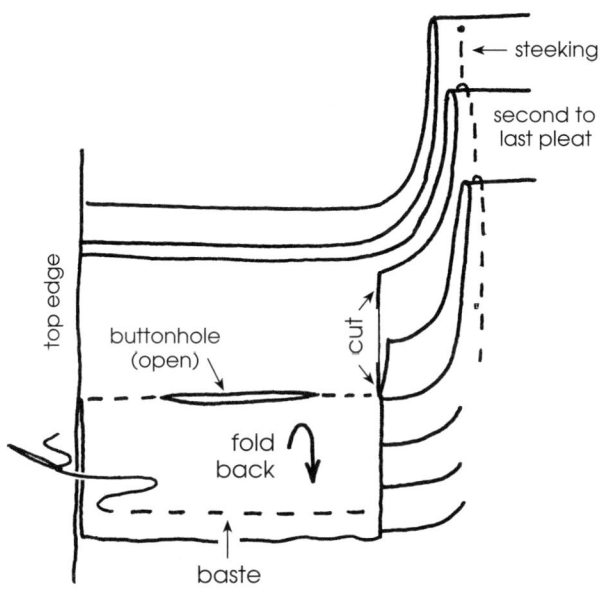

Attaching the stabilizer

In order to keep the waistline in the pleats from stretching, you will need to attach a stabilizer made from a straight grain piece of cotton fabric.

1 Cut a piece of broadcloth about 1 1/4" to 1 3/8" wide and the approximate measurement of the waistline between the buttonhole and the center of the inverted pleat. A straight grain scrap of lining material will do nicely.

2 Turn the kilt over to the wrong side, with the top edge to the left. Fold under one raw end of the stabilizer strip, and center the stabilizer on the waistline, with the end pinned at the line of heavy stitching along the edge of the buttonhole seam allowance. Extend the stabilizer toward you, and pull it snug along the waistline. Lift up the inverted pleat, and fold it toward you out of the way. Trim and fold under the remaining raw end of the stabilizer and line up the end with the center tacking for the inverted pleat. Pin the end.

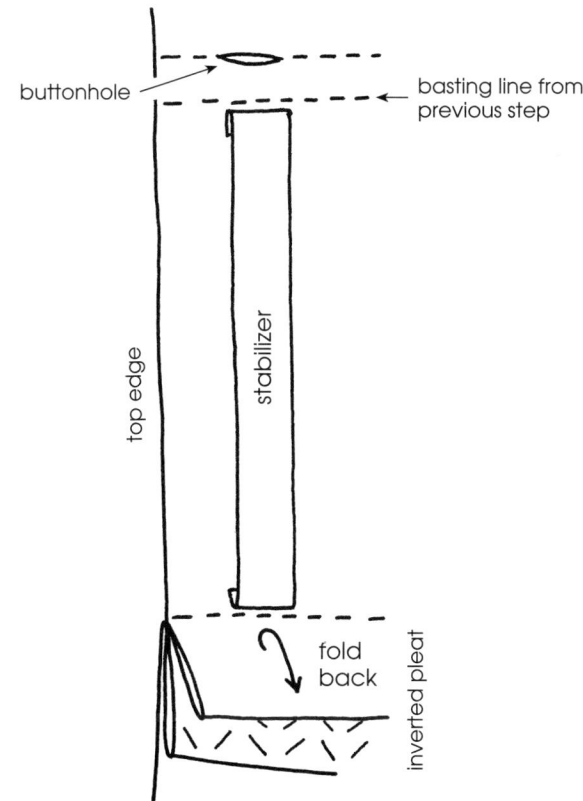

3 Turn the kilt over, and measure the waistline across the pleats from apron edge to underapron edge. Compare this distance with the waist pleats measurement on your record sheet. If the kilt is a little too big in the pleats at the waist, you can shorten the stabilizer a bit to take in the waist. Adjust the stabilizer if necessary, making sure that you don't shorten it so much that the waistline starts to show puckers.

4 Using carpet thread, and starting at the buttonhole end of the stabilizer, stitch the end of the stabilizer to the pleats. As you stitch, check often for dimples or visible stitches. If you find either, pull out the stitches and re-do them. Start with one moderately large stitch at the waistline at the buttonhole end of the stabilizer. Carry the thread to the lower edge of the stabilizer, and take another moderately large stitch. Take another moderately large stitch at the lower edge of the stabilizer. Carry the thread back to the center, and take a fourth moderately large stitch. These four stitches will form an "X" with a stitch above and below.

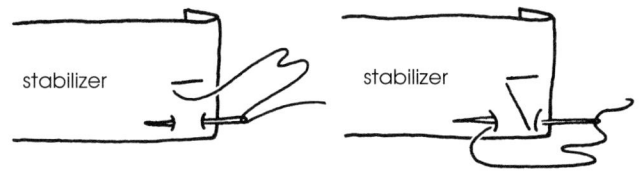

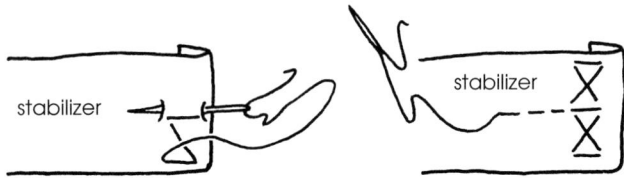

5 Now, carry the thread to the upper edge of the stabilizer, and take a moderately large stitch at the upper edge of the stabilizer. Take a second moderately large stitch at the upper edge of the stabilizer. Then, carry the thread back down to the middle of the stabilizer, and take one final moderately large stitch in the middle. The end of the stabilizer is now stitched with two "X"-shaped stitches with stitches above and below each "X".

6 Take several stitches at the waistline, with every second or third stitch being a back stitch. Every third pleat, repeat the double "X" stitching. Be sure to keep the inverted pleat folded back out of the way, and do one last set of double "X" stitches at the end of the stabilizer.

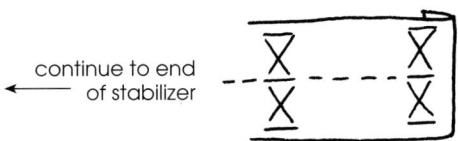

7 Fold the inverted pleat back down over the stabilizer, smooth it down, and use basting thread to tailor stitch it into place above the bottom of the fell.

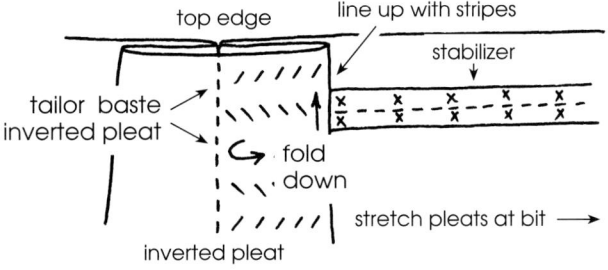

Applying the underapron and apron canvas

Canvas helps stiffen and support the upper edges of the apron and underapron. Be sure to read the tips and hints section on selecting canvas above.

Cutting the canvas

1 Turn the kilt to the wrong side, and measure the underapron from the center of the inverted pleat at the bottom of the fell to the chalk line at the underapron edge. Add two inches. This equals the length of canvas to cut. Measure the distance from the top of the kilt to where the pleats are cut, and subtract an inch. This equals the width of canvas to cut.

2 Cut two pieces of canvas of these dimensions, with the length parallel to the straight grain of the canvas.

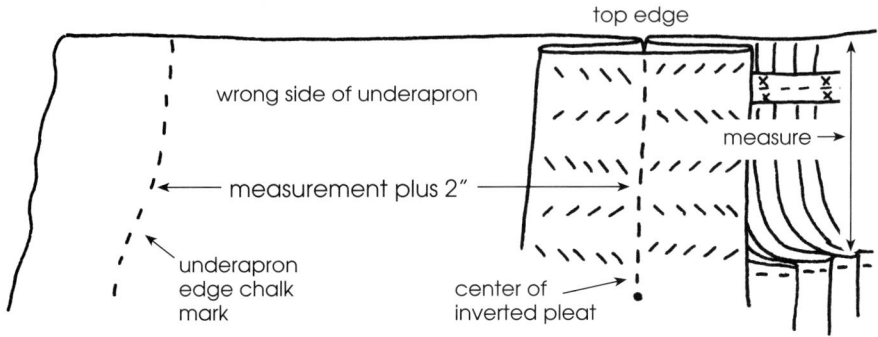

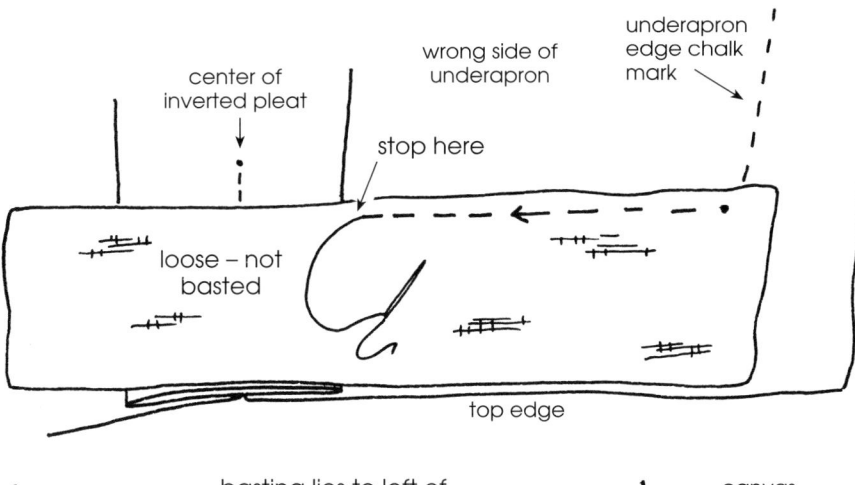

center of inverted pleat

wrong side of underapron

underapron edge chalk mark

stop here

loose – not basted

top edge

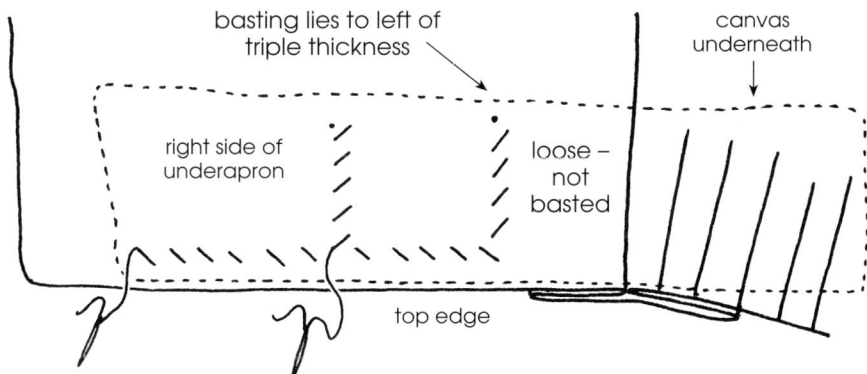

basting lies to left of triple thickness

canvas underneath

right side of underapron

loose – not basted

top edge

Basting the underapron canvas

1 Lay the underapron portion of the kilt wrong side up on a table in front of you with the top of the kilt toward you. Smooth out any wrinkles, and be sure that the stripes are horizontal and not twisted. Lay one piece of canvas on the underapron even with the top edge of the underapron and extending a half inch or so past the underapron chalkline at the right edge. The far edge of the canvas should be parallel to a stripe in the underapron as far as the edge of the inverted pleat. Don't worry about what happens to the left of the inverted pleat edge for the moment.

2 Baste along the far edge of the canvas starting just outside the underapron chalk line and ending before the double thickness of the inverted pleat.

3 Turn the kilt over, and smooth the underapron, making sure the stripes are straight and not twisted. Using basting thread, sew a line of tailor stitching along the center front line. Tailor stitch in a line just on the underapron side of the double thickness, and make a final line of tailor stitching across the top of the kilt, holding the basting about 3/4" down from the top of the kilt so that the basting won't be caught in the top band seam.

Stitching the underapron canvas

1 Turn the kilt over to the wrong side, and put the kilt in your lap, with the top to the left. Thread your needle with carpet thread. Consider using white, rather than black, carpet thread if your lining is white or off-white so that the stitches won't show through the lining.

2 The top edge of the underapron is a straight line, but the top edge of the pleats section is a curve. For portions of the canvas extending into the pleats, you will need to put darts in the canvas that are deeper at the top of the kilt and that taper toward the bottom of the fell in order for the canvas to accommodate the curve of the kilt in the pleats.

3 With the top of the kilt to the left, make a dart in the canvas about 2" toward the center back from the edge of the inverted pleat. The dart should fold away from you and be wider at the left hand side, so that the left edge of the canvas can lie parallel to the top edge of the kilt as it curves. Make sure that the dart is folded at the right hand edge of the canvas as well, rather than tapering to a point.

4 Take your carpet thread, and start the first line of stitching with a moderately large stitch through the dart at the waistline and through as many thicknesses of the kilt as possible without

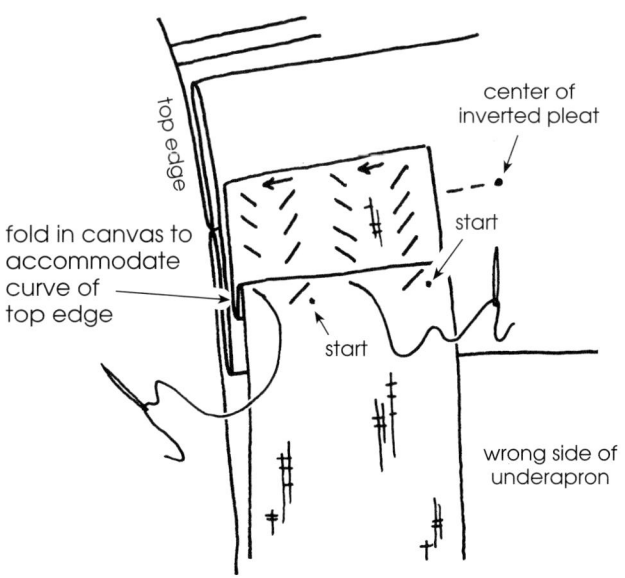

top edge

center of inverted pleat

fold in canvas to accommodate curve of top edge

start

start

wrong side of underapron

causing dimples or visible stitches on the right side of the kilt. Make a line of tailor stitches away from you along the waistline, stopping about 1" past the center of the inverted pleat. If the kilt has a lot of shaping, you may have to add an additional dart. **Check often for dimples or visible stitches on the right side of the kilt.** Tailor stitch toward the top of the kilt, and make another row of tailor stitching toward you along the top edge of the kilt, stopping at the dart. Anchor your thread, and cut it off.

5 Lay the fingers of your left hand flat underneath the pleats, and use carpet thread to make a third line of tailor stitching toward you along the bottom edge of the canvas, starting at the dart. Use your fingers to make sure that the kilt remains flat and smooth underneath. Tailor stitch toward the top of the kilt for 1 $1/2$" or so, and stitch a final row of tailor stitching away from you between rows 1 and 3. End your stitching at the dart.

6 Trim the extra canvas along a line about 1" toward the center back from the center of the inverted pleat.

Basting and stitching the apron canvas

Repeat the process for basting and stitching the apron canvas, basting along the apron side of the deep pleat, placing the dart about 2" toward the center back from the folded edge of the deep pleat, stitching the canvas with carpet thread, and trimming the canvas about 1" toward the center back from the folded edge of the first regular pleat. Work with the top edge of the kilt to your left, and be sure that all darts fold away from you.

Applying the canvas in the pleats

Cutting the canvas

Measure the distance from the top of the kilt to where the pleats are cut. Cut a length of canvas of this width and roughly $3/4$ yard to 1 yard long. If you are making a large kilt, cut a piece at the upper end of the range; if your kilt is small, cut one at the

lower end of the range. If you should misjudge and cut the piece too short, it is a simple matter to piece the canvas as you sew it in.

Stitching the canvas

1 Turn the kilt over to the wrong side, and put the kilt in your lap, with the top to the left. Thread your needle with carpet thread. Consider using white carpet thread, rather than black, if your lining is white or off-white so that the stitches won't show through the lining.

2 Fold under the raw end of the canvas strip, and place the folded edge overlapping the apron canvas slightly and lined up straight with the top edge of the kilt. Make a row of running stitches up the folded edge of the canvas, stitching through as many thicknesses as possible without making dimples or visible stitches on the right side of the kilt.

3 The top edge of the pleats section is a curve, and you will need to put darts in the canvas to shape it across the pleats, just as you did for a portion of the apron and underapron canvas.

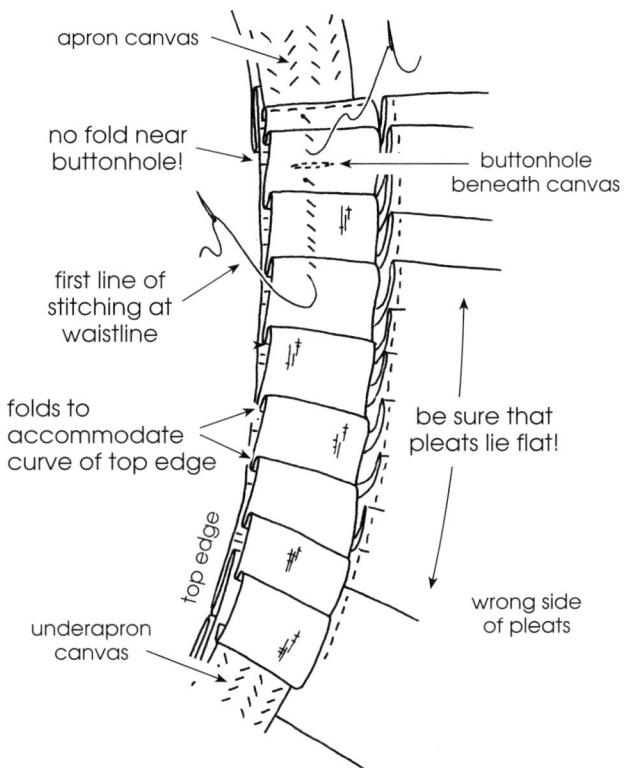

apron canvas

no fold near buttonhole!

buttonhole beneath canvas

first line of stitching at waistline

folds to accommodate curve of top edge

be sure that pleats lie flat!

top edge

wrong side of pleats

underapron canvas

4 With the top of the kilt to the left, make a dart in the canvas within an inch or two of the folded edge. The dart should fold away from you and be wider at the left hand side, so that the left edge of the canvas can lie parallel to the top edge of the kilt as it curves. Make sure that the dart is folded at the right hand edge as well, rather than

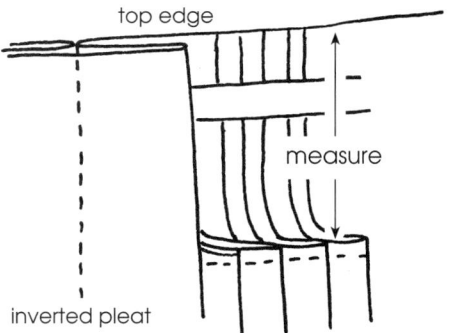

top edge

measure

inverted pleat

tapering to a point. **Be sure to make the dart close to the folded edge of the canvas so that enough clearance remains around the button-hole.**

5 Using your carpet thread, make a line of tailor stitching along the waistline starting at the folded edge, stitching across the dart, and ending about an inch from the buttonhole. Anchor your thread, and cut it off.

6 Smooth the back of the kilt, and continue applying the canvas, adding darts as necessary to curve the canvas so that the top edge remains parallel to the top of the kilt. Be sure to leave clearance for the other side of the buttonhole, and be sure that all of the darts fold away from you and are folded at the right hand edge as well, rather than tapering to a point.

7 Make your first line of tailor stitching along the waistline with carpet thread, starting about 1" toward the center back from the buttonhole. Check often for dimples or visible stitches. At the underapron end of the pleats, trim the excess canvas, fold under the ragged edge, and lap the end of the canvas about an inch over the underapron canvas.

8 If you run out of canvas before you get to the underapron, cut another piece of canvas the same width and the necessary length, fold the ragged edge under, overlap it with the short end of the canvas already stitched to the kilt, and continue your tailor stitching along the waistline. Once you're done, you won't even be able to tell where you added the piece.

9 Make a second line of tailor stitching with carpet thread along the top edge of the kilt, being careful not to make dimples or visible stitches in the right side of the kilt. Stretch the top edge just a little to flare the top edge slightly above the waistline.

10 Lay the fingers of your left hand flat underneath the pleats, and make a third line of tailor stitching with carpet thread along the bottom edge of the canvas, starting at the folded edge. Use your fingers to make sure that the kilt remains flat, smooth, and extended.

11 Run a final line of tailor stitching between rows 1 and 3. If the fell is more than 7" long, consider adding two rows between rows 1 and 3 to hold the canvas.

12 Thread your needle with carpet thread. Starting at the apron edge of the deep pleat, make a single line of stitching about 1/4" down from the top of the kilt all the way across the back of the kilt to the underapron edge of the inverted pleat. Stretch the top a little as you stitch to make sure that the kilt flares a bit above the waistline.

Opening the buttonhole

1 Locate the buttonhole, and make a slit in the canvas directly behind the buttonhole and as long as the buttonhole opening. At each end of the slit, make two diagonal slashes about 1/4"-1/2" long.

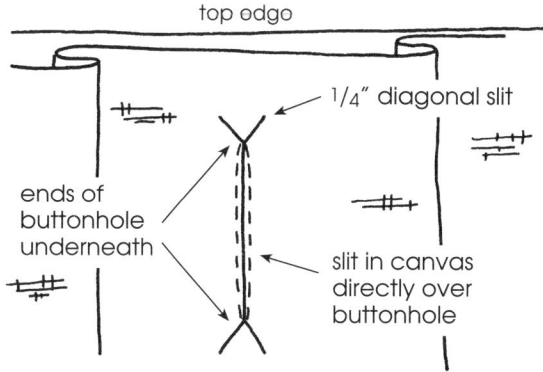

2 Fold the canvas under along the sides and points, and stitch the canvas down using carpet thread and an overcast stitch. Check the right side for dimples or visible stitches.

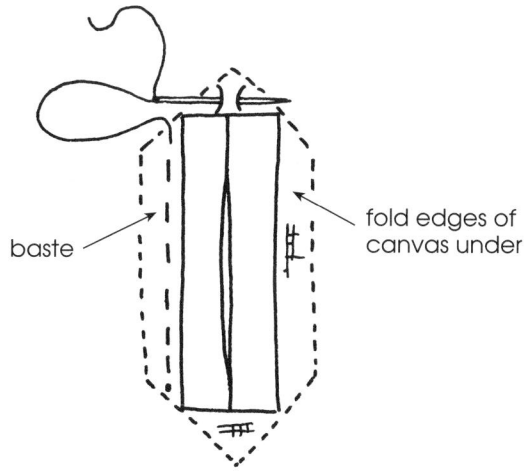

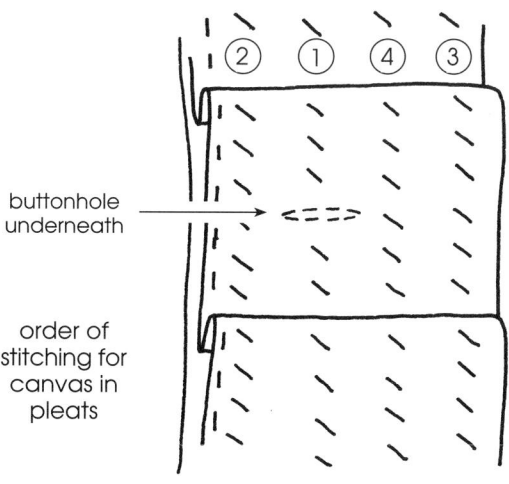

Finishing the underapron edge

1 Turn to the wrong side of the kilt, and put it in your lap with the top edge to the right. Clip the underapron canvas in as far as the underapron chalk line to allow easing.

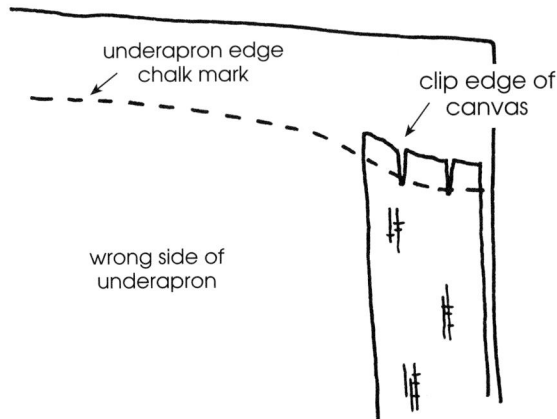

underapron edge chalk mark

clip edge of canvas

wrong side of underapron

2 Flip the kilt over, and hold it with the top to the left. Fold the underapron edge along the chalkline, and baste about $1/4$" from the edge starting at the bottom and ending at the top of the kilt. Be sure to skew and stretch a little to keep the stripes even.

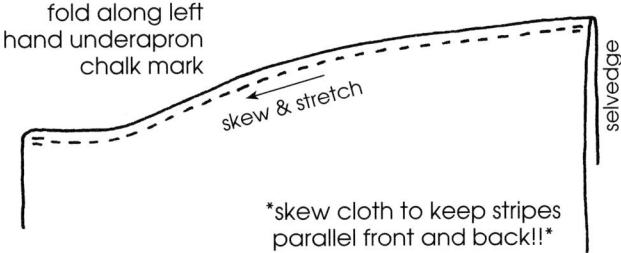

fold along left hand underapron chalk mark

skew & stretch

selvedge

skew cloth to keep stripes parallel front and back!!

3 To make the facing:

– At the top edge, trim the corner just a bit to help the underapron self-facing fold better, but don't remove too much, or you will lose material needed for alterations.

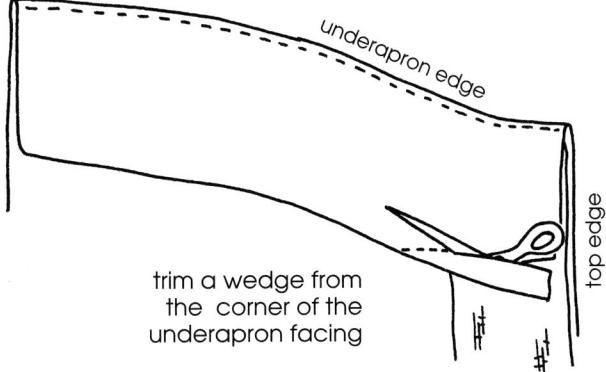

underapron edge

top edge

trim a wedge from the corner of the underapron facing

– Fold the excess fabric at the underapron edge under exactly double to form a self-facing.

– If the kilt has a lot of shaping, turn to the wrong side of the kilt, and add a small dart in the top layer of the facing near the basted edge. Fold the dart toward the edge of the underapron, and baste it from the top edge to the point of the dart through all thicknesses.

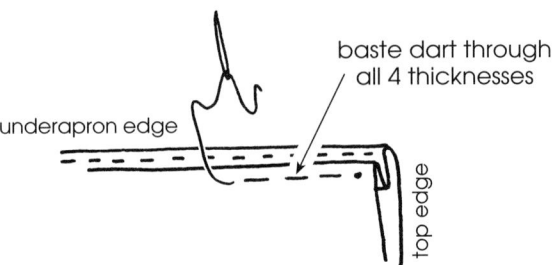

baste dart through all 4 thicknesses

underapron edge

top edge

– Baste the fold from the hem to the top of the kilt along a line about $1/2$" back from the folded edge. Be very careful to match the stripes. If the kilt has a lot of shaping, this will require some stretching and smoothing. At the very bottom of a kilt with a hem, the stripes won't match through the hem allowance area, because the lower hem is turned up on the diagonal.

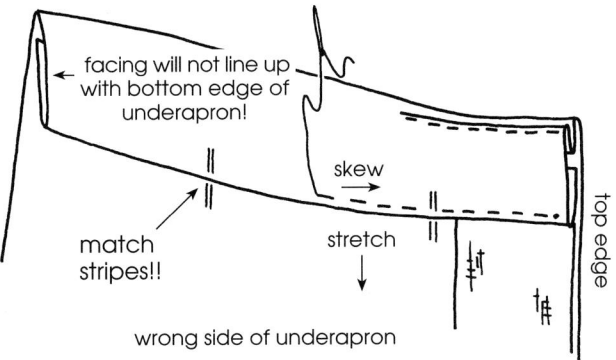

facing will not line up with bottom edge of underapron!

skew

match stripes!!

stretch

top edge

wrong side of underapron

4 Turn to the right side of the underapron, and make several horizontal lines of tailor stitching with basting thread between the bottom of the fell and the top of the kilt to hold the shape for pressing, as you did for the inner edges of the apron and underapron.

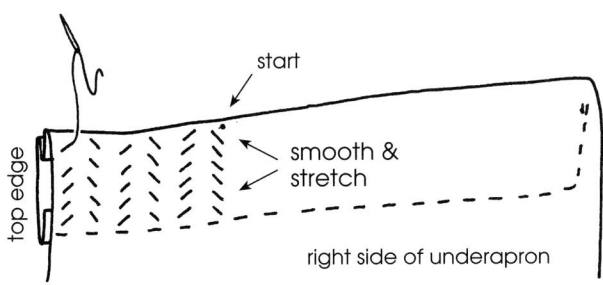

start

smooth & stretch

top edge

right side of underapron

Finishing the apron edge

A properly made kilt has a double fringe. One is a self-fringe of the raw edge of the kilt apron and the other is a fringed scrap inserted along the apron edge and offset slightly from the self-fringe edge. Two thicknesses gives a bit more substance to the fringe.

1   If you have not already done so, pull a $1/2$" fringe on the ragged right apron edge. Be sure not to pull more than $1/2$", because a longer fringe quickly becomes ratty looking.

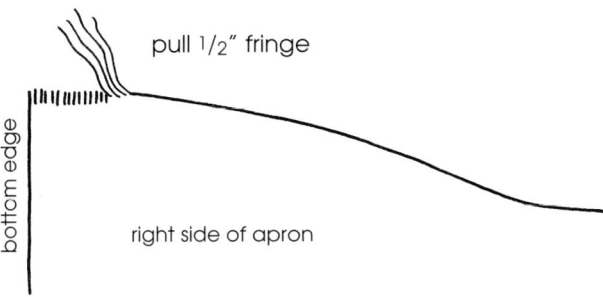

pull 1/2" fringe

bottom edge

right side of apron

2   Take a weft-wise scrap of fabric $1\ 1/2$ to 2" wide left over from trimming the join or the underapron edge, and pull a $1/2$" fringe. Be sure that the fringe scrap is the full length of the kilt *including the hem* (when the kilt must be let down, you don't want to have to piece the fringe...). **Do not** cut this scrap short. Remember that a *warp-wise* scrap is unlikely to match, and each color in the fringe must match exactly.

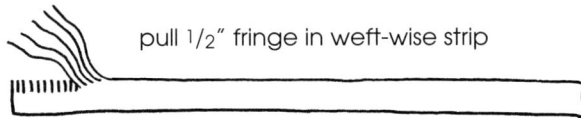

pull 1/2" fringe in weft-wise strip

3   Turn to the wrong side of the apron, and clip the apron canvas about half way down the edge and in as far as the apron chalk line to allow easing.

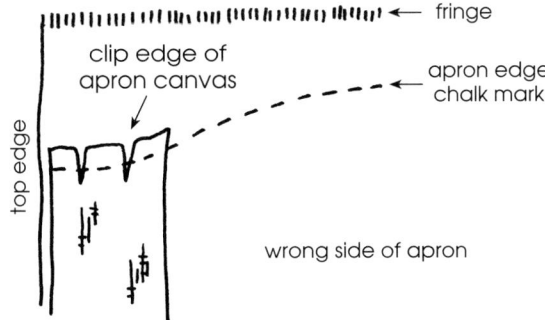

fringe

clip edge of apron canvas

apron edge chalk mark

top edge

wrong side of apron

4   Turn to the right side of the kilt, and put it in your lap with the top edge to the right. Fold the upper edge of the apron along the chalkline, and baste about $1/4$" from the edge starting at the top and ending at the previous basting. Be sure to skew and stretch a little to keep the stripes even. Extend basting to the bottom of the kilt as well, if you have not already done so after putting in a hem.

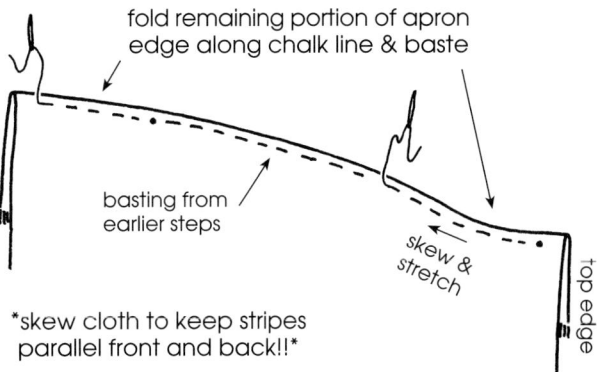

fold remaining portion of apron edge along chalk line & baste

basting from earlier steps

skew & stretch

top edge

skew cloth to keep stripes parallel front and back!!

5   Working from the right side of the apron with the top of the kilt to the right, unfold the apron edge so that the fringed edge is away from you. Lay the fringed scrap on top of the fringed edge of the apron, with the fringed edge of the apron extending outward about $1/4$" farther than the fringe on the scrap. Line up the stripes.

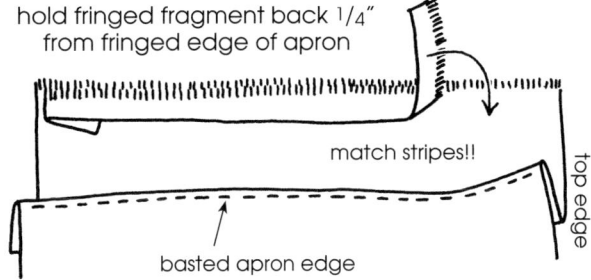

hold fringed fragment back 1/4" from fringed edge of apron

match stripes!!

top edge

basted apron edge

6   Lap the folded edge of the apron over the fringed scrap, sandwiching it between the folded apron edge and the fringed edge. Be sure that the folded edge completely covers all of the fabric of the fringed scrap so that only the fringe shows.

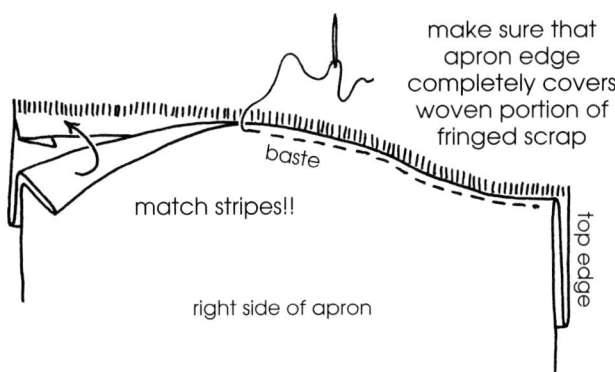

make sure that apron edge completely covers woven portion of fringed scrap

baste

match stripes!!

right side of apron

top edge

7 Baste the edge, making sure that the apron stripes match the colors in the fringe. If the kilt has a hem, don't cut the fringed scrap at the hem edge! Simply fold it over, underfolding it and angling it back slightly under the apron edge so that the non-matching fringe colors in the folded piece don't show. That way, when it's time to let down the hem, the fringe scrap will be long enough. Continue basting to the bottom of the hem.

8 Turn to the wrong side of the apron. If the kilt has a lot of shaping, fold out the facing, and make a small dart in the *underneath* side of the facing to help make the shaping easier. Baste the dart through three thicknesses only!

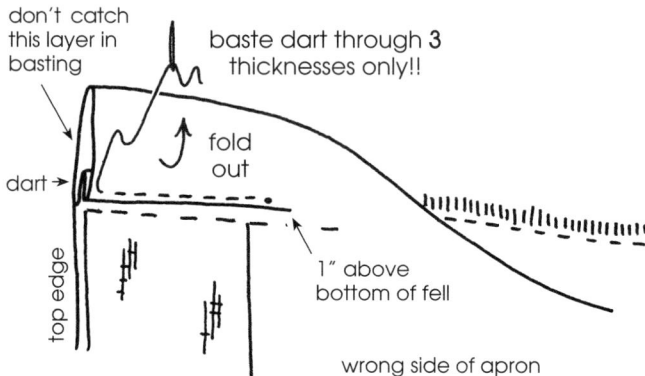

don't catch this layer in basting

baste dart through **3** thicknesses only!!

dart →

fold out

top edge

1" above bottom of fell

wrong side of apron

9 Fold the facing down again, and baste down the inner edge of the facing. Be sure to skew and stretch to make the stripes match.

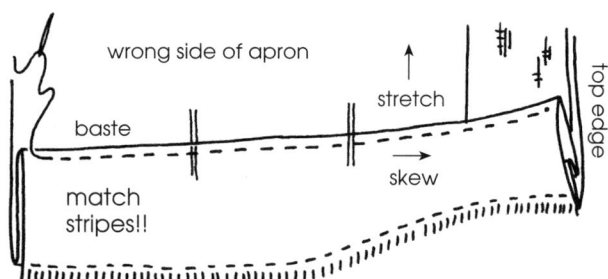

wrong side of apron

baste

stretch

top edge

skew

match stripes!!

10 Turn to the right side of the apron, and make several horizontal lines of tailor stitching with basting thread between the waist and the bottom of the fell to hold the shape for pressing, as

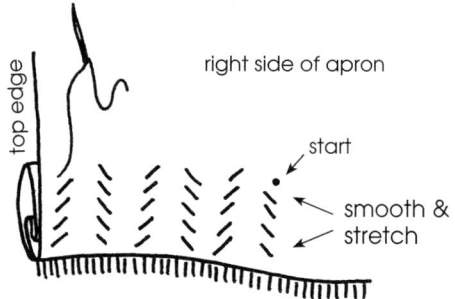

top edge

right side of apron

start

smooth & stretch

you did for the inner edges of the apron and underapron. If you have put in a dart, tailor stitch loosely down the dart. Hold fingers flat underneath as you stitch.

11 The fringe edge is sewn from the right by hand. Select matching thread, and wax it.

– Hold the kilt in your lap right side up, with the top to the right.

– Start with a knot on the back side about $1/2$" down from the top edge of the kilt and about $1/8$" in from the apron edge.

– Sew the edge with *very small back stitches* (see Appendix A) through all thicknesses. The back stitches on the right side should be nearly invisible, and the stitches on the wrong side should be only about $1/8$" or so. Do this stitching very carefully. As with the stitching in the pleats, this is something that really shows if it's done badly.

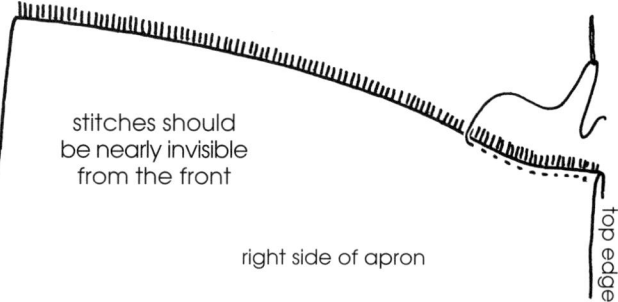

stitches should be nearly invisible from the front

right side of apron

top edge

– Stitch to the bottom of the kilt. Depending upon the locations of colors and the amount of shaping, you may need to change thread colors before you reach the bottom of the kilt.

– At the bottom of the kilt, anchor the stitching with several stitches, and then use a slip stitch to stitch the lower part of the hem together, keeping the center portion of the facing more or less hidden between the apron and back part of the facing.

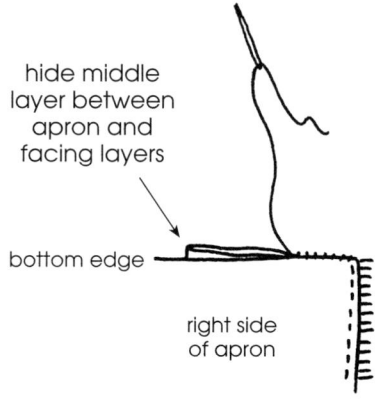

hide middle layer between apron and facing layers

bottom edge

right side of apron

Finishing the facing on the apron and underapron edges

Turn the kilt to the wrong side of the apron. Turn up the very edge of the facing, and use a catch stitch (see Appendix A) and matching waxed thread to stitch down the facing. *Be sure to use a catch stitch, rather than a blind stitch, so that the facing line will not be visible from the right side of the kilt.* Also be sure to do the catch stitch slightly underneath, rather than right at the edge of the facing, so that the stitches don't show from the wrong side of the kilt. Make your stitches small enough that they are nearly invisible from the right side. Catch stitch the facing edge of the underapron as well.

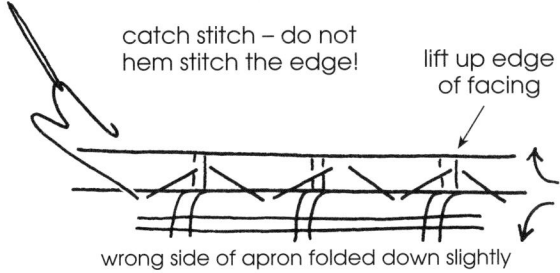

catch stitch – do not hem stitch the edge!

lift up edge of facing

wrong side of apron folded down slightly

Reinforcing the buttonhole

1 Turn to the buttonhole on the outside of the kilt. Select a thread color that matches the kilt at the bottom of the buttonhole, double the thread, and wax it. Make 2-3 bar tacks about $1/2$" long in the same place at the bottom end of the buttonhole.

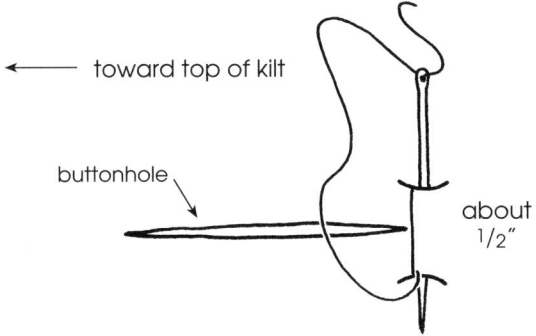

toward top of kilt

buttonhole

about 1/2"

2 Sew buttonhole stitch across the bar tack to reinforce the end of the buttonhole as shown below and above right. Catch in the fabric underneath the bartacks as you make the buttonhole stitch.

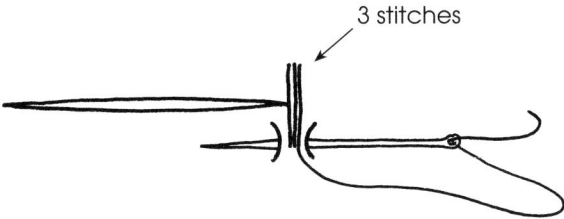

3 stitches

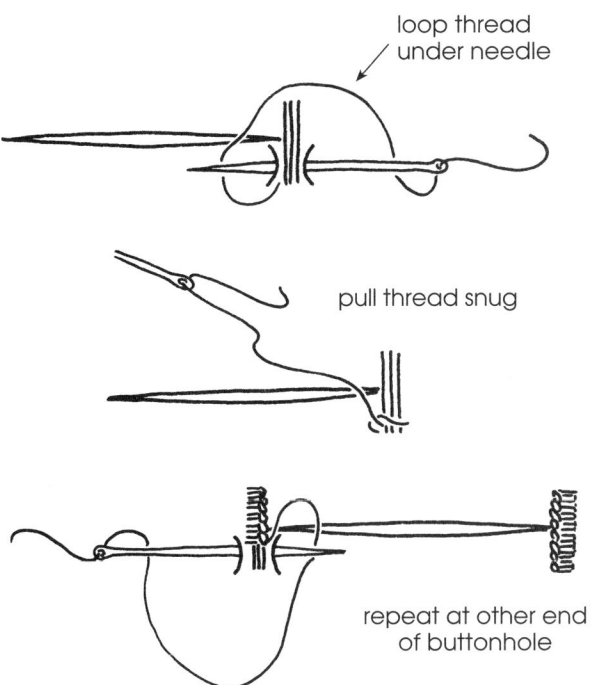

loop thread under needle

pull thread snug

repeat at other end of buttonhole

3 Repeat for the top end of the buttonhole.

4 Take basting thread, and baste the buttonhole closed in preparation for pressing. Use a double-X stitch with a double stitch in the middle.

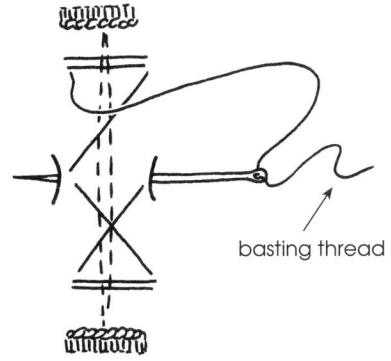

basting thread

Stitching the top band

The top band is the one part of the kilt that may be put on by machine, but it is still basted by hand. The top band may be put on either before or after pressing the pleats and aprons, depending upon when it is convenient for you to press the kilt and let it sit to dry for awhile after pressing. If you wish to press now, go to page 103. Return to this section to apply the top band after pressing.

1 Take a sharp pair of scissors, and trim any canvas that sticks up past the ravelled edge at the top of the kilt. This is particularly important if you are using a brand of canvas such as Tailor's Pride® that has nylon filaments woven in for stiffness. If you have used this type of interfacing, trim the canvas about $1/4$" below the top of the

tartan fabric edge. If you don't, the nylon filaments may poke through the top band, resulting in a line of little prickers sticking out of the top of the kilt. Not very comfortable on sensitive skin! Then, go to the top of the fringed edge, and clip off the fringe from the top edge of the kilt down about $1/2$" to allow room for the top band.

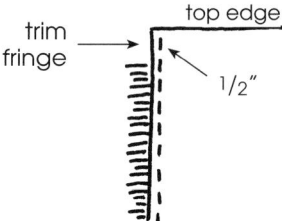

2   Select a warp-wise scrap no more than 3" wide to make the top band. Turn to the right side of the kilt at the apron. Locate the right side of the top band piece (remember that, looking across its width, the diagonal weave pattern should be from lower right to upper left on the right side). Put a chalk mark "X" on the wrong side. Double check, just to be sure – you don't want to discover that the twill goes the wrong way once you've stitched the top band.

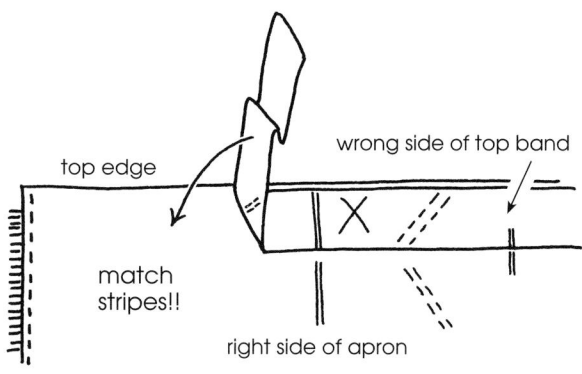

3   The tartan in the top band must match the tartan in the apron. The tartan will not match in either the pleats or the underapron (except by extraordinary coincidence!).

4   Put the band and the kilt *right sides together*, matching the stripe at the apron center front with the same stripe in the top band and having the edge of the top band even with the top of the kilt.

   – Be sure that the top band extends several inches beyond the fringed edge of the apron to allow for alterations.

   – Starting at the apron center front, baste to the *left* along a line slightly less than $1/2$" from the edge, stopping at the fringed edge of the apron.

   – Lift the top band up, and double-check the direction of the twill. With the top band folded up, the diagonal pattern for the kilt and the top band must be identical. If they aren't, remove the top band, turn it over, realign it, and baste again from the apron center to the apron edge. Double-check to see that the tartan matches as well, and, if it doesn't, take the stitches out and re-baste.

   – Extend the top band to the edge of the first pleat, and baste to the *left* from the first pleat back to the apron center front. Double check to make sure that the tartan matches.

   – Extend the top band to the center back, and baste to the *left* from the center back to the first pleat. As you do so, stretch the top edge of the kilt a bit to be sure that the kilt flares above the waistline.

   – Extend the top band to the last pleat, and baste to the *left* from the last pleat to the center back. As you do so, stretch the top edge of the kilt a bit to be sure that the kilt flares above the waistline.

   – Extend the top band to the underapron center, and baste to the *left* from the underapron center to the last pleat.

   – Baste the remainder to the left from the underapron edge to the underapron center.

5   The top band may be stitched either by machine or by hand.

   – **If you sew by machine**, sew a $1/2$" seam exactly parallel to the stripes in the kilt and the top band. As you stitch, keep some tension on the fabric fore and aft in order to keep the top band from skootching and puckering.

   – **If you sew by hand**, use carpet thread, and sew a line of back stitches from the underapron edge to the apron edge about $1/2$" down from the top of the kilt.

6   Cut off the extra waist band length, leaving 2" (leave more if you want to have some for alteration).

7   Turn the kilt to the wrong side, and start at the fringed edge of the kilt. Knot a basting thread. Fold the top band up, and fold the extra on the end along a fold that angles up slightly.

8   Fold the excess back toward the kilt along a fold that angles back slightly toward the kilt.

9   Fold the top band tightly over the top of the kilt, enclosing both the ragged top edge and the extra top band fabric. Baste the top band from the wrong side, folding the top band tightly over the ragged edge of the kilt as you go. Repeat the

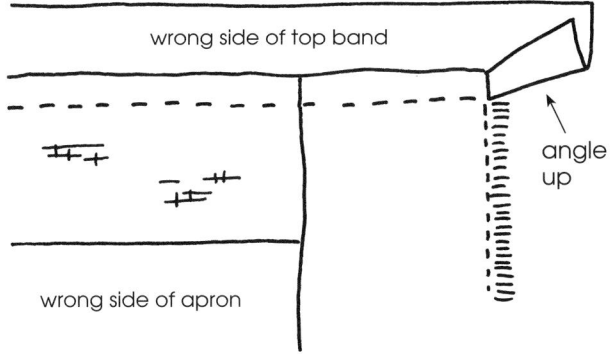

wrong side of top band

angle up

wrong side of apron

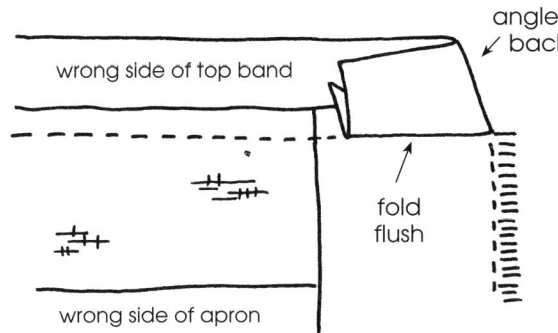

angles back

wrong side of top band

fold flush

wrong side of apron

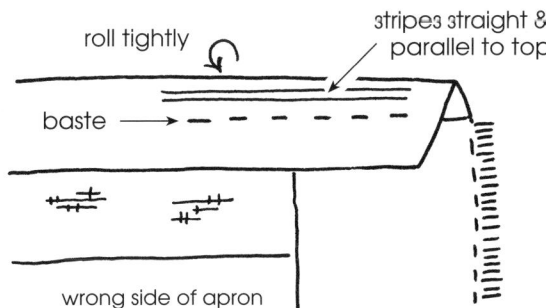

roll tightly

stripes straight & parallel to top

baste

wrong side of apron

same fold for the excess at the underapron end of the top band.

10 Using carpet threat, stitch the top band from the wrong side using a short running stitch with a back stitch every 2 to 3 stitches.

11 Start by stitching the apron end of the band, and continue by stitching more or less "in the ditch", near the top band seam. Be sure that the stitches do not come through to, or dimple, the right side of the kilt. End by stitching the underapron end of the top band.

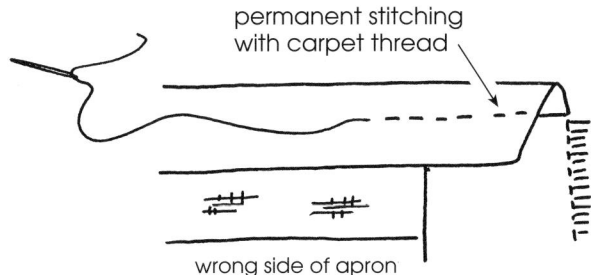

permanent stitching with carpet thread

wrong side of apron

Pressing the kilt

To press your kilt, you will need an iron, a press cloth (a clean old pillowcase is excellent), a spray bottle, and a pressing ham. For all of the pressing, you must have a damp press cloth between the iron and the kilt fabric. Do not iron directly on the kilt fabric, even with a steam iron.

1 Set your iron to wool. If the height of your ironing board is adjustable, lower it about a foot relative to where you normally have it for ironing. You will need to exert pressure on your kilt, and you'll have more leverage if the ironing board is lower.

2 Start with the kilt right side up. Lay the apron edge over the pressing ham. Spray the press cloth with water to dampen it, lay the press cloth on top of the kilt, and press the portion of the kilt that lies on the pressing ham. Press firmly, and rock the iron on the curve of the pressing ham. Don't slide the iron. The press cloth should be damp enough to generate a good amount of steam, because it is the steam that softens the wool for pressing and shaping. You will be amazed at how the bubbly apron edges flatten to a smoothly curved surface!

3 Move another part of the apron edge onto the ham, and press it well, spraying the press cloth to keep it damp. Work your way along both edges of the apron and underapron.

4 With the ham underneath and the damp press cloth on top, work your way along the top band of both the apron and underapron. Then, orient the wide end of the ham toward the bottom of the fell and the narrow end toward the top of the kilt, and press the pleats from the top edge down about 2" below the bottom of the fell. Press firmly.

5 Remove the ham, and drape the kilt over the ironing board with the top edge of the kilt and most of the stitched pleats hanging off the pointed end of the ironing board. Make sure that the pleats are flat and nice and straight. Check to make sure that none of the pleats on the other side are folded the wrong way (which can happen if you slide the kilt across the ironing board). Use the press cloth, and press the pleats from 2" below the bottom of the fell to the bottom of the kilt, paying particular attention to the bottom of the kilt, if the kilt has a hem. The harder you press, the better the creases will be.

6 Turn the kilt over. Use the press cloth, and press the pleats again from the wrong side. Do not press above the bottom of the fell.

7 Lay the kilt as flat as possible, and allow it to dry before proceeding to the buckles and straps.

Sporran loops

If you wish your kilt to have sporran loops (see tips and hints box on this page for a discussion of the pros and cons):

1 Cut two scraps of cloth 1 1/4"x3" to match the tartan at the waistline in two places approximately 2-3" to the right and left of the center back. Roll the pieces lengthwise into a tube, and blind stitch along the long edge.

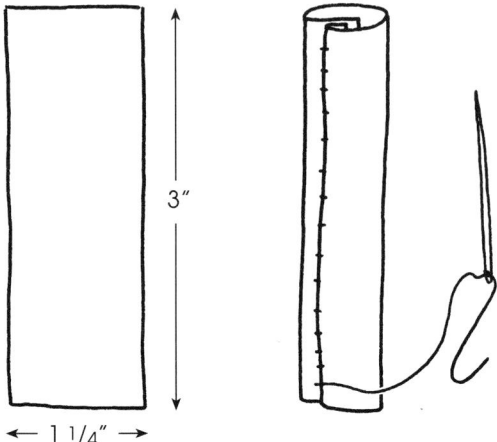

2 Flatten each tube, placing the seam in the center of one side. Place each piece, seam side down, on the kilt, centered on the waistline approximately 2-3" from the center back. Match the tartan, fold the ends under, and stitch the ends invisibly with carpet thread.

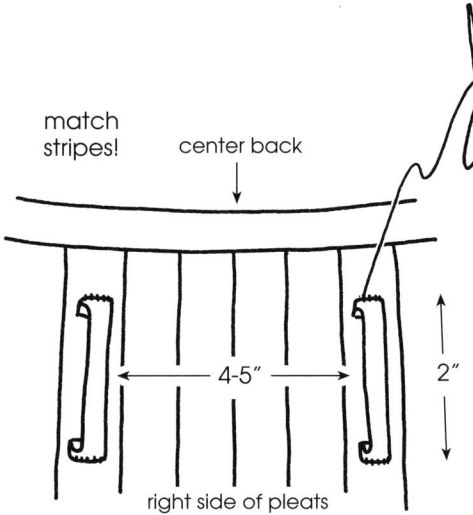

match stripes! center back

4-5" 2"

right side of pleats

Tips & Hints: Loops or no loops?

A man wears a kilt with a sporran and a belt. The sporran strap is worn under the belt and may tend to slip down or to feel to the wearer as if it will slip down. To solve this, a man can loop the sporran strap over the top of the buckles before putting on the belt. The belt, properly lined up with the top of the kilt, will hold the sporran strap in place above the buckles and keep it from slipping down.

Some men prefer sporran loops on their kilts, and you should certainly sew sporran loops on any kilt made for a male dancer.

Sporran loops are not belt loops. The belt is decorative and does not need belt loops. Many men put their kilt belts through the sporran loops, thinking that they are, in fact, belt loops. Doing so eventually distorts the waistline region of the kilt, causing the kilt hem to pull up directly below the loops and to no longer hold a straight hemline.

Despite this, some men insist on loops big enough to put their belts through. If an explanation of the consequences doesn't dissuade them, just smile and sew the loops on.

Attaching buckles and straps

The buckles are not sewn directly to the kilt but rather to a small tab of tartan fabric that is then sewn to the kilt. The stripes in the fabric tab are matched as closely as possible to the kilt at the attachment point.

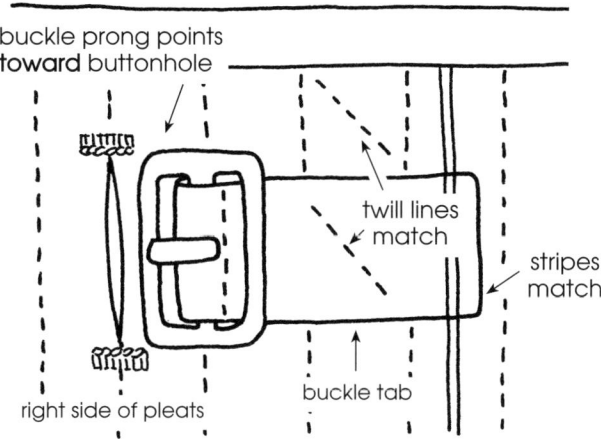

Measuring for the buckles

1 The buckle for the underapron strap is centered on the waistline just behind the buttonhole.

2 To locate the buckle for the apron strap at the waistline, lay the kilt flat on a table with the right side up. Measure a distance equal to the waist measurement plus ½" from the apron edge (not including the fringe) across and into the pleats along the waistline. Make a chalk mark. If there are not enough pleats to add ½" to the waist measurement, make the chalk mark at a distance equal to the waist measurement exactly.

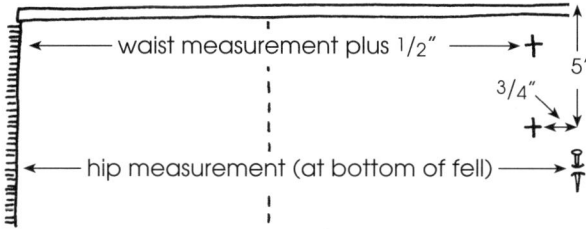

3 If your kilt will have a hip buckle (see the tips and hints box on this page for rules of thumb on numbers of buckles and straps), measure a distance equal to the hip measurement from the apron edge (not including the fringe) across and into the pleats at the level of the bottom of the fell. Mark with a pin, and then place a chalk mark about ¾" to the left of the pin and about 5" down from the top of the kilt. This raises the hip buckle up some, which looks better.

Sewing on the buckles

1 Place the underapron strap buckle on the kilt just behind the buttonhole. **Be sure that the prong is flipped the right way and that the buckle points in the right direction.** The prong of the underapron strap buckle points toward the buttonhole, and the prongs of the buckles for the apron straps point toward the underapron.

2 The buckle tab will be 1 ½" to 2" long and will extend toward the center back from each buckle. Decide which prominent stripe(s) in adjacent pleats you will match in the buckle tab. Look through the leftover tartan pieces and the scraps cut from the pleats. Find an appropriate piece that can be folded to match both the horizontal stripes under the buckle and at least one prominent vertical stripe. Cut a rectangle of fabric a few inches wide and 4" inches long or so from the appropriate part of the scrap. **Be sure that the diagonal weave on the twill will match the diagonal weave on the kilt.**

3 If you have made a kilt with military pleating, it's unlikely that you will have any scraps from which you can match both horizontal and vertical stripes in the buckle tab unless you have a leftover piece that is at least one tartan repeat wide. In most cases, you will not be able to match both horizontal and vertical stripes, so choose whichever you think will look the best. In any event, the kilt straps cover the buckle tabs, so it doesn't much matter anyway.

4 Fold the buckle tab into a tube the width of the opening in the buckle. Slide the tab through the buckle from the back side, and pierce the tab with the buckle prong. **Do not cut a hole for the**

prong. Use your fingernails to work a space between warp and weft threads to slide the prong through.

poke prong through
fabric – do **not** cut a hole

5   Slip the short end of the tab through to the back side of the buckle, and pull it firmly back parallel to the longer top part of the tab.

fold tab back snugly
through buckle

6   Lay the buckle and the tab on the kilt in the proper position, and check the alignment of both horizontal and vertical stripes. Double check to make sure that the diagonal weave lines match the kilt and that the buckle faces the right way. If stripes or twill don't match up, try folding again or piercing the tab in a different spot, or cut a new piece.

7   Once you are satisfied with the stripes in the buckle tab, trim the buckle tab to about 2", and thread your needle with carpet thread. In your left hand, hold the long top part of the buckle tab firmly together with the short lower part. Hold the buckle pointing to the right. Starting at the edge of the buckle that is away from you, stitch the tab closed inside the buckle with a line of running stitches adjacent to the central bar of the buckle. When you get to the bottom of the bar, **do not cut your thread.**

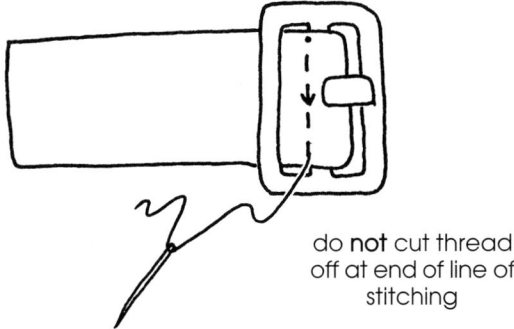

do **not** cut thread
off at end of line of
stitching

8   Place the buckle on the kilt in the proper position and align the stripes. Stitch the buckle to the kilt by sewing back along your first line of

stitching with a running stitch and a back stitch every other stitch. Stitch right through all thicknesses of the kilt and canvas.

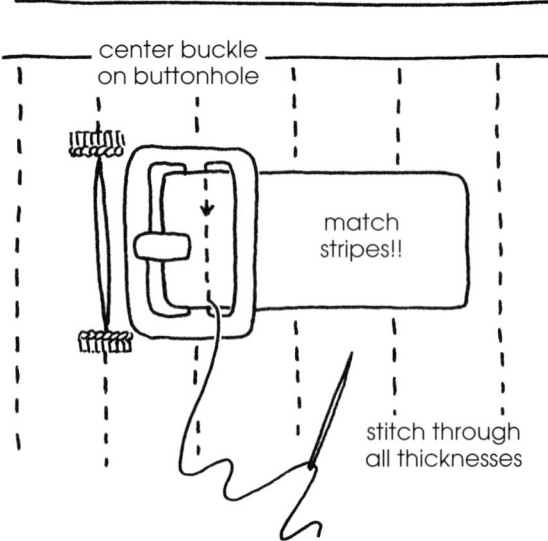

center buckle
on buttonhole

match
stripes!!

stitch through
all thicknesses

9   When you get to the end of the buckle bar, continue on around the tab, sewing it to the kilt with a blind stitch. Fold under the free end, and continue all the way around the buckle tab.

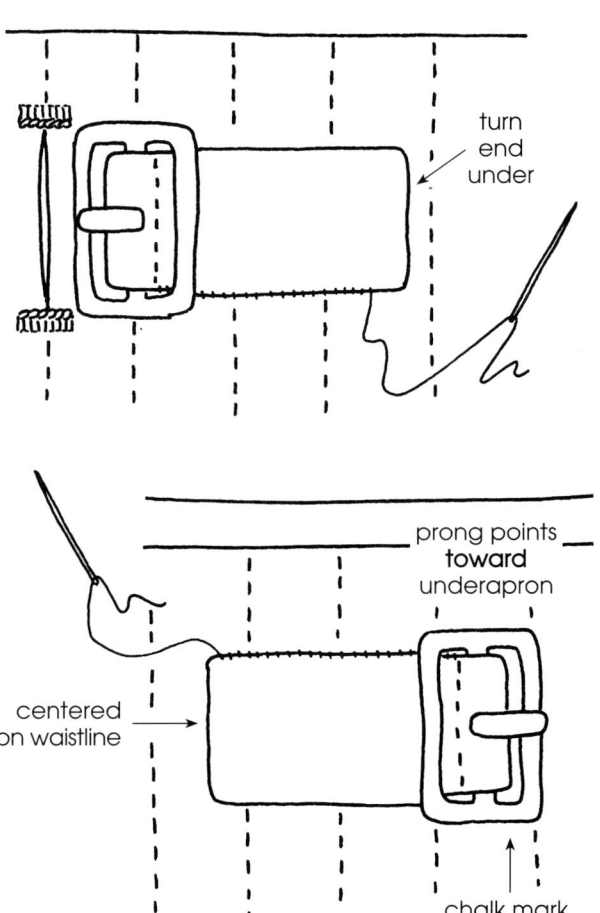

turn
end
under

prong points
toward
underapron

centered
on waistline

chalk mark

10 Repeat for the apron strap buckle(s), lining the prongs up with the chalk marks and making sure that the buckles are facing the apron.

Preparing the straps

1 The kilt straps are much easier to sew on if you first punch small holes to carry the thread. If you don't, you'll be pushing the needle through a thick piece of leather, not an easy job. A saddlemaker's punch with a rotary head is ideal for punching holes, although a mallet and a leather punch tool works satisfactorily.

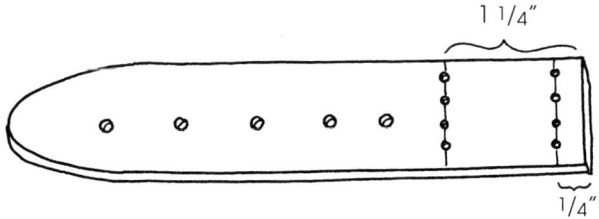

2 Take each of the leather kilt straps, and scribe two lines parallel to the width on each, the first $1/4$" from the square end and the other $1 1/4$" from the square end. Punch four small holes along each scribed line.

3 Remove the basting from the buttonhole.

Attaching the underapron strap

1 The underapron strap is sewn to the front side of the underapron.

2 Lay the kilt out on a table, and fold it in half at the center back with the buckle for the underapron strap facing up. Fold the apron under a bit, and wrap the underapron on *top* of the apron until it lies next to the buckle for the underapron. This is much easier than trying the fit the strap by threading it through the button-hole and will provide an alignment that is just as good.

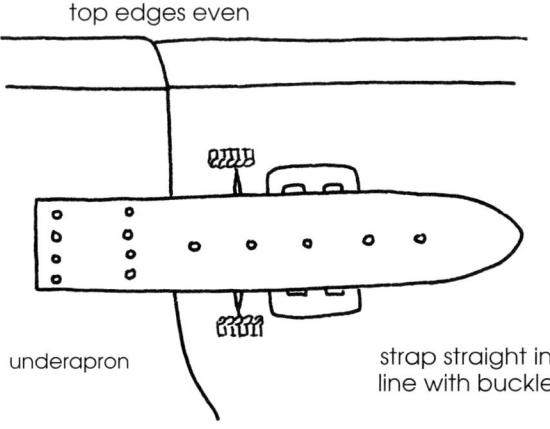

top edges even

underapron   strap straight in line with buckle

3 Lay the strap *on top* of the underapron at the waistline, and align it nice and straight with the buckle. Don't put the end of the strap too close to the underapron edge. Be sure that both lines of stitching for the strap will be covered by the lining on the inside of the kilt.

4 Stitch the strap on with black carpet thread. Pinch the strap tightly to the kilt with your left thumb and fingers, and start with a knot on the under side of the kilt. Start stitching at the right hand end of the line of holes nearest the edge of the underapron, and make two stitches in the right edge hole, stitch the middle holes with back stitches, and make two stitches in the left edge hole.

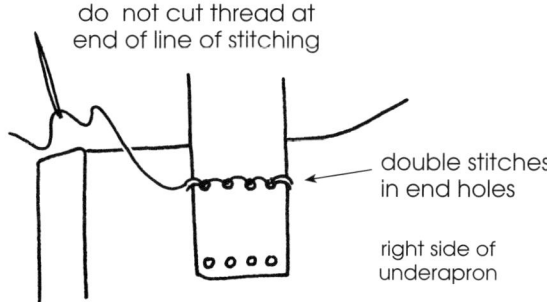

do not cut thread at end of line of stitching

double stitches in end holes

right side of underapron

5 Do not cut the thread. Instead, slide the thread under the strap, and angle it diagonally down to the right end of the second line of holes.

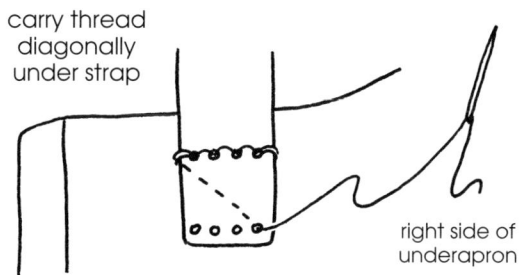

carry thread diagonally under strap

right side of underapron

6 Double-stitch the right edge hole, back stitch the middle holes, and double-stitch the left edge hole. Anchor the thread on the wrong side.

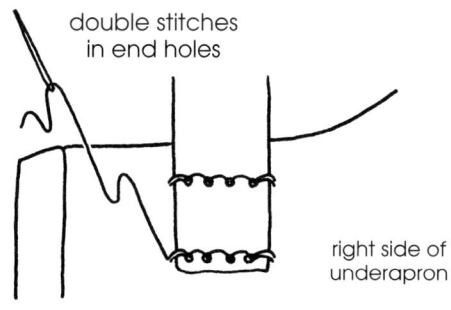

double stitches in end holes

right side of underapron

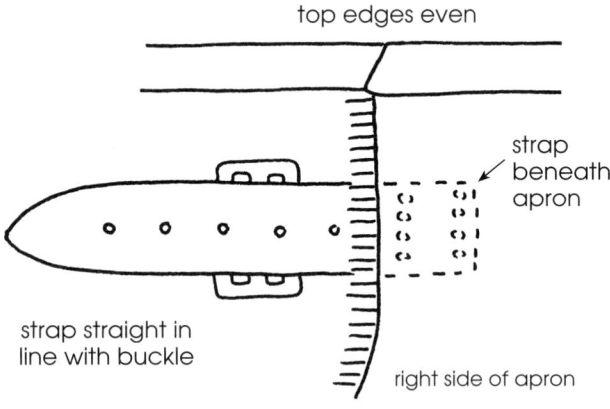

top edges even

strap beneath apron

strap straight in line with buckle

right side of apron

double stitches in end holes

wrong side of apron

Attaching the apron strap(s)

1 The apron strap(s) are sewn to the *wrong* side of the apron.

2 Lay the kilt out on a table, and fold it in half at the center back with the buckle for the apron strap facing up. Fold the underapron under a bit, and wrap the apron around the kilt until the fringe edge lies next to the top buckle for the apron.

3 Tuck the apron strap under the edge of the apron at the waistline, and align it nice and straight with the buckle. Don't put the end of the strap too close to the apron edge. Be sure that the line of stitching nearest the edge of the apron will lie at least 1/4" in from the edge of the apron, not counting the fringe.

4 Stitch the strap on with carpet thread. Choose black or white depending upon the color block that will carry the stitches on the right side of the kilt. Pinch the strap tightly to the kilt with your left thumb and fingers, and turn the edge of the apron over to stitch from the wrong side. Start with a knot on the wrong side of the kilt. Start stitching at one end of the line of holes nearest the edge of the apron. Stitch diagonally through the holes

so that the stitches are tiny on the right side of the kilt. Double the stitches in the two end holes, and back stitch the middle holes.

5 Do not cut the thread. Instead, slide the thread under the strap, and angle it diagonally to the lower end of the second line of holes. Use overhand stitches for the second line of holes, and do not stitch through to the right side of the kilt. Anchor the thread on the wrong side.

6 If your kilt has a hip buckle, repeat for the second apron strap.

Applying the lining

Attaching the apron and underapron lining

1 Turn to the wrong side of the kilt, and measure the distance from the edge of the underapron to the center of the inverted pleat at the bottom of the fell, and add a couple of inches. This equals the length of the lining pieces you will cut. Measure the distance from the top of the kilt to the bottom of the underapron canvas, and add a couple of inches. This equals the width of the lining pieces you will cut. Cut two pieces of lining of these dimensions, with the length parallel to the straight grain of the lining. If possible, use a selvedge edge for one long edge on each

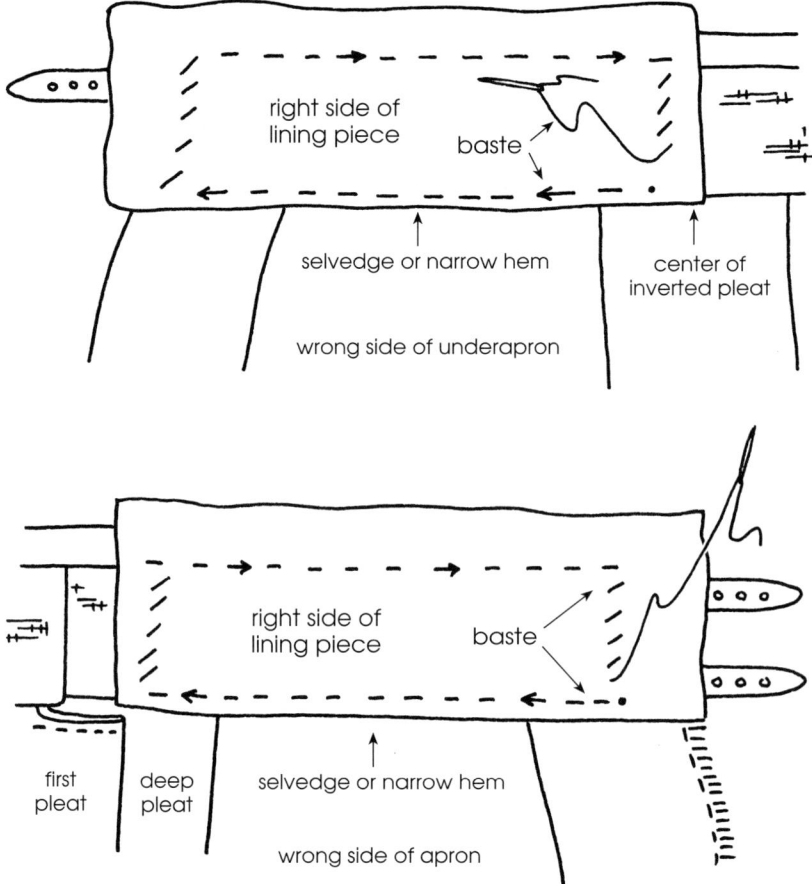

right side of lining piece

baste

selvedge or narrow hem

center of inverted pleat

wrong side of underapron

right side of lining piece

baste

first pleat

deep pleat

selvedge or narrow hem

wrong side of apron

piece. If this is not possible, turn up about $^1/_4$" on one long edge of each lining piece as a hem, and stitch it by machine.

2 Lay the kilt out on a table, and smooth the underapron area. Lay one piece of lining on the underapron with raw edges extending just past the underapron edge and with the selvedge or hem about $^1/_2$" to $^3/_4$" below the edge of the canvas. Be sure that the lining piece is straight and parallel to the stripes in the underapron. The lining will extend to just past the center of the inverted pleat. If it is too long, trim it. The lining piece should also extend past the top of the kilt at least $^1/_4$".

3 Baste the lower edge of the lining from the center of the inverted pleat to the edge of the underapron, stretching the kilt slightly so that the lining is not tight. Baste up the edge of the underapron with tailor stitches held back about an inch from the edge. Baste across the top of the kilt with running stitches held back about an inch from the edge, and complete the basting with tailor stitches along the remaining short side of the lining.

4 Repeat the process for basting the lining to the apron side.

5 The lining is stitched on with a small blind stitch (see Appendix A), and the lining is turned under along a line about $^1/_4$" back from the edge of the kilt as you stitch.

6 For the apron, stitch the lining on counterclockwise, starting at the lower corner near the deep pleat. Blind stitch the lining to one thickness of the pleat, being careful not to stitch through more thicknesses. *Stop stitching at the edge of the pleat, because the lining hangs free across the center of the apron.*

7 Start stitching again at the edge of the facing, and continue stitching up the apron edge, turning the lining under as you go and trimming if necessary. When you get to a strap, run the needle through the uppermost layer of the leather in small stitches to anchor the lining to the strap. Continue around the top of the kilt, trimming and turning under as you go and placing the folded edge of the lining $^1/_8$ to $^1/_4$" below the top of the kilt.

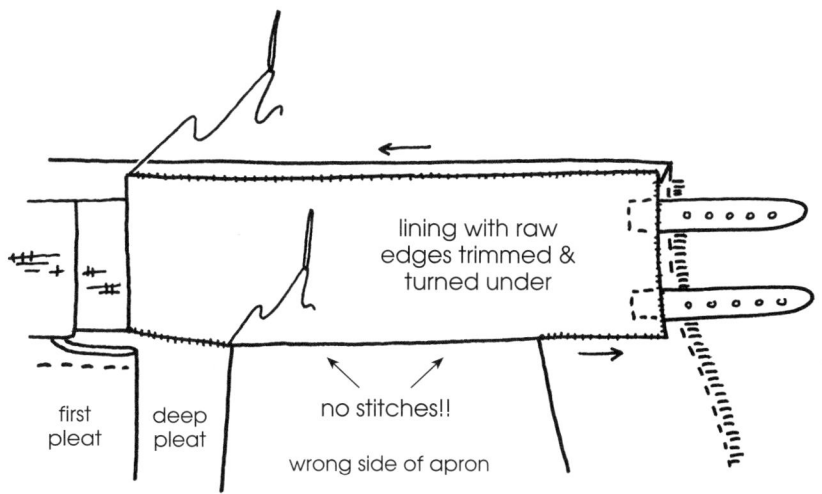

lining with raw edges trimmed & turned under

first pleat   deep pleat   no stitches!!   wrong side of apron

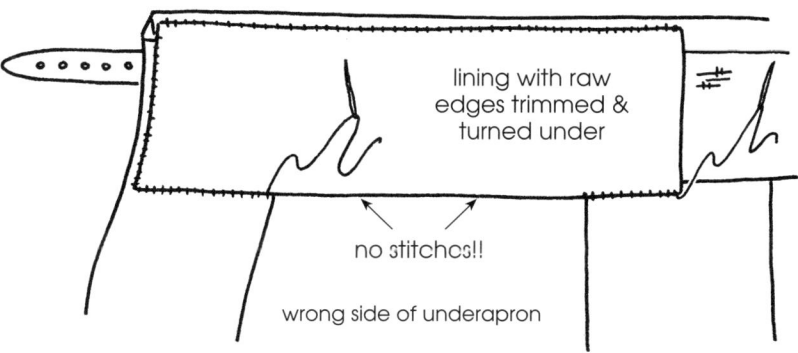

lining with raw edges trimmed & turned under

no stitches!!   wrong side of underapron

8 Stitch the underapron lining in similar fashion, starting along the upper edge at the pleats end and going counterclockwise around the lining. Be sure to leave the lining free across the underapron.

Attaching the back lining

1 Cut a piece of lining as wide as the depth of the fell plus 1" and about a yard long ($^3/_4$ of a yard, if you are making a small kilt).

2 Turn to the wrong side of the kilt, and fold the top of the kilt back at the base of the canvas. Hold the kilt in your lap with the top facing away from you.

Tips & Hints: Selecting lining fabric

Use all-cotton broadcloth or muslin to line a kilt. Even though white or off-white lining will show sweat stains more readily than colored lining, be sure to use white or off-white when lining a kilt made from a dress tartan, because a colored lining may show through the apron of the kilt in the white blocks. Use black or another dark color for kilts having little white.

3   Fold a $1/4$" hem in one short edge of the lining strip, and crease it with your fingernail. Lay the piece of lining right side down below the steeking. Align the long edge of the lining with the steeking, and place the short edge with the crease just to the right of the first pleat.

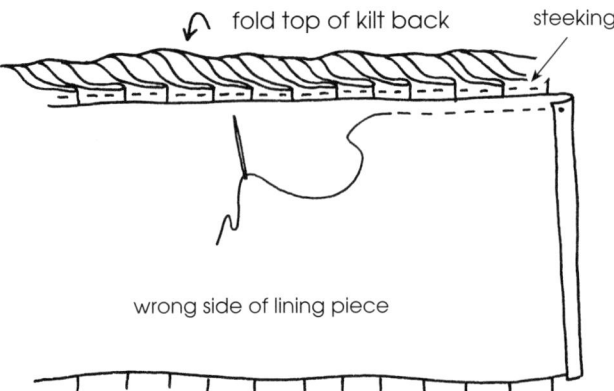

fold top of kilt back   steeking

wrong side of lining piece

4   With carpet thread, stitch the lining to the pleats using a small running stitch with a back stitch every 2 to 3 stitches along a line about $1/4$" down from the steeking. Leave some easement, and be careful not to pull the lining tight. End your stitching at the center of the inverted pleat, trim off all but $1/4$" of the extra lining material, and fold in the edge in a small hem, creasing it with your fingernail.

5   Fold the lining up to hide the stitching, and smooth it flat against the canvas.

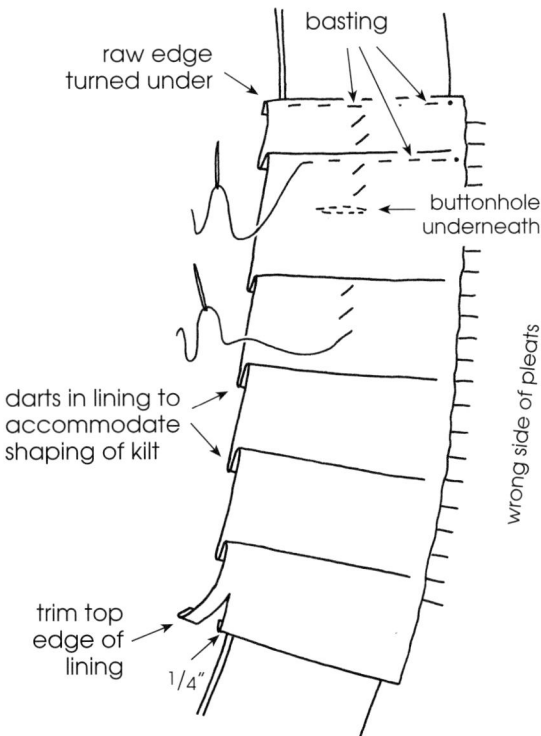

raw edge turned under

basting

buttonhole underneath

darts in lining to accommodate shaping of kilt

wrong side of pleats

trim top edge of lining

$1/4$"

6   Hold the kilt wrong side up in your lap with the top to the left. Straighten the folded edge of the lining, and baste it to the kilt. Starting in the middle of the folded edge, run a line of basting using a tailor stitch down the middle of the lining, folding darts in the lining at regular intervals to accommodate the pleat shaping so that the lining lies flat. Be sure to keep the darts away from the buttonhole.

7   Baste along the edge of each dart, ending each line of basting about 1" below the top edge of the kilt. Trim the top of the lining so that it is only about $1/4$" higher than the edge of the kilt.

8   Use a blind stitch to sew the lining, starting at the bottom end of the folded edge and continuing across the top of the kilt, folding the lining under as you go.

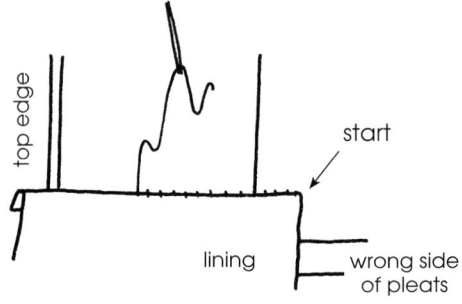

top edge

start

lining   wrong side of pleats

9   As you come to each dart, open out the dart, fold the edge, and re-fold the dart. This makes the edge less bulky than it would be if you made the dart first and then folded the whole dart over.

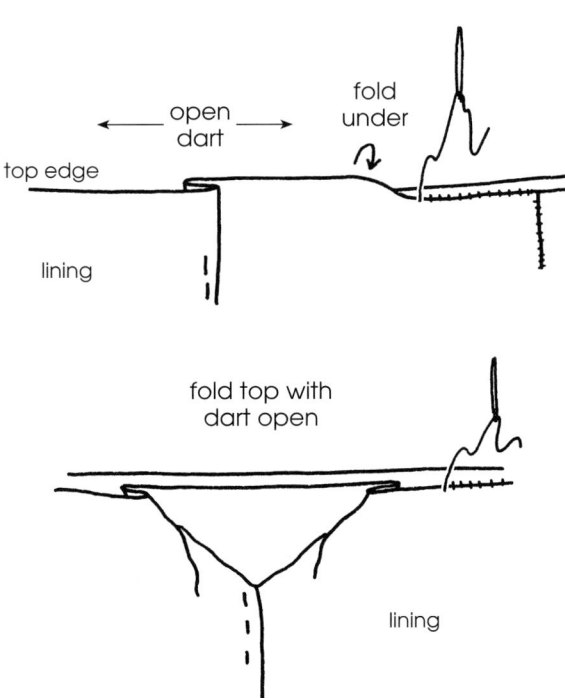

open dart

fold under

top edge

lining

fold top with dart open

lining

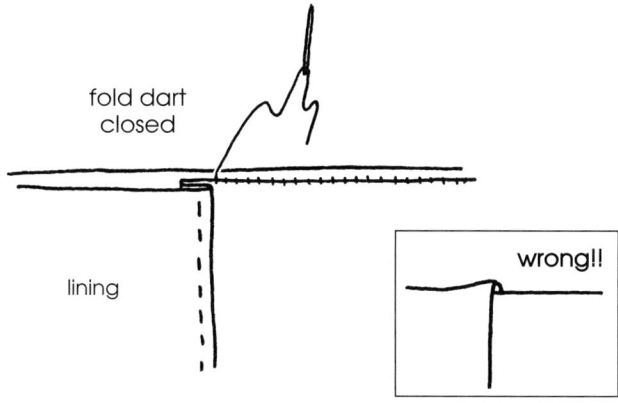

10 Continue stitching across the top of the kilt and down the remaining folded edge.

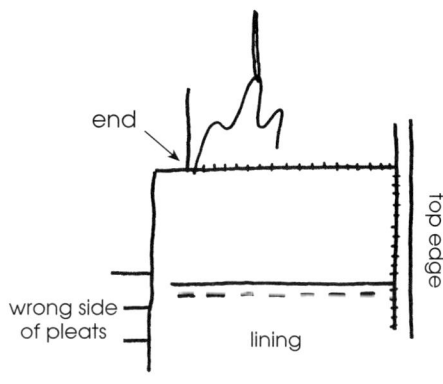

11 Use a blind stitch to stitch each dart, catching a little fabric underneath to stabilize the lining.

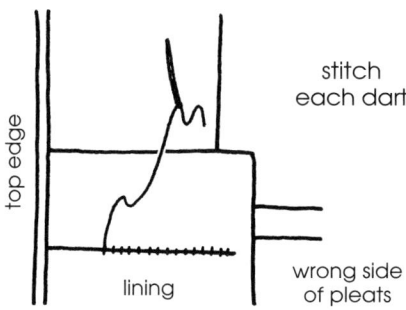

12 Carefully clip the lining at the buttonhole, and slash the corners.

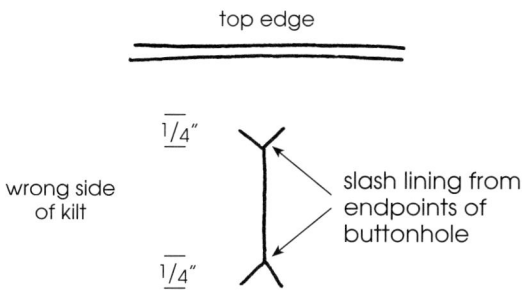

13 Turn back the edges and points of the slashed opening, and blind stitch the lining down around the buttonhole. Be sure that the canvas is hidden.

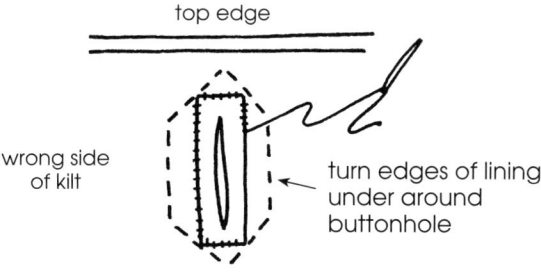

Add a label

Consider adding a label to your kilt that tells who made it. Appendix F lists suppliers for labels of various kinds.

Removing the basting threads

Carefully remove all of the basting threads except the ones holding the pleats. Despite the powerful urge you'll feel to remove the basting stitches as fast as possible, work with care. This would not be the time to snip or snag your beautiful kilt! Although a seam ripper sounds like an ideal tool for removing the basting, it's very easy to snag a kilt with the point. A pair of blunt tweezers or a knitting needle is great for sliding under basting stitches, because neither will snag the kilt.

Cheer, yell, have a glass of champagne, or whatever! You've made your first kilt! Here's to many more.

Tips & Hints: Basting for shipping

If you need to ship the kilt to someone, leave the pleat basting stitches in, and include a note telling the person how to remove the basting. If you do not need to ship the kilt, go ahead and remove the pleat basting. But, don't try the kilt on until you take out the pleat basting! It will feel odd and won't hang right.

Are you a kiltmaker yet?

Does one kilt make you a kiltmaker? Does it take two? Or twenty? There's no one answer, of course, but making a perfect kilt takes some practice. Practice until you can make pleats with perfectly matched stripes and perfectly straight elements all the way across the back without stitches that show. Practice until you can take measurements accurately and until you can make a kilt that matches those measurements precisely. Once you can do these things, you can call yourself a kiltmaker!

Chapter 10

Wearing your kilt properly

A well-made and well-fitting kilt can look dreadful if it is not worn properly. In this chapter, we'll show you how to wear your kilt and accessories properly so that you look your best.

Donning your kilt

Lots of people at Highland games and gatherings don't wear their kilts properly, although they do manage to get the pleats in the back (you may laugh, but we have seen people whose first inclination is to put the pleats in the front!!).

Wear it high enough

Wear your kilt with the waist in the proper place. **Remember that your kilt has a 2" rise above the waistline.** When your kilt is buckled on properly, it will extend 2" *above* your natural waist, with the waistline running through the centers of the buckles and straps. If you try to wear your kilt with the top edge of the kilt at your waistline, the kilt will not lie smoothly at the hips, and the kilt will be too long. Many first time kilt-wearers buckle their kilts on too low, because they aren't accustomed to or simply don't know about the rise. It's just a matter of getting used to a different type of garment. Many men have also forgotten where their waistlines are, because they normally wear their pants well below their waists, particularly if they have a bit of a tub.

Buckle the waist snugly

Wear your kilt buckled snugly at the waist. Pull the underapron strap as tight as you can before buckling the apron strap. Many men don't wear their kilts tight enough, and their kilts tend to sag either in the front or in the back (which is probably the origin of the myth that men's kilts are longer in the back than dancer's kilts...).

If your kilt has a hip buckle, wear the hip strap a bit loose. It's the waist straps and buckles that keep the kilt from falling off. The hip strap just helps keep the fringe edge in place, so there's no need to pull it tight. A hip strap pulled tight looks unsightly on a person with a bit of a corporation, and a hip buckle pulled too tight can contribute to the first pleat flapping open.

Center the stripes

Wear your kilt with the center front stripe centered. Once you've buckled your kilt, check the location of the center front stripe, and give the kilt a twist one way or the other in order to center the stripe. If the kilt fits perfectly, the center back stripe should automatically center when the center front stripe is aligned.

Wearing sporran, belt, and pin

Many first-time kilt owners are unsure about how to wear sporrans, belts, and pins, and many long-time kilt owners, in fact, wear them incorrectly.

Sporran

Put the sporran on first, because the sporran strap is worn *under* the belt at the back of the kilt. The straps of the sporran can be run through the sporran loops, if the kilt has them. If your kilt has no sporran loops, and you are worried about your sporran taking an unexpected excursion to your ankles, loop the sporran strap over the top of the kilt buckles before you put on your belt.

Belt

The belt is purely decorative and is worn over the sporran strap. The top of the belt should be aligned with the top of the kilt. **The belt should not be put through loops on the back of the kilt.** Over time, forcing a belt through what are actually sporran loops distorts the back of the kilt, causing the kilt hem to pull up directly below the loops and to no longer hold a straight hemline. If you don't believe this, surreptitiously examine a number of kilts at the next Highland gathering you attend.

Pin

A kilt pin in the lower right corner of the apron keeps the apron from flapping open in the wind. Highland dancers do not wear pins in competition.

What should I wear under my kilt?

What you wear depends upon how bold you are. The bold go *au naturel*. Most people wear underwear or dark-colored lycra exercise shorts such as bicycle shorts. Dancers wear dark-colored dance trunks, with blouses or shirts tucked into the trunks.

Choosing the right velveteen for a dancer's vest or jacket

The standard Highland competition outfit for girls and women includes a fitted velveteen vest or jacket with metallic braid and diamond-shaped thistle buttons. Consider using cotton velveteen or upholstery velvet rather than rayon velvet, which tends to crush and mat easily.

Choosing a color for the vest or jacket

When selecting the color for a vest or jacket, remember that the outfit will be viewed by judge and audience at a distance of 20 feet or more.

- A color that looks good up close may not be the best color at a distance. For example, matching velveteen to a narrow red stripe in a kilt that consists mainly of green and black is likely to be a bad choice. At a distance, the red stripe will vanish, and everyone will wonder why the dancer is wearing a red vest or jacket with a green and black kilt.

- If possible, take the kilt itself (rather than just a tartan swatch) and several possible colors of velveteen in large swatches (or, better yet, yardage), and view them outdoors from a distance of at least 20 feet in order to choose the best color. The best color choice may turn out not to match *any* of the colors of the kilt individually but rather to go well with the entire tartan at a distance.

- Remember that colors will look darker on an indoor stage or under a competition tent outdoors. Dark shades of blue, green, or even burgundy are likely to look black under such conditions.

- Velveteen will look darker and richer if the vest or jacket is cut so that the nap smooths up the garment toward the top. Velveteen will look lighter in color and slightly shiny if the vest or jacket is cut so that the nap smooths down toward the bottom.

Choosing braid for the vest or jacket

Use gold braid and buttons on a vest or jacket if the kilt has a *prominent* yellow stripe or yellow color block. If the only yellow in a kilt is a narrow stripe that vanishes at a distance, consider using silver braid and buttons instead.

Regional Highland dance champions, each of whom is wearing one of Elsie's kilts, at the 1998 U.S. Inter-regional Highland Dance Championship.

Take good care of a kilt, and it will look nice and last for years. In this chapter, we tell you how to take good care of your kilt and how to deal with the inevitable spots and stains that plague a kilt that is worn often, no matter how lovingly it is cared for.

Keep your kilt looking nice

It's easier to keep a kilt looking nice than it is to deal with spots and wrinkles after having treated it in shabby fashion. The best remedy is a bit of prevention. Here are a few suggestions:

- If you are going to a Highland gathering, wear something else in the car, and put your kilt on when you get there. The pleats will thank you.

- When you sit down, get into the habit of sliding both hands down your backside as you sit, smoothing the pleats flat before you sit. This is a hard habit for men to acquire!

- When you take your kilt off, fold it in half at the waist, right sides together, and then fold it again. Hang it in a good skirt hanger. Folding it inside out keeps the good side out of harm's way.

- When your kilt is sweaty, don't fold it and hang it up in a garment bag. As soon as possible after wearing, lay the kilt out to air and dry thoroughly.

- Store your kilt in a roomy garment bag. Don't jam it in with sixteen other items. The same goes for travelling. Invest in a second garment bag, rather than putting all of your Highland clothing into the same garment bag.

Re-pressing the pleats

Even if you take good care of your kilt, you'll find eventually that you will need to re-press the pleats. If you simply lay the kilt out on the ironing board, the pleats will want to fan out from the bottom of the fell to the bottom of the kilt. If you press the kilt with the pleats fanned, your kilt will look dreadful once you put it on again. If the pleats were fanned when you pressed the kilt, the bottom of each pleat will be wider than the top, and the kilt will hang in waves (kilt below right), rather than hanging nice and straight, as it does in the kilt above right. Unfortunately, once you have pressed the kilt wrong, it is very difficult to press it correctly again.

If your kilt really needs re-pressing, take the time to re-baste the pleats so that each pleat is held absolutely the same width from the bottom of the fell to the bottom of the kilt for pressing. It really doesn't take very long to baste it up, and you will be much happier that you took the time. Refer to the instructions in Basting the Pleats on page 86 for re-basting the pleats and Pressing the Kilt on page 103 for pressing. And remember! Be sure to use a damp press cloth – don't iron directly on the kilt!

a properly-pressed kilt hangs straight down from the bottom of the fell; the pleats were held straight during pressing

an improperly-pressed kilt hangs in waves; the pleats were fanned during pressing

What to do when your kilt gets dirty

Don't have your kilt dry cleaned if you can avoid it. Dry cleaning leaves a subtle residue on the kilt, and your kilt will soil more easily after it has been dry-cleaned. **If you can't avoid having it dry cleaned, at least tell the cleaner NOT to press your kilt.** The pleats are very likely to come back perfectly creased but in the wrong places or with wiggly stripes. Cleaners are notorious for carefully spreading the kilt out along a curve when they press, which will result in splayed pleats as shown on the previous page. It's safer to do the pressing yourself. When you get your kilt back unpressed from the cleaner, baste it (page 87) and press it yourself according to the instructions on page 103.

Alternatives to dry-cleaning

Perspiration stains and odor

- Try airing your kilt first, before you move on to more drastic measures. Airing your kilt periodically will help keep your kilt smelling nice. Prevention also helps – don't put a sweaty kilt into your garment bag. Air dry it thoroughly first. On the way home from a Highland gathering, consider laying your kilt out on top of your luggage in the car to let it air dry on the way home.

- For stains on the lining, put a little ammonia in water, and soak a press cloth in the mixture. Press the lining side with the press cloth between the kilt and the iron.

- The colors on a kilt also perk up when you press with a cloth soaked in a dilute mixture of ammonia and water.

Spots

- For small spot stains, try a Q-tip® with a little ammonia diluted with water.

- For blood and other hard-to-remove stains, try a Q-tip® dipped in an enzyme detergent such as Era®. Be sure to spot-rinse the area well.

A kilt that doesn't fit properly feels awkward and looks a mess. In this chapter, we'll show you how to make a few minor alterations, such as moving the buckles and changing the hem, that can make a big difference in how a kilt looks. We'll also teach you how to make major alterations to a kilt that is too small or too big around.

How do you know when a kilt doesn't fit properly? A kilt should fit tightly – it's too big if you can easily twist the kilt on the body when it is buckled into the tightest holes of the straps. A kilt is too small if the fringe edge of the apron does not completely cover the unpleated fabric of the underapron (Color Figures 5a and 7a). A kilt is too short or too long if the bottom of the kilt does not fall at the top of the wearer's kneecap (Color Figure 4). **When checking the length of a kilt, be sure that the wearer has the kilt buckled at the waistline.** Many are tempted to wear a kilt with the top of the kilt at the waist. This is wrong – remember that the buckles lie at the waist, with the rise extending *above* the waist. When checking the length of a person's kilt, also make sure **that the wearer is looking straight ahead, not down at what you're doing at the bottom of the kilt**.

Moving the buckles

If a kilt is too small or too large, the first plan of attack is to consider moving the buckles. This is a simple job that only requires carefully cutting the stitches of the buckle tabs, moving the buckles, and stitching them down again as described in Sewing on the Buckles on page 105. If you have scraps of tartan, you can make new buckle tabs to match the new buckle positions when re-attaching the buckles. Use carpet thread, and don't sew all the way through the lining to the back of the kilt when you are stitching the buckles back on.

If you have made the kilt smaller by moving the buckles, you will also need to move the underapron strap. Detach the strap, and move it toward the center of the underapron. Reattach the strap using carpet thread.

Changing the hem

Even if you do not know how to make a kilt, you can easily and properly change the hem if you follow our instructions.

Altering the hem in a kilt is a little more complicated than altering a hem in a skirt. You'll need first to undo portions of the apron and underapron stitching in order to take the hem out. Then, after taking the hem out and pressing the kilt well, you will turn the hem back up, but not uniformly everywhere. Here are the details:

1   Remove the catch stitching that anchors the apron and underapron facings up 8" or so from the bottom of the kilt.

2   Remove the stitching on the fringe edge of the kilt (and on the hidden pleat edge of the apron, if the kilt has a hidden pleat) up to 8" or so from the bottom of the kilt. Be particularly careful not to cut the kilt fabric, because these very small back stitches are hard to remove. Don't hesitate to use a magnifier in order to see what threads to pull.

3   Undo the hem stitching, and unfold the hem allowance.

4   Press well to remove the bottom crease from the hem. Be sure to use a spray bottle and press cloth.

5   Mark the new length, and put the hem up according to the instructions in If Your Kilt Will Have a Hem on page 84. If you also have a hidden pleat, follow the instructions in Appendix C for hemming with a hidden pleat.

6   Re-stitch the fringe edge (and the hidden pleat edge, if you have one), and catch stitch the facings down again.

7   Re-baste the pleats according to the instructions in Basting the Pleats on page 87, and press the kilt well (see page 103).

8   If you lengthen the hem by more than 1 1/2 to 2", you must also stitch the fell down farther on every pleat. Use the rule of thumb that the fell should be 1/3 of the total length of the kilt (including the rise) to locate the new bottom of the fell. If you have shortened the kilt, you will have to live with a fell that is too long. Because the pleats are cut out, the fell can't be shortened.

Major alterations

If moving the buckles doesn't fix the problem, or if the underapron shows along the fringe edge, you will need to make major alterations at the edges of the apron and underapron. **The crucial thing to remember is that you must make symmetrical alterations on each side of both the apron and the underapron in order to preserve the center front stripe.** You cannot simply let out the fringe edge, or the center stripe will no longer be centered.

1 Take off the buckles and straps.

2 Undo the linings, and remove the top band at the apron and underapron edges as far back as the back edge of the inverted pleat on the underapron side and the deep pleat on the apron side. Remove the canvas in that same portion.

3 Take out both the apron and the underapron edges, and take out the pleat stitching for the deep pleat and the inverted pleat. Open out the fabric on both sides of the back pleats, and press the apron and underapron well to remove old creases.

4 Using the same centers as before, re-mark the new waist and hip measurements on the apron and underapron of the kilt, and mark the new edges with chalk (pages 55-56 and 64). If you need to enlarge the kilt a good deal, you may need to choose a new center stripe (one closer to the fringe edge) in order to maintain enough fabric in the deep pleat. Check carefully to be sure that you have enough cloth at the fringe edge to do this. Choosing a new center stripe means that the new center front stripe and the older center back stripe will not match, but no one can see the front and back of a kilt at the same time.

5 Follow the instructions in the main part of this book for re-basting the apron edges and re-stitching the deep pleat (pages 71-73) and the inverted pleat along the new apron and underapron lines (pages 85-86).

6 Continue to follow the instructions, reassembling the kilt and adding new canvas as necessary. Don't skimp on the basting and shaping – the alteration should be as well-done as the kilt was originally! You will need to piece the top band at the deep pleat so that the waistband matches the apron across the entire width of the apron. Once you have replaced the top band, baste the pleats, and re-press the kilt. Then, re-do the lining, buckles, and straps.

apron: the unpleated front of the kilt that lies over the underapron. The apron always buckles at the right hip.

arisaid: a tartan shawl. Gaelic: *earisaid*.

asymmetric tartan: a tartan that does not repeat symmetrically about a center line. An asymmetric tartan cannot be divided into halves that are mirror images of one another. Only a few tartans are asymmetric. Synonyms: non-centering, non-matching.

back stitch: a stitch used in a kilt where more secure stitching is needed than would be produced by a running stitch.

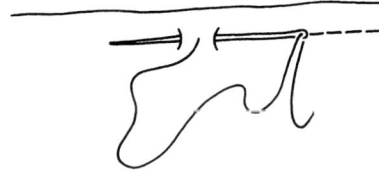

blind stitch: used for the center back join, buckle tabs, and kilt lining. It is not used for the hem or facings!!

catch stitch: used to anchor the edges of the apron and underapon facings.

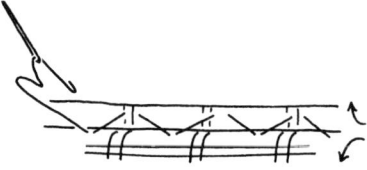

edge stitch: similar to blind stitch but stitched more closely and with a slight back stitch; used to stitch the pleats.

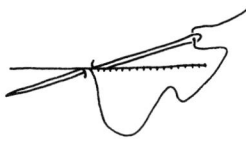

earisaid: see *arisaid*.

feileadh beag: Gaelic, meaning "little kilt"; a modern kilt with stitched and pressed knife pleats. Anglicized to *philabeg*.

feileadh mór: Gaelic, meaning "great kilt"; the traditional Highland dress of the 18th century and earlier, consisting of a large rectangle of tartan pleated loosely in the middle and held at the waist with a belt. The tartan above the waist was worn tucked under the belt, pinned at the shoulder, or wrapped about the shoulders or head.

fell: the stitched portion of the pleats in a kilt.

great kilt: see *feileadh mór*.

guarded: said of a narrow stripe that is edged with black in the overcheck of a tartan; guarding adds definition to stripes in the overcheck.

herringbone stitch: used for the kilt hem.

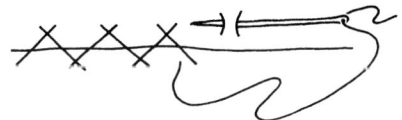

kilting selvedge: a perfectly-woven selvedge that can be used without a hem at the bottom edge of a kilt. Many single-width tartans are woven with only one kilting selvedge, the other selvedge being of lower quality.

military pleating: see *pleating to the stripe*.

non-centering: see *asymmetric*.

non-matching: see *asymmetric*.

overcheck: narrow stripes or sets of stripes superimposed on the large areas of color (the undercheck) of a tartan.

philabeg: see *feileadh beag*.

pivot: a point at which the tartan sett repeats itself in mirror image in a symmetric tartan.

pleat depth: the extent of the underfold for a pleat. The depth of a pleat cannot be seen from the back of the kilt unless a pleat is open.

pleat mark separation: the distance between pleat chalk marks used when marking a self-color kilt.

pleat size: the width of a pleat seen when looking at the back of a kilt. Pleat size at the waist is commonly smaller than pleat size at the hips.

pleating to the sett: a style of pleating in which the tartan is folded in the pleats in such a way as to reproduce the tartan pattern across the back of the kilt. A kilt pleated to the sett looks much the same in the back as it does in the front.

pleating to the stripe: a style of pleating in which the tartan is folded to show the same stripe in every pleat. Also called *military pleating*. A kilt pleated to the stripe looks very different front and back.

rise: the extension of the kilt above the waistline, originally to keep the abdomen and middle back warm when worn with the traditional short jacket. Kilts were formerly made with rises of 3" or more. Modern kilts are made with a rise of 2".

running stitch: used for basting the kilt and for some permanent stitching that does not need strength.

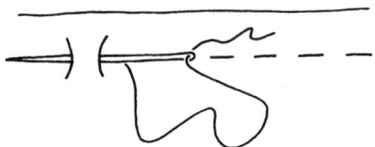

self-color kilt: a kilt made from wool in a solid color. Self-color kilts are typically navy, khaki, saffron, or green.

selvedge: the finished (non-ravelling) edge of a length of fabric. The selvedge lies parallel to the warp of the cloth and is formed during weaving as successive weft threads wrap around and enclose the warp threads at both edges of the fabric on the loom.

sett: the precise proportion and sequence of colors repeated to produce a tartan. In tartan, both warp and weft have identical setts.

steeking: a line of stitching done with heavy thread on the wrong side of the kilt to stabilize the pleats just above the bottom of the fell. From the Scottish word *steek*, meaning to stitch.

symmetric tartan: a tartan that repeats symmetrically about a point, or pivot. A symmetric tartan can be divided into halves that are mirror images of one another. Most tartans are symmetric.

tailor basting: used for stitching the canvas and to hold the shaping for pressing.

tramline: double narrow black lines in the overcheck of many Black Watch-based tartans.

twill line: a diagonal pattern line characteristic of straight twill weaves; the line is not a color line but rather a subtle pattern line produced as weft threads pass over and under two warp threads at a time.

underapron: the unpleated front of the kilt that lies beneath the apron. The underapron always buckles at the the left hip.

undercheck: the large areas of color underlying the smaller stripes and bands in a tartan.

warp: the threads of a piece of fabric that run the length of the fabric and parallel to the selvedge. The warp threads are wound onto the loom before weaving.

web: the crossing warp and weft threads that together form a piece of fabric.

weft: the threads of a piece of fabric that lie across the width of the fabric and perpendicular to the selvedge. The weft threads are carried on a shuttle and woven across the warp threads to produce the web of the fabric.

Splitting measurements: some examples

#1	inches	apron	pleats
waist	20″	10 1/2″	9 1/2″
hips	27″	13″	14″

#2	inches	apron	pleats
waist	22 1/2″	12″	10 1/2″
hips	26 1/2″	13″	13 1/2″

#3	inches	apron	pleats
waist	23 1/2″	12″	11 1/2″
hips	25 3/4″	12 3/4″	13″

#4	inches	apron	pleats
waist	23 1/2″	12 1/2″	11″
hips	29″	14″	15″

#5	inches	apron	pleats
waist	23 1/2″	12 3/4″	10 3/4″
hips	31 1/2″	15 1/4″	16 1/4″

#6	inches	apron	pleats
waist	24 1/4″	12 3/4″	11 1/2″
hips	29″	14″	15″

#7	inches	apron	pleats
waist	24 1/2″	13″	11 1/2″
hips	31 1/2″	15 1/4″	16 1/4″

#8	inches	apron	pleats
waist	24 1/2″	13″	11 1/2″
hips	36 1/4″	17″	19 1/4″

#9	inches	apron	pleats
waist	26″	14 1/2″	11 1/2″
hips	40″	19″	21″

#10	inches	apron	pleats
waist	26 1/2″	14 1/2″	12″
hips	35 1/2″	17 1/4″	18 1/4″

#11	inches	apron	pleats
waist	27″	14 1/2″	12 1/2″
hips	34 1/2″	16 3/4″	17 3/4″

#12	inches	apron	pleats
waist	28″	14 3/4″	13 1/4″
hips	32″	15 3/4″	16 1/4″

#13	inches	apron	pleats
waist	28″	15 1/2″	12 1/2″
hips	38 1/2″	18 3/4″	19 3/4″

#14	inches	apron	pleats
waist	28 1/2″	15 1/4″	13 1/4″
hips	35 1/2″	17 1/4″	18 1/4″

#15	inches	apron	pleats
waist	29″	16″	13″
hips	42 1/2″	20 1/2″	22″

#16	inches	apron	pleats
waist	30 1/2″	16″	14 1/2″
hips	35 1/2″	17 1/4″	18 1/4″

#17	inches	apron	pleats
waist	30 1/2"	17"	13 1/2"
hips	42 "	20 1/2"	21 1/2"

#18	inches	apron	pleats
waist	30 3/4"	16 1/4"	14 1/2"
hips	39"	19"	20"

#19	inches	apron	pleats
waist	31 1/2"	17"	14 1/2"
hips	37 1/4"	18 1/4"	19"

#20	inches	apron	pleats
waist	31 3/4"	17 1/2"	14 1/4"
hips	39 1/2"	19 1/4"	20 1/4"

#21	inches	apron	pleats
waist	32"	17"	15"
hips	40"	19 1/2"	20 1/2"

#22	inches	apron	pleats
waist	33"	17 1/4"	15 3/4"
hips	38"	18 1/2"	19 1/2"

#23	inches	apron	pleats
waist	34"	18"	16"
hips	40"	19 1/2"	20 1/2"

#24	inches	apron	pleats
waist	36 1/2"	19"	17 1/2"
hips	40 1/2"	20"	20 1/2"

#25	inches	apron	pleats
waist	37"	19 1/2"	17 1/2"
hips	42 1/2"	21"	21 1/2"

#26	inches	apron	pleats
waist	38"	20"	18"
hips	45"	22 1/2"	22 1/2"

#27	inches	apron	pleats
waist	39"	21 1/2"	17 1/2"
hips	43"	21 1/2"	21 1/2"

#28	inches	apron	pleats
waist	42"	21 1/2"	20 1/2"
hips	44"	22"	22"

#29	inches	apron	pleats
waist	51"	25 1/2"	25 1/2"
hips	50"	25 1/2"	25 1/2"

Notes about the splits in Appendix B

Most of the splits in this appendix follow the general rule of assigning about an inch more to the pleats in the hips than is assigned to the apron. Several of the examples depart from the general rule, and a brief explanation will help you choose how to make the splits for your kilt:

- Examples 8, 9, and 15 show kilts with 1 1/2 - 2 1/4" more in the pleats than in the apron at the hips. Each of these kilts is for a woman with a large waist/hip differential, and a little extra in the pleats at the hips will help reduce the apron shaping and help the kilt to fit more smoothly around the buttocks.

- Examples 2, 3, 12 and 24-29 show kilts with either equal apron and pleats measurements at the hips or at most 1/2" more in the pleats than in the apron. Each of these kilts is for a child or a man with a prominent tummy. These kilts need to keep more in the apron at the hips so that the kilt hangs well in the front. Person #29 has a bigger waist than hips, so the kilt will be made with the same measurement at the hips as at the waist (51"), even though the actual hip measurement is smaller (50").

Adding a hidden pleat

I n this appendix, we will teach you how to add a "hidden pleat" of extra fabric to the left hand apron edge. If you want to add a hidden pleat to the kilt you are making, you must do so at the time you mark the apron and pleats. You cannot add one later.

A hidden pleat in the wrong side of the left apron edge can be added to a kilt for a number of reasons:

- if you want to hide extra fabric for alteration

- if, in laying out the apron and pleats, you decide that the deep pleat would be overly large

- if you want to add weight in a light weight kilt to the left apron edge that is comparable to the weight of the apron on the fringe edge, making the left apron edge less likely to flap in the wind during competition.

Leaving enough room for a hidden pleat

1   Once you have finished marking the apron and the pleats between the center back and the apron edge, but before you mark the remaining pleats to the left of the center back, measure the distance along the selvedge from the lower left apron corner approximately to the edge of the first pleat (be sure that the selvedge still faces away from you).

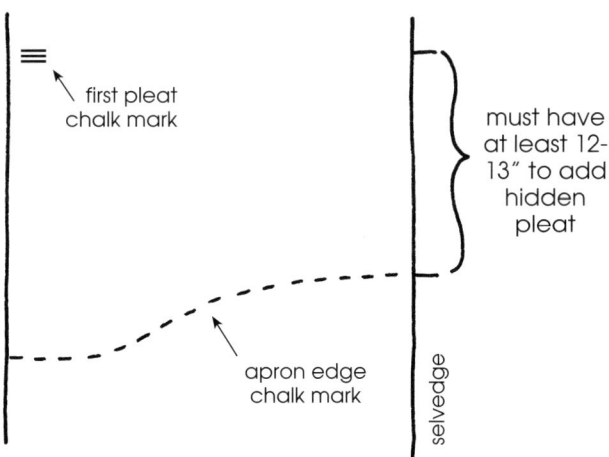

first pleat chalk mark

must have at least 12-13" to add hidden pleat

apron edge chalk mark

selvedge

2   If this distance is less than about 9-10", you can't put in a hidden pleat. You need a distance of *at least* 12-13" to put in a hidden pleat (and you can accommodate a distance of 14-16"), otherwise too

much cloth will go into the hidden pleat, and the deep pleat won't be deep enough. If you don't have enough distance between the apron edge and the last pleat, eliminate the last pleat that you have marked, and measure the distance along the selvedge between the apron edge and the lap line for the new last pleat.

3   If you have eliminated a pleat, be sure to use the new number of pleats to the right of the center when you figure out how many pleats you will mark total!

4   Go back to where you left off in the regular instructions, and continue marking the kilt. When you get to Stitching the Pleats on page 72, stop, and return to these instructions.

Basting the hidden pleat

1   After basting the left apron edge, measure the distance along the selvedge between the basted apron edge and the lap point for the first pleat. Subtract 10" from this measurement (subtract 8" or 9" instead, if you are making a very small kilt). This is the amount that you will reserve for the deep pleat.

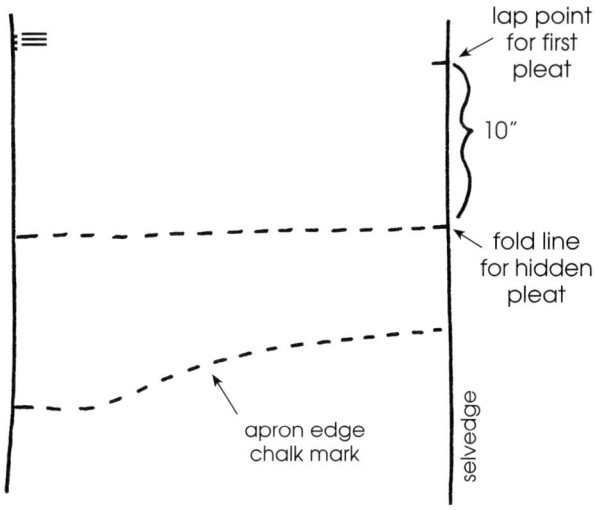

lap point for first pleat

10"

fold line for hidden pleat

apron edge chalk mark

selvedge

2   Take the remainder, and measure from the chalk mark at the edge of the apron toward the first pleat, and make a chalk mark at the selvedge. Fold the kilt *wrong* sides together along a straight stripe from the selvedge to the top of the kilt at this mark, and baste from the bottom of the kilt to the top edge. If the kilt will have a hem, start basting 6" up from the selvedge, if you don't want to have to remove basting stitches before sewing the hem.

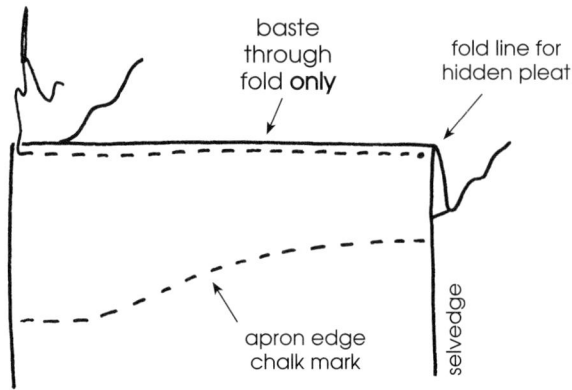

3   Hold the kilt right side up with the top to the right. Lay the edge of the hidden pleat you have just basted on top of the back side of the apron edge, holding the folded edge of the hidden pleat back about $1/8$" from the edge of the apron. Line up the stripes, and baste the folds together from the selvedge to the top of the kilt. If the kilt will have a hem, start basting 6" above the the selvedge, if you don't want to have to remove basting stitches before sewing the hem.

4   Return to Stitching the Pleats on page 72.

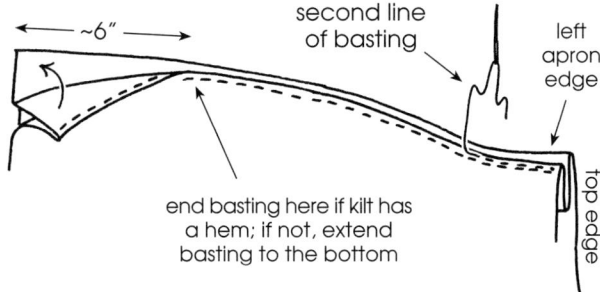

Finishing the bottom edge of the hidden pleat

Stop when you get to Finishing the Bottom Edge on page 83. Turn the kilt to the right side, and go to the left edge of the apron. Bring the edge of the apron/hidden pleat at the lower edge of the kilt to the lap line on the first pleat (which will be straight down the tartan from the bottom of the fell). Pinch and hold the apron/hidden pleat at the lap line, and

locate the middle of the deep pleat behind the apron edge. Mark both the lap line and the midpoint of the deep pleat with pins. If your kilt will not have a hem, skip to Option B below.

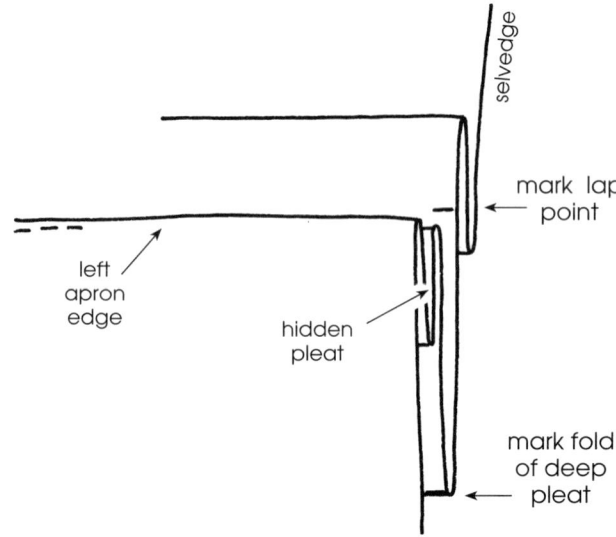

Option A: If the kilt *will* have a hem

1   Baste the hem as instructed on page 84 as far as the deep pleat.

2   When you are within a few inches of the first pleat, turn the kilt to the wrong side, and open up the deep pleat. Turn up the hem with an extra $3/8$" at the middle of the deep pleat. Taper to the regular hem allowance at the apron edge of the *hidden pleat*. The "dip" keeps the point of the deep pleat from sagging below the top apron.

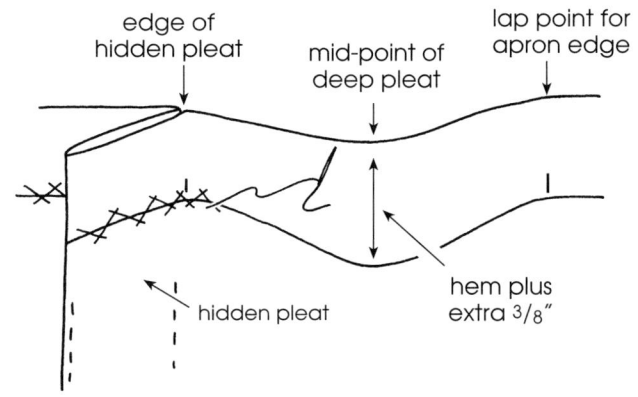

3   Continue basting across the dip, being sure to baste the hidden pleat itself at the regular hem depth. Baste the remaining hem at the exact hem length. The right edge of the top apron is not basted on a taper. Stitch the hem with a herringbone stitch (see the Glossary in Appendix A).

4   Skip Option B, and go to Finishing the Edge of the Hidden Pleat on the next page.

Option B: If the kilt will *not* have a hem

Turn the kilt to the back, and open up the deep pleat. Fold a dip in the bottom of the kilt to the inside that tapers from nothing at the apron edge of the *hidden pleat* to about $3/8$" at the midpoint of the deep pleat, to nothing again at the lap line for the apron. Baste, and then stitch with a herringbone stitch (see Appendix A). Do not turn up the hidden pleat itself. The "dip" keeps the point of the deep pleat from sagging below the top apron.

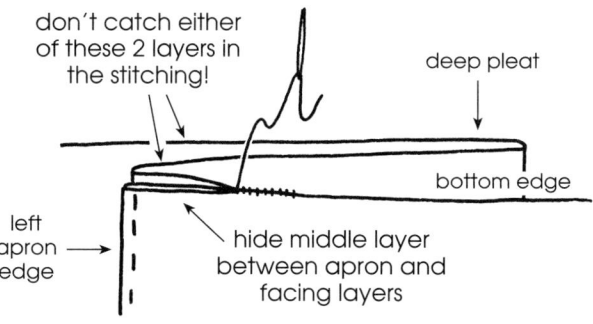

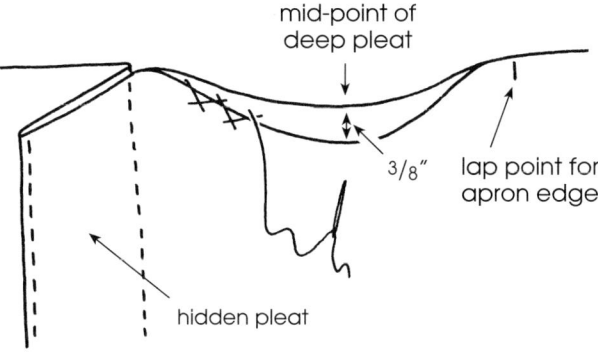

Finishing the edge of the hidden pleat

Stitch the underapron edge that has the hidden pleat.

- Select a matching thread, and wax it.

- At the bottom of the kilt, use a slip stitch to stitch the hidden pleat to the lower apron edge, being sure to stitch *only three thicknesses together* (don't catch in the deep pleat!!) and keeping the center portion of the hidden pleat hidden between the apron and back part of the hidden pleat.

- When you reach the apron edge, continue up the edge of the kilt. Sew the edge with *very*

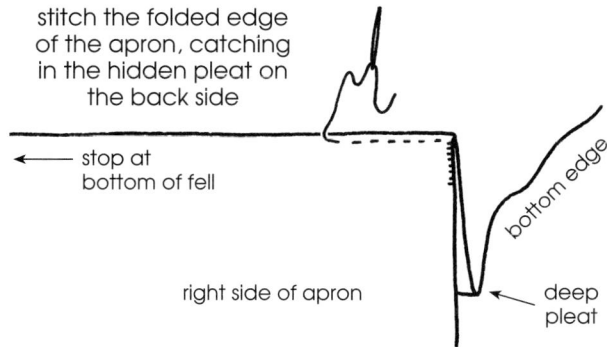

small back stitches (see Appendix A) through all thicknesses. The back stitches on the right side should be nearly invisible, and the stitches on the back should be only about $1/8$" or so. Do this stitching very carefully. As with the stitching in the pleats, this is something that *really* shows if it's done badly.

- Stitch to the bottom of the fell. Depending upon the locations of colors and the amount of shaping, you may need to change colors before you reach the bottom of the kilt.

- Return to Completing the Inverted Pleat on page 85.

Constructing a self-color kilt

A self-color kilt is one made from solid color wool, rather than from tartan. In this appendix, we will show you how to modify the instructions in the main part of the book if you wish to make a self-color kilt.

A self-color kilt is constructed in exactly the same way as a kilt made from tartan. The only difference comes in marking the pleats.

1 Follow the instructions in Chapter 5 for selecting materials and preparing to make the kilt. Be sure to select high quality wool in twill weave, rather than plain weave. Yardage woven with a twill weave has a prominent diagonal pattern to the weave. Select a hard woven worsted to avoid problems with fuzzing and pilling.

2 Follow the instructions in Chapter 7 for ripping the fabric, marking the apron and center back, ignoring any references to tartan stripes. Mark a center line for the apron at a distance from the fabric edge equal to at least half the apron hip measurement plus 7-9". Locate the approximate center back either in the center of your length of fabric (if you are working with single width fabric) or along a line at least 2 $^1/_2$" in from the raw edge, if you are working with two pieces ripped from a double width piece of fabric.

Determining the number of pleats and marking the pleats

In place of the sections on marking pleats in Chapter 7, do the following:

1 Consult your record sheet, and determine how many inches you assigned to the pleats at the waist. Multiply this number by 2 and round down to the nearest whole number (*e.g.*, 14" x 2 = 28 pleats). This is the *maximum* number of pleats that you can put into the back of your kilt, because you do not want to have pleats that are any smaller than $^1/_2$" across at the waist. You can also choose to have fewer pleats than this number. If you choose fewer pleats, each pleat will be more than $^1/_2$" across at the waist. Don't, however, choose a smaller number of pleats than the number of inches you assigned to the pleats in the hips (*e.g.*, 19 pleats for a hip split of 22") – that would make each pleat more than 1" across

at the hips. Remember also that the more pleats you have, the shallower each pleat will be. The fewer pleats you have, the deeper each pleat will be. See Chapter 4 if you don't remember the relationships.

2 Decide how many pleats you want to have across the back of your kilt, and record the number on your record sheet.

3 Lay out the piece of fabric on which you have already made the apron and center back markings, with the selvedge away from you.

  – Measure the distance along the selvedge between the approximate center back and the chalk mark at the lower left edge of the apron. Subtract about 10". Double this distance and write it down (*e.g.*, 180"). This is the total length of cloth available for pleats.

  – Divide this total available length by the number of pleats in the kilt to determine the distance between center marks for the pleats (*e.g.*, 180" ÷ 27 pleats = 6 $^2/_3$"). Write this distance down as the pleat mark separation.

4 Go to the chalk mark at the lower left edge of the apron. Measure about 10" to the left, and make a small chalk mark at the selvedge. Move

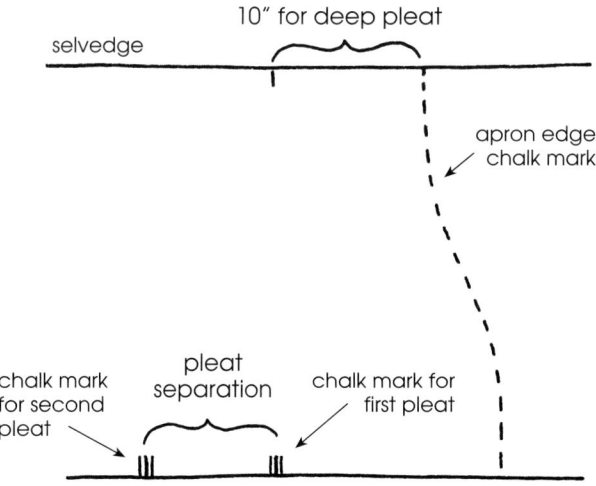

to the top of the kilt, and mark a chalk line perpendicular to the raw edge exactly opposite the chalk mark you made at the selvedge. This line will form the center of the first pleat to the left of the apron. The distance between the apron edge and the first pleat allows the apron to be underlain by a deep pleat to help the kilt hang well. Placing the first pleat too close to the apron edge will not allow enough fabric for the deep pleat.

5 **If you wish to include a hidden pleat at the edge of the underapron for added weight or for growth, see Appendix C for instructions on placement and marking. You must mark the hidden pleat before you mark the first pleat – it cannot be added later.**

6 Be sure that the fabric is laid out with the selvedge away from you. Starting at the center chalk line for the first pleat next to the apron, measure a distance equal to the pleat mark separation to the left, and draw a second chalk mark. This line marks the center of the second pleat to the left of the apron. Continue measuring and marking the centers of pleats until you have marked as many pleats as you need. If you are working with two pieces of fabric that will be joined at the back, be sure that the center of the last pleat at the left edge of the first piece of fabric is no closer than 2 $^1/_2$" to the raw edge. This will allow the join seam to be hidden inside the pleat. Be sure to start the first pleat on the second piece of fabric at least one full pleat mark separation to the left of the raw edge in order to have enough fabric to make a full-size pleat and successfully sew the join.

7 Double-check that you have marked the correct number of pleats.

8 Proceed to the regular instructions beginning with Marking the Underapron on page 64.

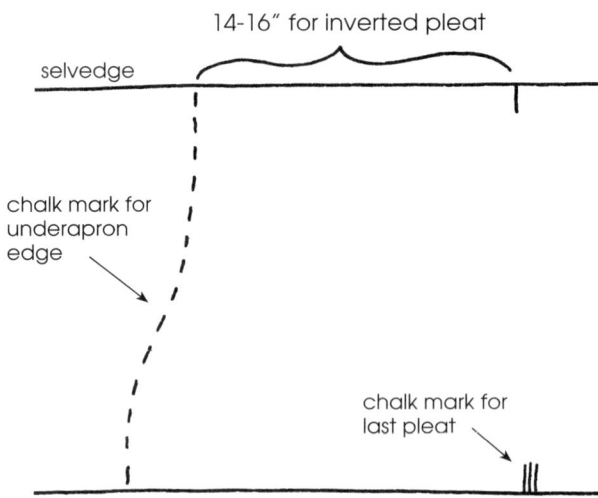

Follow the instructions for marking the underapron, but mark a center line for the underapron that is at least half the underapron hip measurement plus 14-16" from the lower edge of the last pleat. This will leave enough cloth to make the inverted pleat at the right hand edge of the underapron and still allow for alterations. Make sure that the lower left edge of the underapron will fall at least 6" from the raw edge of the fabric in order to leave enough cloth for self-facing and alterations. If the left apron edge will be too far to the left, move the center chalk mark to the right, and make the inverted pleat shallower.

9 Continue with the remaining instructions in Chapter 7.

Completing the kilt

Finish the kilt according to the remaining instructions for tartan kilts in chapters 8 and 9. Ignore any references to tartan stripes.

Evaluating and marking asymmetric tartan

It is possible to have a double width of asymmetric tartan from which it is literally impossible to make a kilt. Before cutting or marking a piece of asymmetric tartan, use this appendix to figure out whether, by some stroke of bad luck, you have such a piece of tartan.

As discussed in Chapter 3, very few tartans have asymmetric (non-centering) setts. This appendix applies only if you are making a kilt from one of the following commonly-available tartans: Buchan, Buchanan and Hunting Buchanan (but not Old Buchanan or Dress Buchanan), Campbell of Argyll, Dress Campbell, Drummond of Strathallen, MacAlpine, Dress MacDonald, Old Macmillan, Malcolm, Hunting Stewart, and the Ontario and Québec provincial tartans) and ONLY if you are using a double width of fabric.[1]

If you work through the following steps and discover that you cannot make a kilt from the piece of tartan you have, at least you won't have cut your piece of tartan and can save it for something else.

Analysis of the problems introduced by tartan asymmetry

As with any kilt made from a double width of fabric, you'll need to split your piece of tartan lengthwise and make the kilt from two pieces of cloth joined together at the back of the kilt. **Before making any cuts, though, let's work through the problems asymmetry poses in a double width piece of fabric.**

A kilt made from a double width of asymmetric tartan *must* have a hem

- The two illustrations above right show a piece of double width fabric opened out flat and right side up and the same piece split lengthwise into the two halves for the kilt.

- In order to make a kilt and match the tartan at the center back join, piece #1 and piece #2 must be joined along the line marked X-Y-Z, with X matching X and Z matching Z. Piece #2 **cannot** be rotated or flipped. If it is rotated to match the

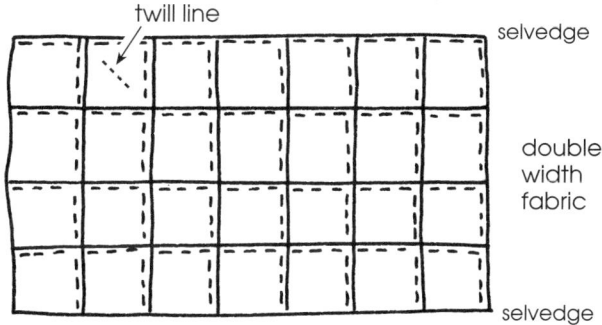

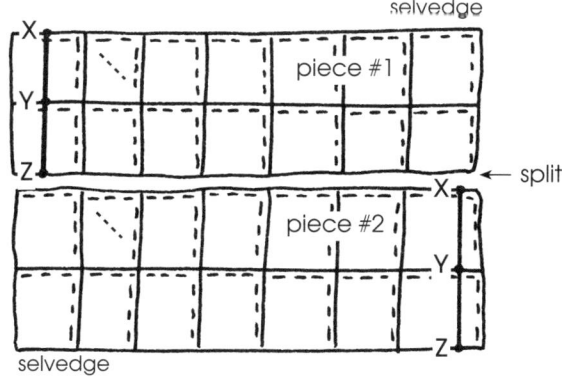

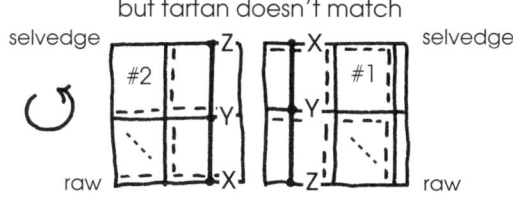

#2 rotated to match selvedges, but tartan doesn't match

selvedges, the tartan will be a mirror image and won't match, because the tartan is asymmetric. If piece #2 is flipped, the twill line and tartan won't match.

- To make a full-length piece for the kilt, pieces 1 and 2 must be slid *without* rotating until X, Y, and Z match. Because piece #2 is not rotated, the

---

[1] Occasionally, a mill will weave a double width of asymmetric tartan with a reverse in the sett at the fold, making the two halves mirror images of one another. Examine your tartan carefully. If the sett does, in fact, reverse at the fold, you're in luck. Go back to the regular instructions on page 53, and lay your kilt out according to the regular instructions for double width fabric.

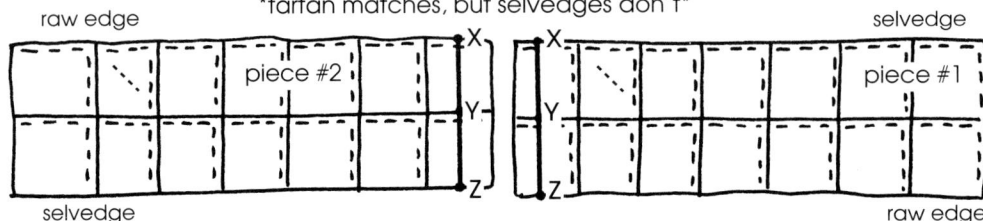

raw edge — piece #2 — X Y Z — selvedge

X Y Z — piece #1 — selvedge — raw edge

selvedge edge of piece #1 lines up directly with the raw edge of piece #2. **There is no way around it – this kilt must have a hem**. If the person you're making the kilt for doesn't want a hem, you're dead in the water.

It may, in fact, be impossible to match the tartan at the join

- Far more serious than the hem problem is the problem of matching the tartan. In a kilt made by joining two pieces of fabric at the back, the tartan **must** match horizontally across the seam, otherwise the kilt looks ridiculous.

- Let's go back to the illustration above. It is highly **unlikely** that lining up the selvedge and the raw edge will also match the tartan stripes at the center back. Consequently, you will very likely need to shift piece #2 up or down some in order to match the tartan.

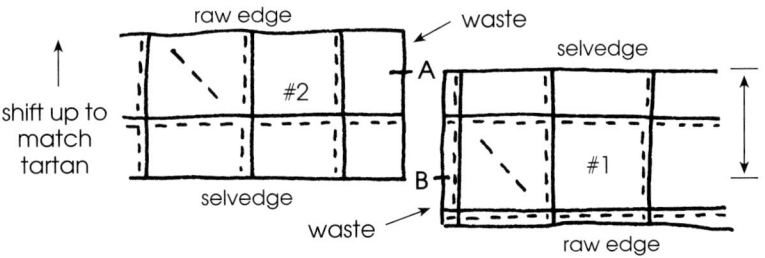

raw edge — waste — #2 — shift up to match tartan — selvedge — waste — A — selvedge — #1 — B — raw edge

- **You must use the overlap region (between points A and B above) for making the kilt. The strips outside the overlap region will be waste.**

- **You must have enough depth in the overlap region for the kilt, including the rise and the hem.** If you had to offset the pieces a large amount to match the tartan at the join, you may find that the overlap region is so narrow that you simply don't have enough depth to make the kilt.

How to test before cutting the tartan to see whether you have enough depth in the overlap region to make the kilt

1 Open out your fabric, and lay it right side up on a table in front of you. Fold the fabric in half width wise so that the two raw edges are aligned to your right and so that the top layer is offset to the left just a little. Mark the centers of the two

raw edges with small chalk lines on the right side of the fabric.

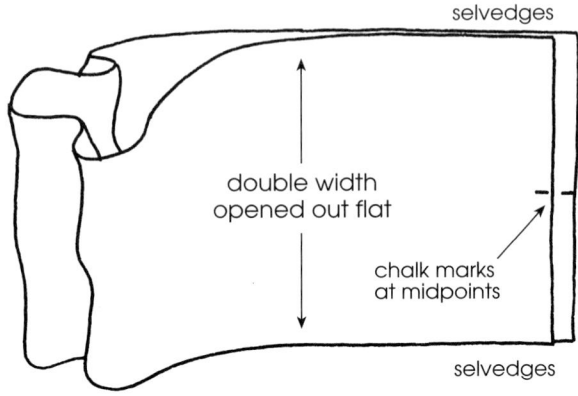

selvedges — double width opened out flat — chalk marks at midpoints — selvedges

2 Slide the upper layer away from you until the center line chalk mark on the upper layer lines up exactly with the far selvedge of the piece underneath. If, by chance, the stripes of the tartan match exactly, you're in luck, and you can return to the instructions in chapter 7 and proceed with the instructions for how to mark a kilt with a hem.

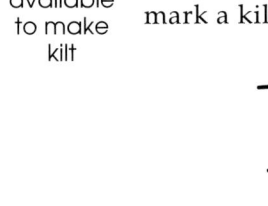

depth available to make kilt

selvedge — Yey! The tartan matches when chalk marks are aligned with the selvedges (rare!!) — midpoint chalk mark — selvedge — selvedge — midpoint chalk mark — selvedge

3 If the stripes in the tartan don't match (a far more likely scenario), slide the upper layer either away from you or towards you until the tartan does match. Slide in whatever direction minimizes the amount of offset you need to make.

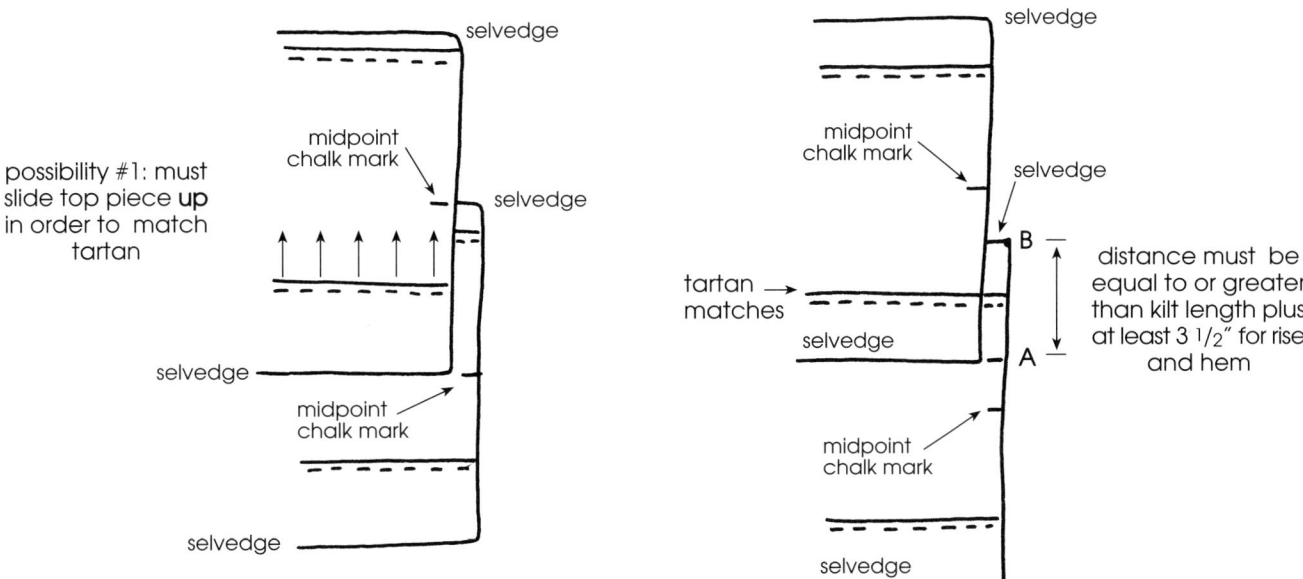

Possibility #1: If you must slide the upper layer away from you in order to match the tartan (above left), your fabric should look like the illustration above right. Make a chalk mark at the edge of the lower piece of fabric at the level of the selvedge edge of the upper piece (point A). Measure the distance from point A along the raw edge to point B, at the selvedge of the lower piece. Write down this measurement.

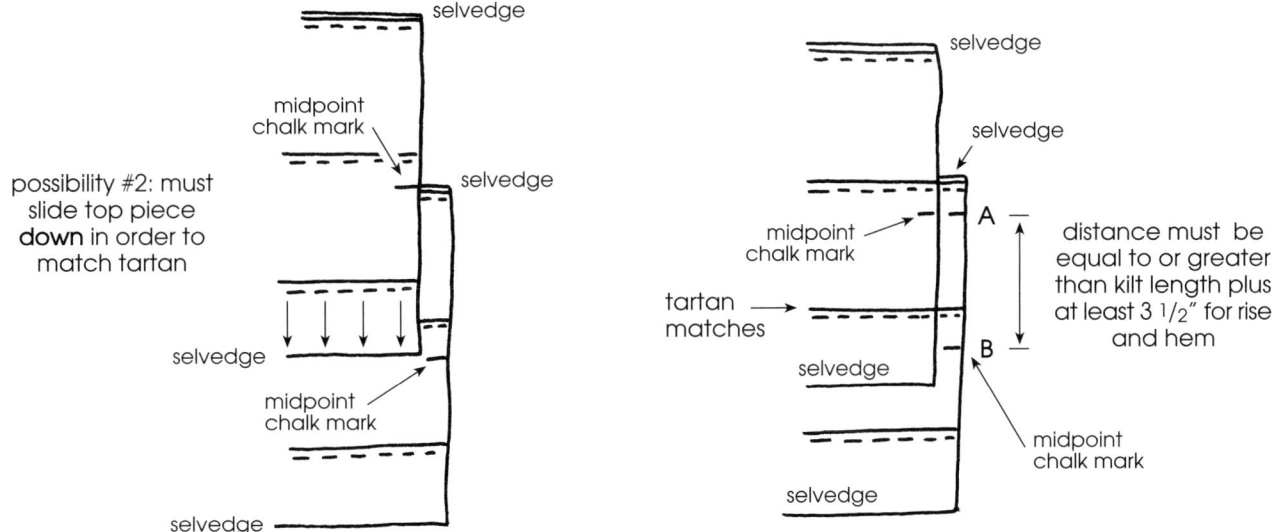

Possibility #2: If you must slide the upper layer toward you in order to match the tartan (above left), your fabric should look like the illustration above right. Make a chalk mark at the edge of the lower piece of fabric at the level of the center chalk mark of the upper piece (point A). Measure the distance from point A along the raw edge to point B, at the center chalk mark on the lower piece. Write down this measurement.

---

4 Go to your record sheet, and get the length measurement you made. Add 2" for the kilt rise plus a minimum of 1 ¹/₂" for a hem (*e.g.*, 21 ¹/₂" + 2" + 1 ¹/₂" = 25"). This is the minimum total depth of fabric you will need for your kilt.

5 Compare the minimum total depth needed for the kilt with the distance that you measured from A to B in #1 or #2 above. **The distance from A to B must be equal to or greater than the mini-**mum total depth needed for the length plus rise plus hem.

6 **If the distance from A to B is less than you need, your kilt project with this piece of tartan has just ground to a halt. There is *nothing* you can do to make the kilt from this piece of fabric, but at least you won't have ruined the fabric by cutting it, and you can save it for another project.**

If your fabric passed the test: marking the length of the kilt and ripping the fabric

The directions for marking the tartan and ripping the fabric are slightly different depending upon whether you slid the top layer away from you (go to Option A below) or toward you (go to Option B on page 133) when you matched the tartan in step 3 on the previous two pages.

Option A: If you slid the top layer away from you to match the tartan:

1   Arrange your fabric again as shown below, making sure that the tartan is lined up. Be sure that chalk mark A along the right raw edge is still clear and is lined up with the near selvedge edge of the upper piece.

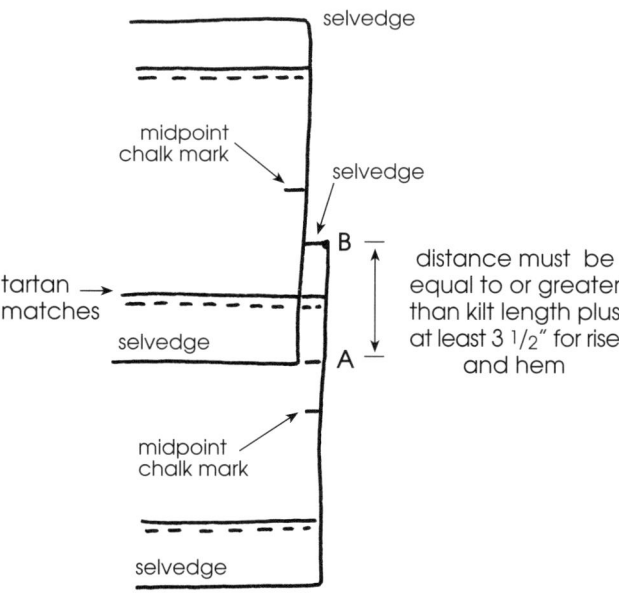

2   You must lay out your kilt between chalk mark A and the far selvedge of the lower piece.

3   As illustrated in the kilt parts diagram on page 34, a kilt is made with a rise, or an extension above the waistline. While kilts used to be made with a 2 $^1/_2$" or even a 3" rise, most kilts today are made with a 2" rise.

The total length of a kilt is the length measurement from the waist to the top of the knee cap plus 2" for the rise.

4   Add 2" to the length measurement that you recorded. This is the total *finished* length of the kilt. Record this on your record sheet.

5   Decide how much hem you will put into the kilt. Use the guidelines in the tips and hints box (page 53). Record the total finished length plus the hem on your record sheet.

6   Starting at the far selvedge of the lower piece of fabric, measure the total length of the kilt *plus the hem* toward you from the selvedge edge along the right hand raw edge, and mark with a short chalk line at the edge of the fabric. Double-check to be sure that this mark lies **between** point A and the far selvedge and that the mark is at least $^3/_4$" from the center line chalk mark. This will leave a warp-wise piece wide enough for the top band. You cannot use a weft-wise strip cut from the end of the fabric to make the top band (see tips and hints on page 54), so you **must** leave a strip along the center of your fabric for the top band.

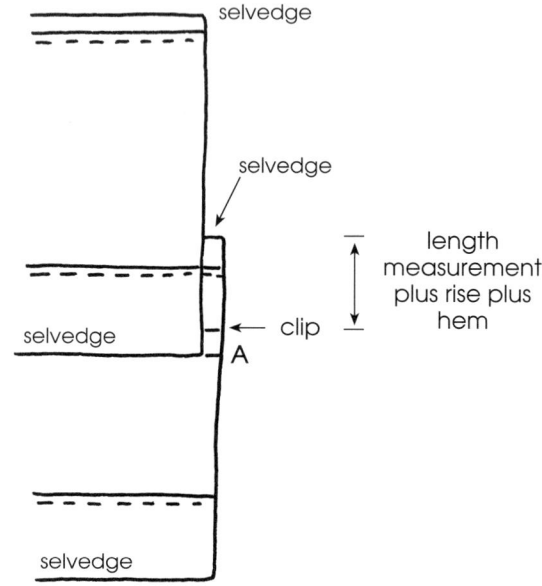

7   **Measure again**, and check to be sure that you have added both the hem and a 2" rise to the original length measurement and that you have left enough material for the top band.

8   Take a pair of sharp scissors, and clip the edge of the fabric two threads outside the chalk line to allow for fraying.

9   Measure again, and double check that you have added the rise and the hem. This is not the time to make a mistake! Once you rip the cloth, it's too late to remember that you forgot to add the rise and hem or to discover that you measured wrong.

10 **Rip** the length of the cloth, rather than cutting. Ripping is preferable to cutting, because ripping will produce an absolutely straight edge.

11 You now have two pieces of fabric, one wider than the other. Lay the narrower piece down right side up with the selvedge edge away from you. Lay the wider piece on top of it, also right side up, double-checking that the twill line slants

from lower right to upper left in both pieces. The top piece should have the selvedge edge toward you.

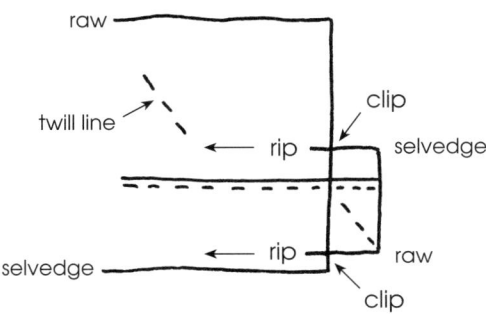

12 Line up the tartan along the right hand edges. Make two chalk marks on the wider piece, one at the selvedge edge of the narrower piece and one at the raw edge of the narrower piece.

13 Clip the edges two threads toward the edge at each chalk mark. Double-check, and rip the two edges off the wider piece, which will now have two raw edges.

14 **Be sure to save the wider ripped-off strip for the top band.** Breathe a sigh of relief and congratulate yourself that you have survived this nerve-wracking step.

15 Pull the stray threads from the ripped edge. Once you've removed the few loose threads, the edge won't ravel anymore. Don't bother serging or zigzagging it. Return to the regular instructions in Marking the Top Apron on page 55.

Option B: If you slid the top layer toward you to match the tartan:

1 Arrange your fabric again as shown below, making sure that the tartan is lined up. Be sure that the center line chalk mark and chalk mark A along the right raw edge are still clear and that chalk mark A is lined up with the center line chalk mark of the upper piece.

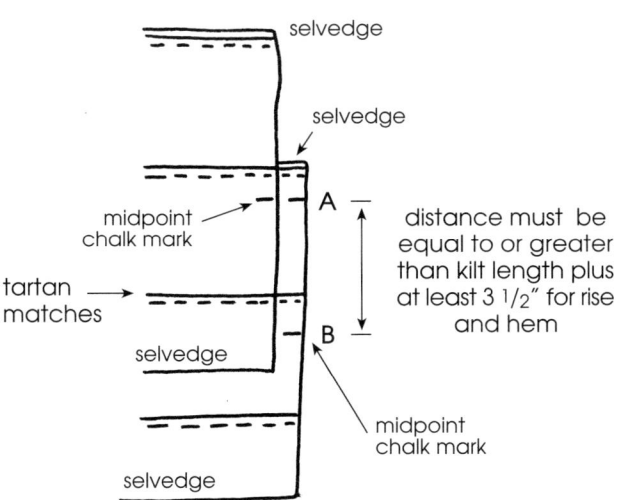

2 You must lay out your kilt between chalk mark A and the center line chalk mark.

3 As illustrated in the kilt parts diagram on page 34, a kilt is made with a rise, or an extension above the waistline. While kilts used to be made with a 2 $1/2$" or even a 3" rise, most kilts today are made with a 2" rise.

The total length of a kilt is the length measurement from the waist to the top of the knee cap plus 2" for the rise.

4 Add 2" to the length measurement that you recorded. This is the total *finished* length of the kilt. Record this on your record sheet.

5 Decide how much hem you will put into the kilt. Use the guidelines in the tips and hints box (page 53). Record the total finished length plus the hem on your record sheet.

6 Starting at the centerline of the lower piece of fabric, measure the total length of the kilt *plus the hem* away from you along the right hand raw edge toward the far selvedge, and mark with a short chalk line at the edge of the fabric. Double-check to be sure that this mark lies **between** the center line and point A and that the mark is at least 1 $1/2$" from the far selvedge. This will leave a warp-wise piece wide enough for the top band. You cannot use a weft-wise strip cut from the end of the fabric to make the top band (see tips and hints on page 54), so you **must** leave a strip along the selvedge of your fabric for the top band.

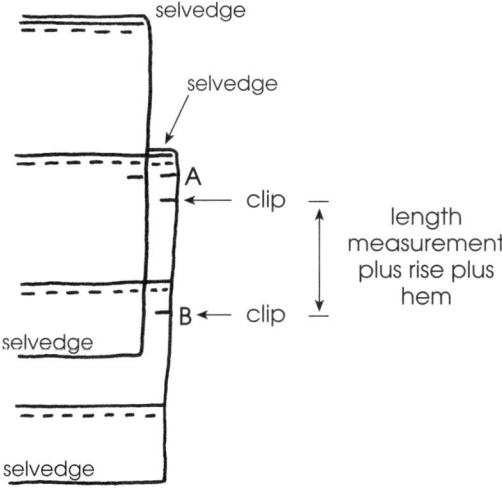

7 Measure again, and check to be sure that you have added both the hem and a 2" rise to the original length measurement and that you have left enough material for the top band.

8 Take a pair of sharp scissors, and clip the edge of the fabric in two places, once at the chalk mark made in the previous step and one at the center

line chalk mark. Clip two threads outside each chalk line to allow for fraying.

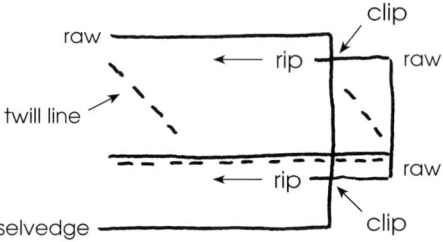

9 **Measure again**, and double check that you have added the rise and the hem. This is not the time to make a mistake! Once you rip the cloth, it's too late to remember that you forgot to add the rise and hem or to discover that you measured wrong.

10 **Rip** the length of the cloth at both clip marks, rather than cutting. Ripping is preferable to cutting, because ripping will produce an absolutely straight edge. **Be sure to save the narrower ripped-off strip for the top band.**

11 You now have two pieces of fabric, one wider than the other. Lay the narrower piece down right side up. Lay the wider piece on top of it, also right side up, double-checking that the twill line slants from lower right to upper left in both pieces.

12 Line up the tartan along the right hand edges. Make two chalk marks on the wider piece, one at each of the raw edges of the narrower piece.

13 Clip the edges two threads toward the edge at each chalk mark. Double-check, and rip the two edges off the wider piece, which will now have two raw edges. Breathe a sigh of relief and congratulate yourself that you have survived this nerve-wracking step.

14 Pull the stray threads from the ripped edge. Once you've removed the few loose threads, the edge won't ravel anymore. Don't bother serging or zigzagging it. Return to the regular instructions in Marking the Top Apron on page 55.

Suppliers and sources

Woollen mills that supply tartan

The suppliers listed below typically sell tartan at lower cost than local retail stores, but customers will pay shipping charges and may pay duty, depending upon the location of the business.

Lochcarron of Scotland, Ltd.: Lochcarron of Scotland, Ltd. weaves an outstanding range of tartan in a variety of weights. Their Braeriach weight (13 ounce) and Strome weight (16 ounce) tartans make up into superb kilts. Braeriach weight fabric is available double width in over 200 tartans, if one counts all of the modern, ancient, and weathered varieties. Strome weight fabric is available in double width for over 100 of the more common tartans and in single width for over 570 additional tartans, again counting all of the modern, ancient, and weathered varieties. Lochcarron, Ltd. carries over 520 tartans in Reiver weight , including the Canadian provincial tartans, several Irish tartans, and a selection of 25 dress dancers' tartans. While Reiver weight (10 ounce, 59" wide) is on the light side for a kilt, this weight may be your only choice for some tartans if you are not prepared for the expense of a custom weave. Reiver weight does not have a kilting selvedge. Lochcarron, Ltd. also weaves Spring weight (9 ounce) tartan in plain weave for various sewing projects other than kilts. They are the weavers of the McLlennium (National Millennium tartan) and the Diana, Princess of Wales commemorative tartan (although the latter is available only as finished goods and is not available as yardage).You may place inquiries and orders by e-mail, and they accept credit card payments.

> **Lochcarron of Scotland, Ltd.**
> Waverly Mills
> Huddersfield Street
> Galashiels
> Scotland TD1 3AY
>
> Phone: 011-44-1-896-661211
> Fax: 011-44-1-896-758833
> e-mail: exportsales@lochcarron.com
> http://www.lochcarron.com

D.C. Dalgliesh, Ltd.: D.C. Dalgliesh, Ltd. weaves primarily light-medium weight tartans. Their K/7 light-medium weight fabric (11-12 oz.) is available in double width in a wide range of modern, dress, reproduction, and ancient tartans. Dalgliesh, Ltd. has the best selection of popular dress tartans for dancers and currently offer over 75 dress tartans in a weight slightly heavier than that of dress dancers' tartans available from other mills. Their K/7 tartan makes up into a superb light-weight kilt that holds a good press. The mill also weaves heavy weight tartan (16 ounce) with either a hard finish (K/1) or a softer finish (F/1). The range of heavy weight tartan available is very limited, and you must call Dalgliesh to find out what is in stock. The mill does custom weaving, and any tartan is available custom woven in single width in either 11-12 or 16 ounce weights. Unlike most other mills, Dalgliesh will weave single kilt lengths on a custom basis. Dalgliesh, Ltd. does not take credit cards, nor does the company have a web site or e-mail. Customers must pre-pay orders in pound-sterling money orders.

> **D.C. Dalgliesh, Ltd.**
> Dunsdale Mill
> Selkirk, Scotland TD7 4EB
>
> Phone: 011-44-1-750-20781
> Fax: 011-44-1-750-20502

House of Edgar, Ltd.: House of Edgar, Ltd. weaves a wide range of tartans in several weights. Their lightweight fabric (10-11 ounce) is available in about 50 tartans, with no kilting selvedge. Their medium weight (13 ounce) fabric is available in over 170 standard tartans, 32 Irish county tartans, over 30 Scottish district tartans, and 15 plain matching twills. They weave heavy weight fabric (16 ounce) in 32 Irish county tartans and 55 clan and district tartans. They also weave 6 tartans in ultra-heavy regimental weight. Their medium, heavy, and ultra-heavy weight tartans have kilting selvedges. House of Edgar also sells silk yardage in over 50 tartans for other types of projects. Customers should call or fax for current prices and payment options.

> **House of Edgar Woolens, Ltd.**
> Tower House, Ruthvenfield Rd.
> Inveralmond
> Perth, Scotland PH1 3UN Scotland
>
> Phone: 011-44-1-738-609060
> Fax: 011-44-1-738-604010

Fraser and Kirkbright Weaving Co. (formerly West Coast Woolen Mills): West Coast Woolen Mills closed in the summer of 2000 and have re-opened in the fall of 2000 under new ownership as Fraser and Kirkbright Weaving Company. They weave light-weight (11 ounce) tartans, including the Canadian provincial tartans, and offer them at low cost. Tartantown in British Columbia (see below) will contract with them to weave dress dancers tartans, and those tartans will be available through Tartantown but not directly from the mill. The dancers' tartans will be woven in 12 ounce weight with a kilting selvedge.

Fraser and Kirkbright Weaving Co.
2938 East 27th Avenue
Vancouver, BC Canada V5R 1N8

Phone: 1-604-436-1951
Fax: 1-604-436-1947

Retail stores that supply tartan

Most retail stores specializing in imported items from Scotland can supply tartan and are willing to order whatever tartan they do not carry in stock. If you order locally, you will likely pay full retail price, as well as sales tax. We have listed only a few of the many retail stores, two in Canada and three in the U.S.

Tartantown: Tartantown is a Canadian retail company specializing in Scottish regalia, piping and drumming supplies, and outfits for dancers. They can find just about any tartan for you and are very helpful about sending samples. In addition to offering at retail prices a wide selection of Scottish-woven tartans, Tartantown has offered about 20 dress tartans woven in Canada by West Coast Woolen Mills, which is now out of business. The quality of this tartan is a bit variable, with early batches woven in lighter weight (11 ounce) with a poor selvedge and later batches woven in 12 ounce weight with a good selvedge. Tartantown will likely have stocks of these tartans at least for awhile, so it would be best to inquire specifically about the weight and selvedge of particular pieces if you order tartan woven by West Coast Woolens. Tartantown will likely continue to contract with the successor company (Fraser and Kirkbright Weaving Company, see above) to provide a number of Canadian-woven tartans. These tartans will be in 12 ounce weight with a kilting selvedge. If you choose to buy tartan retail in the U.S. or Canada, these tartans have been and probably will continue to be less expensive than the retail prices on imported tartan woven in Scotland. Tartantown is also very good at selecting samples of velveteen to go with various tartans.

Tartantown
555 Clarke Rd.
Coquitlam, BC V3J 3X4 Canada

Phone: 604-936-8548
Fax: 604-936-8502
e-mail: info@tartantown.com
http://www.tartantown.com

Burnett's and Struth: Burnett's and Struth is a Canadian retail company specializing in Scottish regalia. Like many retail stores, they can find just about any tartan you want. American customers will likely be charged duty. Burnett's and Struth also carries nicely-made, reasonably-priced Highland dancing shoes manufactured by their subsidiary The Highland Shoe Company.

Burnett's & Struth Scottish Regalia, Ltd.
61 Patterson Road
Barrie, Ontario L4N 3V9 Canada

Phone: 705-728-3232
Fax: 705-728-2962

Scotland by the Yard: Scotland by the Yard is an American retail company specializing in Scottish imports. They can find just about any tartan for you, although the prices are generally retail prices. If you are of Scottish heritage and join the St. Andrew's Society of Vermont ($25 to join and $10/year afterwards), however, Scotland by the Yard offers a discount of 25% on Highland regalia, including tartan.

Scotland by the Yard
8828 Woodstock Road
Quechee, VT 05059

Phone: 1-802-295-5351
Fax: 1-802-295-5135

The Scottish Lion: The Scottish Lion is an American retail company specializing in Scottish regalia. Like many retail stores, they can find just about any tartan you want. Their mail order catalog has a very nice set of color thumbnail pictures of over 500 tartans, making the catalog worth it for that alone. The illustrations contain very few thumbnails of dress tartans, however.

The Scottish Lion Import Shop
P.O. Box 1700
3424 White Mountain Highway
North Conway, NH 03860-1700

Phone: 800-355-SCOT
Fax: 1-603-356-9032
http://www.scottishlion.com
e-mail: scottishlion@landmarknet.net

Highland Heritage, Ltd.: Highland Heritage is a another retail company specializing in Scottish regalia. Like many retail stores, Highland Heritage can find just about any tartan you want.

Highland Heritage, Ltd.
1601 Concord Pike, Suite 69
Wilmington, DE 19803

Phone: 1-302-656-4007
Fax: 1-302-656-4008
http://highlandheritage.com
e-mail: info@highlandheritage.com

Suppliers for canvas, chalk, & tailoring supplies

Oregon Tailor Supply: This company can provide hard-to-find tailoring items. They carry Tailor's Pride® canvas, open-top tailor's thimbles in various sizes, and tailor's chalk. If you order tailor's chalk from them, be sure to specify dust-off (clay) chalk. Their JEMS brand chalk comes in yellow and "white" (which is really a very pale gray that shows up just well enough on dress tartans).

Oregon Tailor Supply Co., Inc.
P.O. Box 42284
Portland, OR 94242

Phone: 1-800-678-2457
Fax: toll free 1-877-233-9621
http://www.oregontailor.com

G Street Fabrics: This company carries Tailor's Pride® canvas by the yard.

G Street Fabrics On Line
http://www.gstreetfabrics.com

Alpha Impressions: This company makes sew-in labels of various kinds for garments.

Alpha Impressions, Inc.
P.O. Box 3156
Los Angeles, CA 90051-1156

Phone: 1-800-834-8221
Fax: 1-213-234-8215

Chef's: If you plan to make many kilts, a lightweight ironing board will not hold up to the stresses of pressing kilts. This company carries heavy duty ironing boards and steam pressers. A steam presser does a beautiful job on the pleats and is worth the cost, if you plan to make many kilts.

Chef's
P.O. Box 620048
Dallas, TX 75262

Phone: 1-800-338-3232
Fax: toll free 1-800-967-3291
http://www.chefscatalog.com

Chlotilde: A good light source is a must for sewing a kilt. Ott-Lite® lamps by Environmental Lighting Concepts, Inc. are cool, daylight balanced lamps made specifically for close work, and they are ideal for sewing. The portable Ott-Lite® is particularly nice, because it folds compactly, protecting the bulb for transport. Chlotilde carries several varieties of Ott-Lites®, as well as many other sewing notions.

Chlotilde
B 3000
Louisiana, MO 63353-3000

Phone: 1-800-772-2891
Fax: toll free 1-800-863-3191
http://www.chlotilde.com

Atlanta Thread Supply: This company can provide hard-to-find tailoring items. They carry Tailor's Pride® canvas, open-top tailor's thimbles in various sizes, and tailor's chalk, including JEMS clay chalk in white (see Oregon Tailor Supply at left for description). They also carry threads and heavy duty steam irons and ironing boards.

Atlanta Thread Supply
695 Red Oak Road
Stockbridge, GA 30281

Phone: 1-800-847-1001
Fax: 1-404-389-9202
http://www.atlantathread.com/

Suppliers for other items

The following suppliers offer other items, including buckles and straps, buttons and braid, dancing shoes, custom-made Highland dancing outfits, Highland regalia, argyll (tartan) hose, and many other Scottish items

Highland Xpress
P.O. Box 901574
Kansas City, MO 64190

Phone: 816-746-6750
Fax: 816-746-6904
http://members.tripod.com/~highxpress/

Tartantown
555 Clarke Rd.
Coquitlam, BC V3J 3X4 Canada

Phone: 604-936-8548
Fax: 604-936-8502
http://www.tartantown.com

Burnett's & Struth Scottish Regalia, Ltd.
61 Patterson Road
Barrie, Ontario L4N 3V9 Canada

Phone: 705-728-3232
Fax: 705-728-2962

Tartan hose

The following two companies custom knit beautiful tartan hose to go with any kilt. Contact them about instructions for measuring, and include a sample of the tartan to insure an accurate color match. Turn-around time is a minimum of three weeks in house, plus shipping time.

Kilkeel Tartan Hose
Proprietor Kurt Sekules
44 Newry Rd.
Kilkeel, Northern Ireland BT34 4DU

Henderson Highland Hose
9 Lovaine Terrace
Berwick-upon-Tweed
United Kingdom TD15 1LA

Phone & fax: 011-44-1-289-302831

Other sources for instructions on making and wearing kilts

--------, *Scottish Kilts and Jackets*, Folkwear Pattern #152.

Cannonito, Janet, 1991, *Kiltmaking: The Making of a Scottish Kilt*, Irvine, CA, Tartan Patch, 64p.

Gemmell, C.R. and Chegwin, Colin R., 1996 (rev. ed.), *Kiltmaking*, Checro, 32p.

Glover, Robert, 1978, *Kiltmaking*, Farnborough, UK, privately published, 22p.

Stewart, Ann, 1991, Making a Kilt: *Threads*, v. 33 (February/March), p. 54-60.

Thompson, J. Charles, 1989 (3rd rev. ed.), *So You're Going to Wear the Kilt*, Arlington, VA, Heraldic Art, 120p.

Relevant websites

Thousands of sites exist on the World Wide Web that are related to kilts, tartan, and Scottish traditions. We have listed below the URLs for only five sites that are particularly relevant to the topic of this book and that are likely to remain stable for a long period of time. Web addresses for particular suppliers are listed with their descriptions on the previous pages of this appendix.

The Official Registry of All Publicly Known Tartans, with color images of thousands of tartans:

> http://www.tartans.scotland.net/

How to pleat and wear a great kilt http:

> http://www.tartanweb.com/tweb/greatkilt/index.htm

The Tartan Finder, with color images of tartans

> http://www.house-of-tartan.scotland.net/house/

Listing of Highland Games and Gatherings worldwide

> http://www.maclachlans.org/games.html

Scottish Internet links

> http://www.scotlands.com/

Dr. Barbara Jarvis Tewksbury has an unlikely background for an author and illustrator of a book on kiltmaking. She has a PhD in Geology and has been professor of geology at Hamilton College in Clinton, New York for close to 25 years. She has received national recognition for teaching and curriculum development, having served as President of the National Association of Geoscience Teachers and having been named 1997 Professor of the Year in New York State by the Carnegie Foundation for the Advancement of Teaching. Geology is not her whole life, however. Barb has a lifetime of interest in hand crafts and construction projects of all kinds. She is a skilled seamstress whose projects have won many awards, including numerous blue ribbons and a Best in Show prize at the New York State Fair. When her daughter, Carolyn, attended her first Scottish Highland dance camp in 1996, Barb went along to learn kiltmaking from Elsie Stuehmeyer. In five short days, Barb was hooked. The precision and complexity of the process appealed to her more than any other hand craft ever had. As a result, she has been making kilts ever since, squeezing time for making custom-made kilts into the spaces of a life already crammed with a family and a full-time professorship. Elsie was impressed by Barb's commitment to traditional kiltmaking, her meticulous work, and her rather excessive note-taking during the kiltmaking course. She asked Barb if she would be willing to help her write a book on kiltmaking, with Barb translating Elsie's expertise into instructions for a neophyte. The rest is history.

Elsie Scott Stuehmeyer is without doubt the pre-eminent kiltmaker in North America, and her experience in making and fitting kilts is truly staggering. She has quite literally made thousands and thousands of kilts over the past 50 years in every imaginable tartan for people of all shapes and sizes. She is so well-known as a kiltmaker that people book her a year in advance when they know that they will need new kilts. Her kilts have been worn by beginning dancers and by champions, by commoners and royalty. She made a kilt for Prince William of Britain, and she has a picture from Everest base camp of a Sherpa, who had summitted Everest, wearing the kilt she had made for him. She learned the art of kiltmaking at age 15 as an apprentice at Thomas Gordon's in Glasgow in 1949. She remembers quite clearly that she would have much preferred being a telephone operator but that her parents insisted that she apprentice in a trade. She spent five long years as an apprentice kiltmaker, where she learned the traditional art of kiltmaking at the very best company in Scotland. Since leaving Scotland in 1973, she has made a career of kiltmaking in the United States. In addition, she has patiently taught kiltmaking to scores of students over many years, and she tempers her insistence on correct methods and meticulous sewing with a lively personality and a vast collection of hysterically funny stories told with a delightful accent. If you should pass through Petaluma, California, keep your eye out for Elsie's unmistakable license plate – KILTMKR.

Postscript

This book is dedicated to the pipers, dancers,
drummers, athletes, artisans, and enthusiasts
whose interests and talents keep Scottish
traditions alive.